The MAILBOX — The Education Center

SUPERBOOK

Grade 3

Everything You Need for a Successful Year!

- **Language Arts**
- **Math**
- **Science and Health**
- **Social Studies**
- **Graphic Organizers**

- **Centers**
- **Games**
- **Differentiation Tips**
- **Bulletin Boards**
- **Arts and Crafts**

And Much More!

Revised and Updated!

Managing Editor: Debra Liverman

Editorial Team: Becky S. Andrews, Kimberley Bruck, Karen P. Shelton, Diane Badden, Thad H. McLaurin, Jennifer Bragg, Amy Erickson, Marsha Erskine, Peggy Hambright, Sherry McGregor, Amy Payne, Gerri Primak, Hope Taylor Spencer, Karen A. Brudnak, Juli Docimo Blair, Hope Rodgers, Dorothy C. McKinney

Production Team: Lori Z. Henry, Pam Crane, Rebecca Saunders, Jennifer Tipton Cappoen, Chris Curry, Sarah Foreman, Theresa Lewis Goode, Greg D. Rieves, Eliseo De Jesus Santos II, Barry Slate, Donna K. Teal, Zane Williard, Tazmen Carlisle, Marsha Heim, Lynette Dickerson, Mark Rainey

www.themailbox.com

TABLE OF CONTENTS

Table of Contents

Holidays and Seasonal Activities

Back-to-School

Boarding Pass
for the
Third-Grade Express

signed _Amanda Lipscomb_

Welcome Aboard!

Boarding Pass
for the
Third-Grade Express

signed _Mark Williams_

Welcome Aboard!

Blake   Harris

★ I am...   ★ ★

funny
creative
tall
smart
fast

I like...

tractors
baseball
basketball
drawing
horses

★

All Aboard!

Invite students to climb aboard the "Third-Grade Express" with the patterns on page 7. A week before the big day, mail each of your new students a special boarding pass to your classroom. Program the "Scheduled Stops" card with a preview of projects, themes, and events that will take place in the first few weeks of school and tuck one into each envelope. Students' interest will be piqued, and parents will appreciate the information about your curriculum plans.

High-Flying Students

The year will be off to a soaring start with these personalized kite projects. Give each student a copy of a simple kite pattern. Have the student complete each section of the kite with information about himself as shown. The student then colors the kite, cuts it out, and attaches a length of yarn as a tail. Provide time for each student to share his creation with the class. Display these high-flying projects in the classroom to help students become better acquainted.

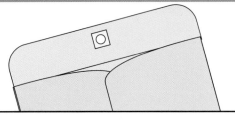

Room Preparations		Teacher Preparations	
makes nametags	☑	copy math lesson	☑
make seating chart	☐	make spelling list	☑
	☐	get reading books	☐
	☐		☐
	☐		☐
	☐		☐
	☐		☐
	☐		☐
	☐		☐
	☐		☐

munications (office, pare ts, etc
run ies of information p cket

Check the Details!

The first few days before school can be a flurry of activity as you attend to the many details of getting your room ready, making lesson plans, and securing materials. Stay on top of things with the checklist on page 8. Make a copy of the list and fill in the tasks you need to accomplish. With a glance, you will be able to see what progress you have made and what tasks still lie ahead as the big day draws near!

					June 4 Gail	
				May 28 Mike	June 9 Bill	
	February 28 Mark		April 5 Myra	May 5 Shelly	June 1 Kay	July 11 Tracy
January 3 Tina	February 4 Sara	March 11 Phil	April 19 Tommy	May 1 Dawn	June 7 Tina	July 15 Ben
Jan.	Feb.	March	April	May	June	July

Birthday Graph

This first-day activity will also serve as a birthday-graph display. Before the first day of school, draw a blank graph on bulletin board paper. Label the bottom of the graph with the months of the year. Staple the graph to a bulletin board and add a decorative border. Make a class supply of cupcake cutouts and place one on top of each student's desk. As each student arrives on the first day, instruct him to write his name and birthday on the cutout. Have the student staple his completed cupcake to the appropriate section of the graph. Extend the activity by asking students to volunteer information about the results of the graph.

Organized Information

Be prepared for the many types of communications that will come across your desk in the beginning days of school. Prior to the first day, purchase a large three-ring binder and a package of pocket-type dividers. List the types of papers you need to keep on file during the year, such as faculty memos, parent correspondence, schedules, and policies. Label a divider page for each section and arrange the sections alphabetically in the binder. When important information arrives at your desk, file it in the appropriate divider section. You'll keep track of all your important papers and have a comprehensive record of the school year.

Teacher Trivia

Welcome your new students with a display that lets them get to know you. Create a display on a sheet of poster board of family pictures, craft projects, awards, and other personal information. Write a question under each item, such as "What kind of dog do I own?" or "Where did I go on vacation this summer?"

After students have had time to examine the display, ask them to venture a response to each question. Verify correct answers; then ask students to contribute a little information about themselves. Within minutes, students will feel more comfortable because they have some background information about their new teacher and classmates.

before hand your Raise speaking

do best Always your

everyone with Treat respect

Scrambled Rules

One challenge children face every fall is learning the rules of their new classroom. Make this task an enjoyable activity by creating a list of scrambled rules. Rearrange the words in each classroom rule so that they are in random order. Write each scrambled rule on a sentence strip or on the board for students to decipher. After a designated time period, ask student volunteers to rewrite each rule correctly on the board. Discuss the rules with your students.

Homework Hangers

Promote the importance of a proper homework setting with an activity that reinforces good study habits. Have your students brainstorm a list of habits for homework time, such as working in a well-lit place, avoiding distractions like television and radio, keeping necessary supplies on hand, and referring to an assignment sheet for information. Give a copy of the form on the bottom of page 9 to each student to compose a homework plan. Then have students create a doorknob hanger to let family members know when homework time is in progress. Provide each student with a copy of the pattern on the top of page 9. Have the student create a message and illustration to remind his family that quiet time is needed. Laminate the completed hangers before sending them home with your students.

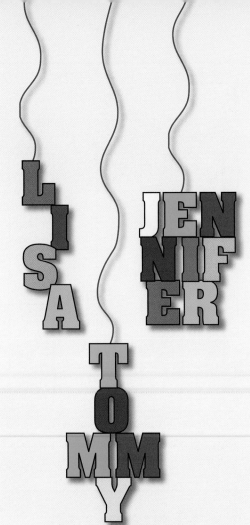

Name-Droppers

This first-day art project will not only decorate your classroom but will also help students learn one another's names! Provide a set of tagboard die-cut letters for students to use as stencils and an assortment of colored construction paper. Instruct each student to trace the letters of her name onto different colors of construction paper. Have the student cut out the letters and glue them together in an arrangement that spells her name. Use a length of yarn to suspend the personalized project from the ceiling above the student's desk.

Boarding Pass
for the
Third-Grade Express

signed _____

Welcome Aboard!

Scheduled Stops
for the
Third-Grade Express

During the next few weeks, we will

- _____

- _____

- _____

- _____

Glad to have you aboard!

Room Preparations	Teacher Preparations

Communications (office, parents, etc.)

Note to the teacher: Use with "Check the Details!" on page 6.

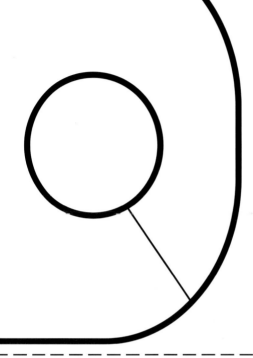

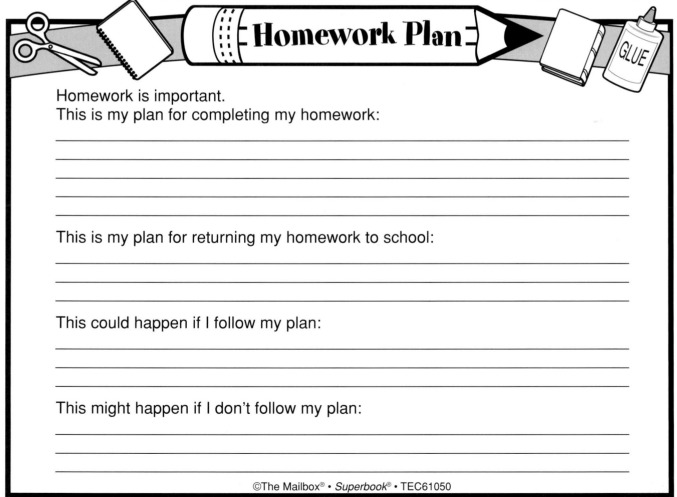

Homework is important.
This is my plan for completing my homework:

_____
_____
_____
_____
_____

This is my plan for returning my homework to school:

_____
_____
_____

This could happen if I follow my plan:

_____
_____
_____

This might happen if I don't follow my plan:

_____
_____
_____

Note to the teacher: Use with "Homework Hangers" on page 6.

9

Reading

Prereading Predictions

Before reading a selection with your class, create a list of important vocabulary words from the story. Include people, places, events, objects, and descriptions that are important to the story. Display the list and have students use the words as clues to predict possible characters, plots, and settings. Record students' predictions; then read the story together. Afterward refer to the predictions and compare them to the actual characters and events in the story. **Predictions**

What's Behind That Door?

Explain to students that making a prediction before reading is like looking at a closed door and guessing what's behind it. Next, have each child fold a sheet of unlined paper in half and draw a door on the front. Guide the student to list on the door her name; the story, chapter, or book title; and her predictions. After reading, direct each child to review her predictions, open the door, and summarize her reading on the inside. **Predictions**

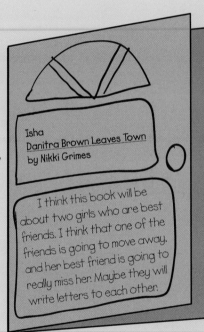

Isha
Danitra Brown Leaves Town
by Nikki Grimes

I think this book will be about two girls who are best friends. I think that one of the friends is going to move away, and her best friend is going to really miss her. Maybe they will write letters to each other.

This is a book of poems. The two girls, Danitra and Zuri, are best friends, but Danitra doesn't move. She just goes to visit family for the summer. At first Zuri is really mad, but she gets over it when Danitra writes her a letter. They write letters that are really poems about summer to each other.

Starter Strips

Here's a simple tip for helping students make and revise predictions as they read. Program a sentence strip for each student with the starter "I predict." Then laminate the strips and give one to each child along with a wipe-off marker. Before reading, guide each student to record on the strip his prediction and place it on his desk. To revise his prediction, the child simply wipes the strip clean and records his new idea. **Predictions**

I **predict** that Amelia Bedelia will make a crazy cake.

Follow the Signs

Want your students to stop and think about unfamiliar words in their reading rather than just skip over them? Try this! As a child reads, direct him to list each word that he does not recognize and its page number on a copy of the bookmark pattern on page 26. Guide the student to also record what he thinks the word might mean. When he finishes reading, have the child look up each word in a dictionary to confirm or revise the meaning. Then have the student reread the text, keeping his bookmark handy and paying special attention to the words he wondered about during his first reading. **Predictions for unknown words**

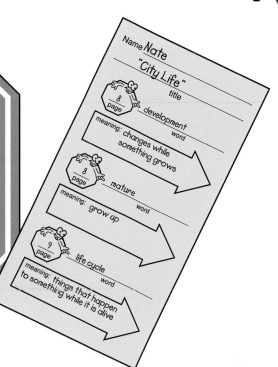

Narrowing It Down

Help students make and revise predictions. Before reading a selection, have each child list a prediction about the selection's main idea on a copy of the bottom half of page 26. After reading about one third of the selection, guide the student to review and clarify her prediction. Direct the child to repeat this step after reading the next third of the selection. When she finishes reading, have the student review her predictions and then list the selection's main idea at the bottom of the page. **Predictions**

Name Sandra

Predictions

"Through Grandpa's Eyes"
title

I think the main idea will be that a grandpa tells his grandchild stories about when he was young.

The main idea may be that the child is telling about his grandpa's house and his blind grandpa.

The main idea may be that the child is telling about the things he does with his grandpa.

The main idea is that the child is learning how rich his grandpa's world is.

Setting Explorations

Before reading a story, share with students the story's time and place. Next, lead students to discuss what they know about the setting, adding facts and details that will help other students better understand the story. Then guide each student to keep the setting in mind while he makes predictions about the story. **Predictions**

We See When We Read!

The part I remember most is when he built his house.

Billowy Thinking

Remind students to visualize with this fun-to-create display! Have each student draw a self-portrait and then post it on a bulletin board, leaving several inches around it. Title the board "We See When We Read!" Then, after a class reading, guide each student to draw a picture about the most important thing he pictured during the reading. Next, the child trims the picture into a cloud shape and posts it above his portrait. He glues several cotton balls between the two pictures as shown. For each new class reading, each student simply replaces the thought bubble with his new one. **Visualizing**

Picturing the Story

The Day Jimmy's Boa Ate the Wash
by Trinka Hakes Nobel and Jasmin

Have each student fold and staple three sheets of unlined paper to make a booklet as shown. Next, begin reading aloud a picture book without showing students the pictures. Stop reading after a few minutes and guide each student to draw on the first page inside her booklet what she imagined while you read. Then continue reading, stopping five more times to have students draw. After reading, direct each student to list on her booklet's cover the story's title, its author, and her own name as illustrator. Have students share their versions of the story in small groups. **Visualizing**

Act It Out

During your next class reading, instruct each student to close his eyes to better picture the story as you read it aloud. After stressing that students remain seated, guide them to act out the characters' actions as you read. For example, if a character is climbing a ladder, the student might move his arms and legs in climbing motions. After reading, have students open their eyes. Then guide the class to retell the story, recording students' ideas on the board. Reread the story, guiding the class to compare it with their retelling. **Visualizing**

What Did You Observe?

Help students enhance their comprehension with this multisensory web. Before reading, have each student draw a web as shown. Next, as she reads, guide the child to use words and pictures to record her impressions for each sense. Then have the child use her web to summarize her reading. **Visualizing**

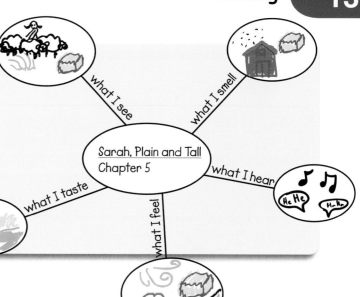

Roll 'Em!

Inspire students to create movies in their heads when they read. After reading a story, have each child draw on a copy of the strip on page 27 pictures of the story's beginning, middle, and end. Then guide the student to cut out the strip, the theater screen, and the slits as shown. Have the child slide his strip through the slits and then share his movie with a small group. **Visualizing**

Advertise!

For a fun twist on book talks, have students promote books and the visual images they inspired. After a child finishes reading a self-selected book, have her create a poster that advertises her book as if it were a movie. Direct the student to list the book's title and author and then vividly announce and recreate the pictures she imagined as she read. Display the posters along a common hall to attract new readers from all around the school! **Visualizing**

Key Events

After your class has read a story, discuss the key events that form the story's main idea. Write each event on chart paper. Use the key patterns on page 28 to provide each student with three keys. Tell her to select three events listed on the chart. Have the student describe and illustrate one of the selected events on each key pattern. Then have her punch a hole in each key and thread the keys on a yarn ring. Display the projects on a bulletin board titled "The Keys to Our Story." **Important Events**

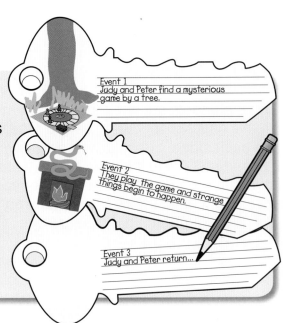

Event 1
Judy and Peter find a mysterious game by a tree.

Event 2
They play the game and strange things begin to happen.

Event 3
Judy and Peter return...

Main Idea to Go

To make this portable center, collect short, interesting articles from newspapers or children's magazines. Cut off each article's title and then glue the pieces to tagboard. Laminate and cut apart the pieces. Next, place five sets of titles and articles in a resealable bag. When a student has a few minutes, he takes the bag and reads each article. Then he identifies the article's main idea and finds its matching title. **Main idea**

New Dinosaur Fossil Discovered!

Local Artist to Help Plan City Park

Dog Helps Family Find Lost Cat

Robot Pets?

Our All-Star Team Is Going to Nationals!

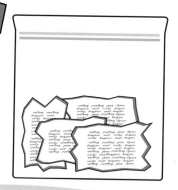

3, 2, 1

Remind students to keep track of important ideas and details by counting back from three! Each time a student completes a reading assignment, guide her to list three important details, two interesting details, and then the main idea—3, 2, 1! **Main idea**

Full Steam Ahead!

For this activity, enlarge the train cars on page 29. Next, guide students to define *main idea,* recording the class's definition on the engine. Place the engine on the board and point out that the main idea needs supporting details. Lead students to brainstorm types of details that can support the main idea, recording their ideas on the remaining train cars. Add the cars to the train. Then direct each student to read a selection and record its main idea and supporting details on a copy of page 29. After the child finishes, have him cut out and post his work on a display titled "Tracking With Supporting Details." **Supporting details**

Pass It On

Here's an activity that gives students practice identifying a paragraph's main idea. Select four different paragraphs from grade-level nonfiction text. Number and copy the paragraphs, making a set for every four students. Next, have students bring journals and pencils and sit in a circle. Then hand out the paragraphs. On your signal, direct each student to read his paragraph and record its main idea. After three to five minutes, call out, "Pass!" Have each child pass his paragraph to his left and repeat the process with the new paragraph. Continue with the remaining paragraphs and then lead students to share their main ideas, discuss any differences, and come to a consensus about each one. **Main idea**

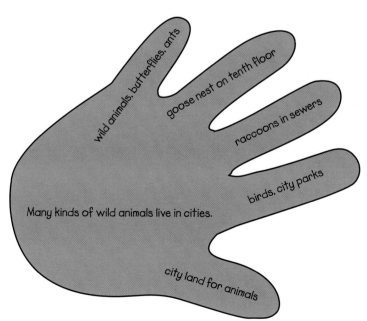

wild animals, butterflies, ants

goose nest on tenth floor

raccoons in sewers

birds, city parks

Many kinds of wild animals live in cities.

city land for animals

Notes at My Fingertips

Before reading, have each student trace her hand on a sheet of paper. As she reads, have the child jot important words or phrases in the fingers. When she finishes reading, guide the student to review her notes, identify the selection's main idea, and list it in the palm. Then have her use the hand-shaped organizer to describe the selection's main idea and supporting details. **Main idea**

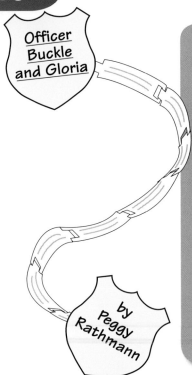

Story-Sequencing Chains

For this project students can use a story from their independent reading or a book they have read together as a class. Give a copy of the link patterns on page 30 to each student. Instruct the student to write a key event from the story on each link pattern. Then direct each student to cut out each link. To assemble the chain, have the student arrange the events in the correct order of occurrence. Then have him thread the end tab from each link through the opening in the adjacent link and glue it in place. While the glue is drying, give each student one large sheet of construction paper. Instruct the student to fold his paper in half and sketch a shape relevant to the story. Have him cut out the shape so that two are created. Instruct him to write the title of the book on the first cutout and the name of the author on the second cutout. Complete the project by gluing a cutout to each end of the chain. Hang the completed chains around the room for an eye-catching display.
Sequencing

Summarized Stories

Select a chapter book that the students have read together. Create a group for every chapter in the book and place an equal number of students in each group. Instruct each group to reread the designated chapter and write a paragraph summarizing its important events. Challenge students to summarize the chapter in five sentences or less, using the word *and* no more than twice. Tell the group to also create an illustration for the chapter. Compile the resulting pages into a book and ask a student volunteer to design a cover. Arrange for the groups to take turns sharing the book with a younger grade or with other classes who have read the book. **Summarizing**

Sequenced Story Cards

After reading a story together, place students in groups of two or three. Instruct each group to write and illustrate a sentence detailing an event from the story on a 5" x 8" notecard. Call on each group to share its completed card with the class. After the sentence has been read, have the group place its card on the chalk rail in random order. When each group has shared its work, ask the class to help you arrange the cards in the order that they occurred in the story. Compile the sequenced cards into a booklet that summarizes the story. **Sequencing**

Flip It!

For this clever sequencing project, guide each student to fold a sheet of unlined paper horizontally, leaving a half-inch strip along the bottom as shown. Have the child record the story's title and author and her name on the strip. Next, have her cut the top flap into three sections. Direct the student to illustrate the most important events from the story's beginning, middle, and end on each section. Then have her flip the flaps and briefly summarize each event. **Sequencing**

Dr. De Soto is a mouse dentist who helps a lot of animals. He takes care of little animals and big animals. But he never takes care of animals that might eat him.

Doctor De Soto by William Steig

Middle

End

Ahmad

Craft Stick Sequencing

Follow up a class reading by giving each pair of students a craft stick numbered one through ten, depending on the number of students in your class. Then call on the duo holding number one to retell an event from the beginning of the story. Repeat for each remaining number, recording students' responses on sentence strips. After the twosome with the last craft stick retells the final event, guide students to check the strips and revise the order as necessary. **Sequencing**

Mrs. Rogers leaves a list of jobs for Amelia Bedelia.

A String of Events

Help students order events from a chapter book with a timeline approach. After reading, assign one chapter to each small group of students. Have the group list on separate index cards the chapter's four most important events. Direct the group to flip the cards and number them in order. Next, have the group shuffle its cards and pass them to another group. Guide each group to arrange the cards in order before flipping them to check. Repeat until the groups have all ordered the main events of each chapter. To display students' work, suspend a length of string and have each group paper-clip its cards in order along the string. Place a clothespin between each chapter if desired. **Sequencing**

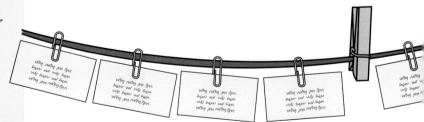

Opinions in Advertising

Show your students how persuasive opinions can be. Cut out a collection of advertisements from newspapers and magazines. Place students into small groups and distribute several ads to each group. Instruct students to look at the wording of each advertisement and make note of statements that offer opinions instead of factual information. Point out to students that the pictures in the ads can also convey an attitude or opinion about the product. After students have had time to make observations, provide time for each group to discuss its findings with the class.

Fact and opinion

Show Us the Facts and Opinions!

Incorporate a fact-and-opinion lesson with a favorite student event—show-and-tell! As each student takes a turn showing an object to the class, she must tell three facts and one opinion about the item. Ask student volunteers to identify which statement was an opinion. Extend the activity by having classmates offer facts and opinions about each item.

Fact and opinion

Fact Standoff

Use a student-generated supply of statements for an activity in recognizing facts and opinions. After the class has read a story or chapter together, have each student write one fact or opinion about the story on a slip of paper. Collect the papers and place them in a container. Draw out one paper at a time and read the statement to the class. If the statement is a fact, each student stands up by her desk. If it is an opinion, the student sits down. Continue until all the statements have been read aloud.

Fact and opinion

That's a Fact-o

For this quick game, have each student fold a sheet of paper in half four times to create 16 rectangular spaces. Next, direct the child to write "fact" or "opinion" in each of the spaces. Then read aloud a statement and guide students to decide whether it is a fact or an opinion. Have each student put a marker on an appropriately labeled space. Continue reading statements until a student marks four spaces in a row to make a Fact-o. Have students clear their boards and play again as time allows! **Fact and opinion**

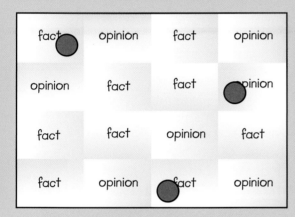

fact	opinion	fact	opinion
opinion	fact	fact	opinion
fact	fact	opinion	fact
fact	opinion	fact	opinion

Flowery Decisions

For this center, copy, cut out, and laminate the flower patterns on page 31. Also write "fact" on five craft sticks and "opinion" on five more craft sticks. Next, glue the loop side of a small Velcro fastener onto the back of each flower and the hook side of a small Velcro fastener onto each craft stick. At the center, a student reads each statement, decides whether it is a fact or an opinion, and attaches the correct craft stick. **Fact and opinion**

Roses smell the best.

opinion

Flipping Over Cause and Effect

Select a story that the class has read together and write four events from the story on the board. Pair students and give two copies of the patterns on page 32 to each pair. Instruct each team to think of a cause-and-effect situation for each event listed on the board. Have the partners write the information in the appropriate spaces on the pattern and then cut out each shape. Fold each shape in half and place a dot of glue on the back of each section. Press the right half of the cause section to the left half of the matching effect section. Then glue each unattached end to a sheet of construction paper. Provide time for students to share their completed projects with the class. **Cause and effect**

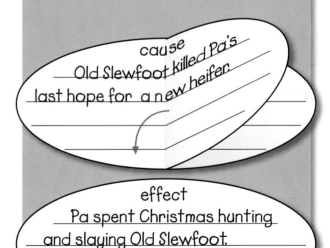

cause
Old Slewfoot killed Pa's last hope for a new heifer.

effect
Pa spent Christmas hunting and slaying Old Slewfoot.

Weather Effect

Review the concept of cause and effect each day with a quick weather report. Announce the day's forecast and then guide students to brainstorm a list of things that could be affected by the weather.
Cause and effect

There is an 80 percent chance of rain this afternoon.

I will have to wipe my dog's muddy feet before she can come inside.

We won't go outside for recess.

Water will come in the window that I left open.

Domino Topple

For this hands-on exploration, provide access to dominoes and 1½" x 2" sticky notes that have been cut in half. Then have each pair of students identify a chain of causes and effects in a current reading. When the pair has identified the chain of events, have the twosome list each event on a sticky note and stick it onto a domino. Finally, direct each duo to share its chain by reading aloud each event before lining up and then knocking over its domino chain. **Cause and effect**

Mr. and Mrs. Mallard are looking for a place to build their nest.

They are flying all over.

They get tired.

They stop at a pond in the Public Garden in Boston.

People on a boat throw peanuts into the water.

Mr. and Mrs. Mallard decide to stay.

Chain of Hints

Help students better identify cause and effect with a clever reminder to look for clue words. List clue words, such as those shown on the sentence strips, and introduce them to students. Then loop each strip to make a supersize paper chain of cause-and-effect clues. Post the chain in the classroom for everyday reference. **Cause and effect**

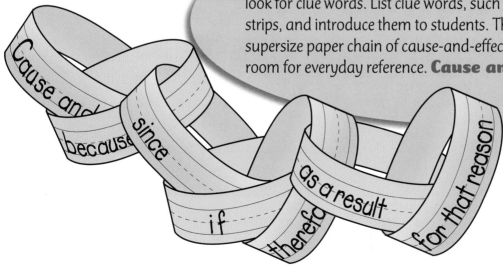

Cause and
because
since
if
therefore
as a result
for that reason

Reading Links

Here's a model idea for guiding students to make connections while they read. Label four foam balls as shown. Connect them using pipe cleaners cut in half and use a pipe cleaner loop to hang the model. Before a class reading, display the model and also draw a web, as shown, on the board. As you read, list on the web any connections that you make. Then keep the model on display and guide students to draw the web and record their connections each time they read. **Connections**

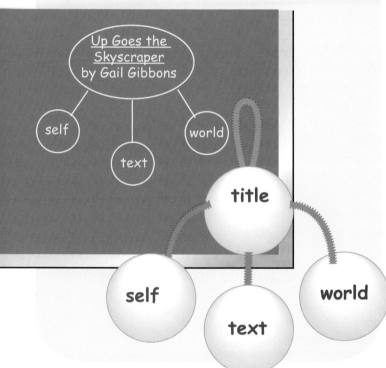

Inverted Notes

Have each student turn her reading journal upside down and backward and write from the back toward the front about the connections she makes when she reads. For each entry, the student describes the connections she made. Next, she writes about how that connection helps her under-stand, enjoy, learn from, or ques-tion her reading. Finally, each student labels the connec-tion *(text-to-self, text-to-text,* or *text-to-world)* in the page's top margin, which is now at the bottom of the page. Connections

September 10

text-to-text

Make It Meaningful

To help students use their text connections to better understand what they read, teach them to take three-part notes. Before reading, have each child create a three-column table as shown. Then, as he reads, lead him to jot down each story event that inspires a connection, the connection he makes, and an explanation of how it helps him better understand the text. Connections

Text	What it makes me think about	How it helps me understand what I'm reading
Fern wants to keep Wilbur as a pet.	I wanted to keep a dog that we found at the park.	I understand how Fern feels about keeping Wilbur.
Fern daydreams about Wilbur while she is at school.	Last week, I kept thinking about my new bike.	When I was thinking about my bike, it seemed like that was all I could think about. So I know how much Fern cared about Wilbur.

Raise Your Hand

Give students a hand in making text connections! Copy and cut apart the patterns on page 33 for each group of four students. Next, glue the patterns to large craft sticks and place each set of sticks in a cup. Before a class reading, give each group a cup of sticks. Then, as you read, have each student who makes a connection choose the appropriate stick and raise it. When you call on the child, she reads the sentence starter and then explains her connection. **Connections**

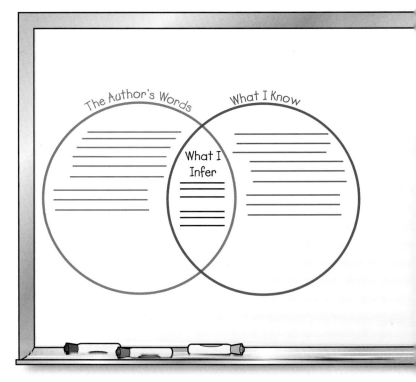

Getting Ready

Before beginning a unit of study or a class reading, list several topic-related terms in the left section of a Venn diagram labeled as shown. Next, point out that good readers use what they know and the author's words to make inferences. Then challenge students to make inferences or predictions about the upcoming reading. Record each comment in the diagram's center section and guide the child to explain his reasoning. Refer back to the organizer after reading to help students elaborate or refine their ideas. **Inferences**

Stuck on the Story

To encourage students to make inferences as they read, provide a supply of large sticky notes trimmed into speech bubble shapes. As each child reads, guide him to note on a speech bubble shape each inference he makes and place it beside the text. Then lead a discussion of the reading material, encouraging students to share and explain their inferences. Inferences

Alexander says that it isn't fair that his brothers still have money after he spent all of his. I think that Alexander knows he will always spend his money even though his brothers will save some of theirs. He thinks it's not fair because he can't help spending his money.

INTERESTING INFERENCES

Use everyday situations to help students infer how story characters might react to a situation or resolve a problem. After reading a book together, discuss how the characters responded to certain events in the story. Then have students use what they know about the characters to decide how each character might react to the situations listed below. Have each student select two or three situations and write paragraphs telling how the character might respond. **Inferences**

What would the character do...

⭐ if he found a lost dog on the highway?

⭐ if his best friend ignored him on the playground?

⭐ if, while playing a game, he saw another player cheating?

⭐ for fun on a rainy day?

⭐ if he forgot his mother's birthday?

⭐ if he found a wallet full of money?

⭐ if he left his homework on the bus?

⭐ to show he was sorry for something he had done?

Picture Book Conclusions

To teach students to draw conclusions, read aloud the beginning and middle of an unfamiliar picture book. Next, guide each student to draw and write what he thinks will happen in the ending. Then have each student share his conclusion with the class before reading the book's actual ending. **Conclusions**

Bon Voyage!

Have students use their inferring skills to send a story character on vacation! Ask each student to select a character from a story you have read together or from his independent reading. Remind him to consider the likes and dislikes of the character in determining the vacation spot. Have each student write a paragraph explaining his choice of destination and then jot down an itinerary for the character. Give a sheet of drawing paper to each student and instruct him to sketch a suitcase shape. Tell him to fill the suitcase with drawings or magazine cutouts showing items that the character would pack. Finally, have each student draw several snapshots of the character enjoying the vacation. Then set aside a special time for each student to present his vacation package to the class. **Inferences**

The Power of One Minute

Here's an activity that shows students how practice makes them better readers! Copy several short comprehension passages and give each child one. Direct each student to begin reading. Have the student stop after one minute and circle the last word that she read. Next, instruct each student to read the complete passage to three other students. Then have the student read for one minute and circle the last word that she reads this time. The benefits of practice will be clear! **Fluency**

I know how

there is

all together

A Few Words at a Time

Help students improve their reading fluency with flashy phrase cards. Copy and cut out the cards on page 34 for each pair of students. Direct the duo to read the phrases together. Then have each student flash the cards one at a time for his partner to read. Challenge students to flash the cards faster each successive round to help them read groups of words instead of single words. Fluency

See-Through Analysis

Try this tip to encourage students to assess their own fluency! Set up a listening center with a blank tape, a transparent sheet, and a wipe-off marker. Each student who visits the center brings a passage to read aloud and records her reading. Then the child rewinds her recording and places the transparent sheet over her passage. The student plays her recording, reading the passage as she listens. If she notices a mistake, the child circles it on the transparent page. Then she wipes the transparent page clean and tries again! **Fluency**

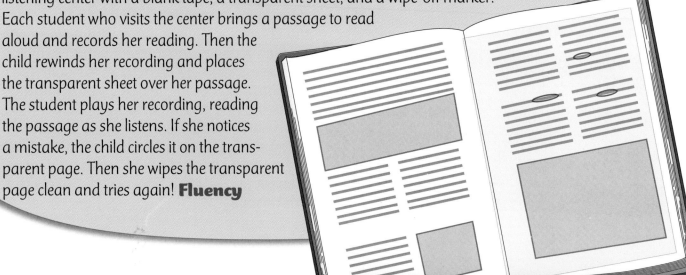

Live!
From the Pacific Coast,
Leo, a California sea
lion, is born. Leo weighs
15 pounds.

The Latest News

For this fluency-building activity, collect a student news magazine for each pair of students. Have each twosome choose an article from its magazine to present as late-breaking news. Instruct the partners to read and summarize the article. Next, have the pair make cue cards by copying its summary in large letters on construction paper sheets. Guide the partners to divide the summary into two parts and then practice reading their parts to each other, focusing on fluency, accuracy, and expression. Once students are ready to present their summaries, clear off a table to make a news desk and videotape each "live" news report. **Fluency**

Lots of Lists

Here's an idea that has students reading all kinds of words! To begin, display several categories of words (see examples). Next, challenge each student to find at least ten words that fit one of the categories. Once each student has made a list, have her read it to you. Correct any pronunciation errors and direct the child to memorize her list. Then set aside time for each student to present her list with dramatic flourish or sound effects. Post students' lists on a board titled "Got a Minute? Read a List!" **Fluency**

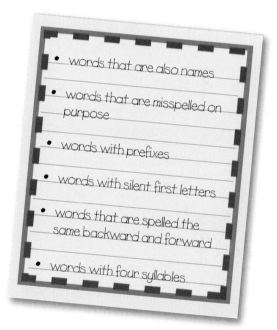

- words that are also names
- words that are misspelled on purpose
- words with prefixes
- words with silent first letters
- words that are spelled the same backward and forward
- words with four syllables

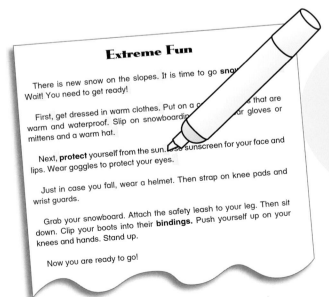

Extreme Fun

There is new snow on the slopes. It is time to go **sno**... Wait! You need to get ready!

First, get dressed in warm clothes. Put on a ... that are warm and waterproof. Slip on snowboardi... r gloves or mittens and a warm hat.

Next, **protect** yourself from the sun. ...e sunscreen for your face and lips. Wear goggles to protect your eyes.

Just in case you fall, wear a helmet. Then strap on knee pads and wrist guards.

Grab your snowboard. Attach the safety leash to your leg. Then sit down. Clip your boots into their **bindings.** Push yourself up on your knees and hands. Stand up.

Now you are ready to go!

Highlighting Help

To help students focus on appropriate phrasing, have them plan their pauses. Give each child a copy of a grade level–appropriate selection. Next, have the child silently read the selection, highlighting the commas and ending punctuation marks as he reads. Then lead students to chorally read the selection, helping them recognize each punctuation mark's pause. Have students practice reading the selection with partners before leading the class to chorally read the selection again and listen for phenomenal phrasing! **Fluency**

Check out the skill-building reproducibles on pages 35–38.

Bookmark Pattern

Use with "Follow the Signs" on page 11.

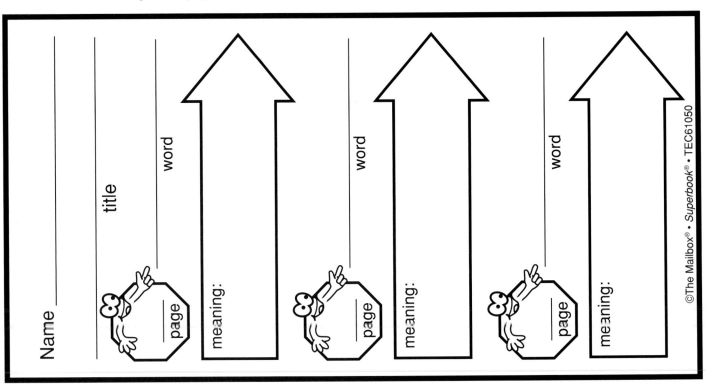

Name _____

title _____

word _____

page _____

meaning: _____

word _____

page _____

meaning: _____

word _____

page _____

meaning: _____

Name_____ Predictions

title _____

I think the main idea will be _____
_____

The main idea may be _____
_____

The main idea may be _____
_____

The main idea is _____

Note to the teacher: Use with "Narrowing It Down" on page 11.

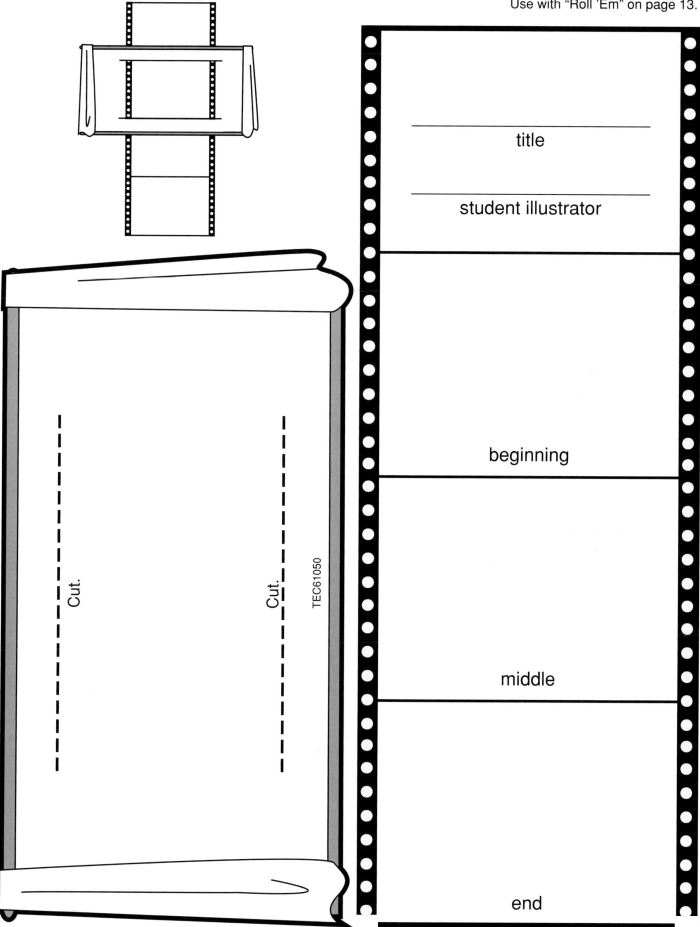

title

student illustrator

beginning

middle

end

Cut.

Cut.

TEC61050

Key Patterns
Use with "Key Events" on page 14.

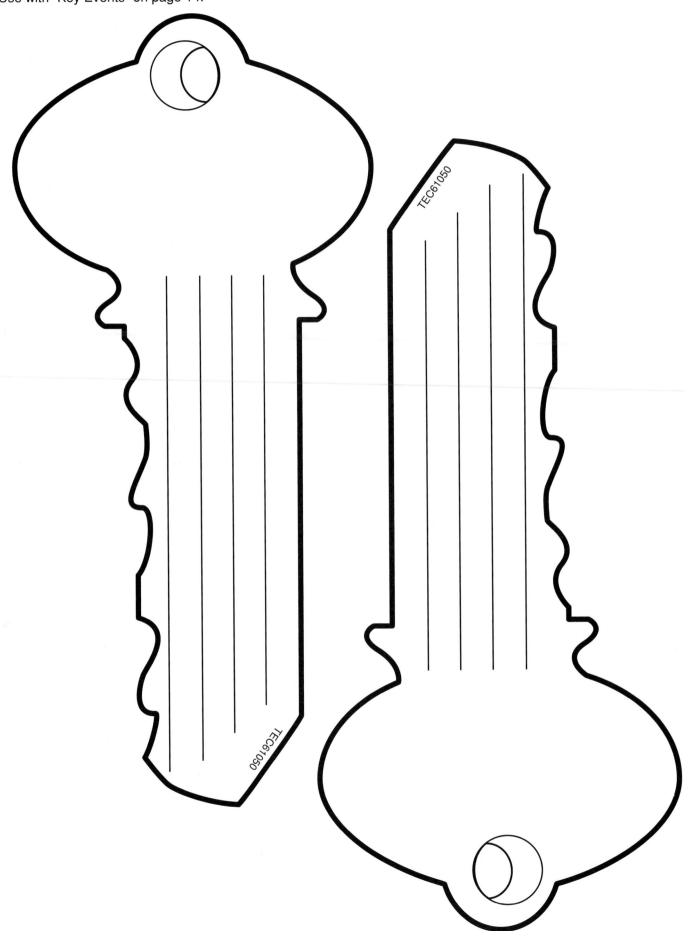

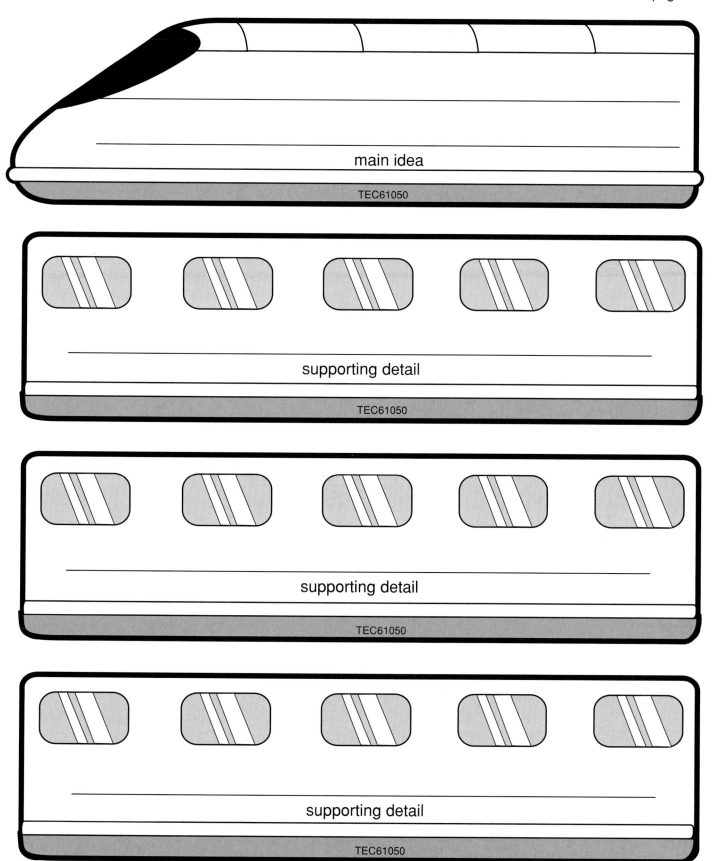

main idea

TEC61050

supporting detail

TEC61050

supporting detail

TEC61050

supporting detail

TEC61050

Link Patterns

Use with "Story-Sequencing Chains" on page 16.

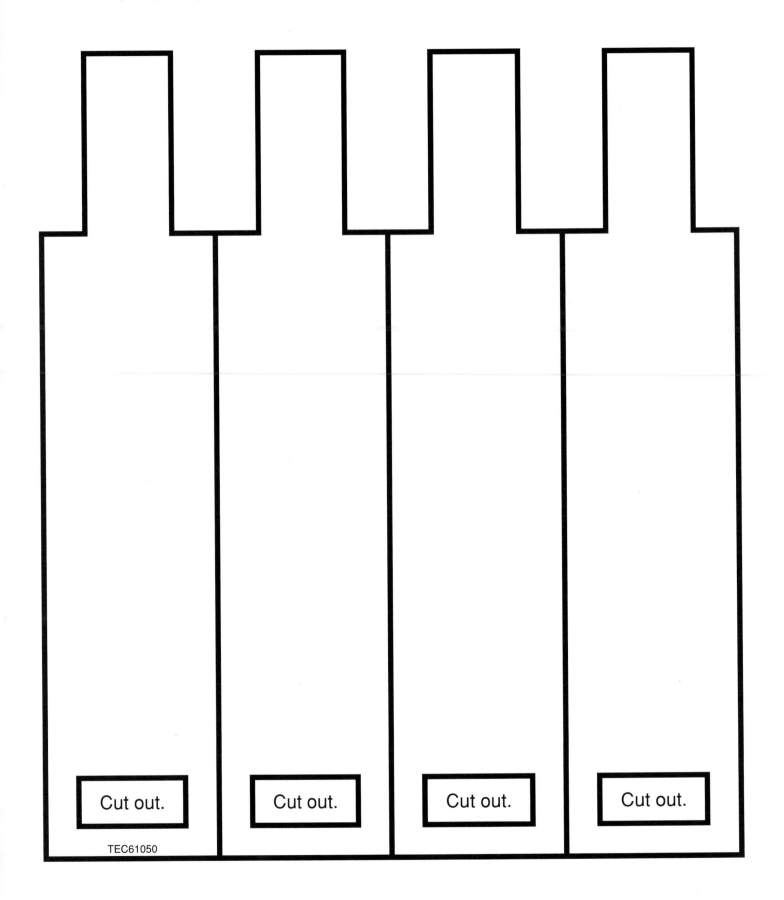

Cut out.

Cut out.

Cut out.

Cut out.

TEC61050

Roses smell the best.
TEC61050

Tulips are the most colorful flowers.
TEC61050

It is hard to grow pretty flowers.
TEC61050

There are too many kinds of flowers.
TEC61050

The best flowers are the ones that grow wild.
TEC61050

Sunflowers are better than daisies.
TEC61050

Many people decorate with flowers.
TEC61050

There are about 250,000 kinds of flowering plants.
TEC61050

Every flower's job is to make seeds.
TEC61050

All flowers used to be wild.
TEC61050

Flowers grow on almost all plants.
TEC61050

Some flowers only open at night.
TEC61050

Cause-and-Effect Patterns

Use with "Flipping Over Cause and Effect" on page 19.

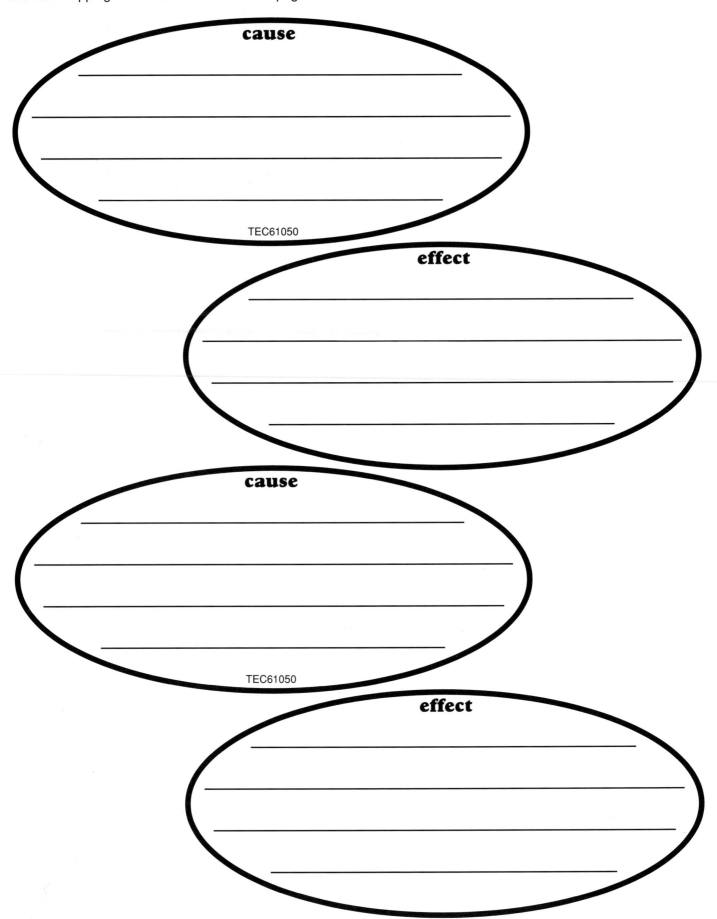

cause

TEC61050

effect

cause

TEC61050

effect

Connection Stick Patterns
Use with "Raise Your Hand" on page 22.

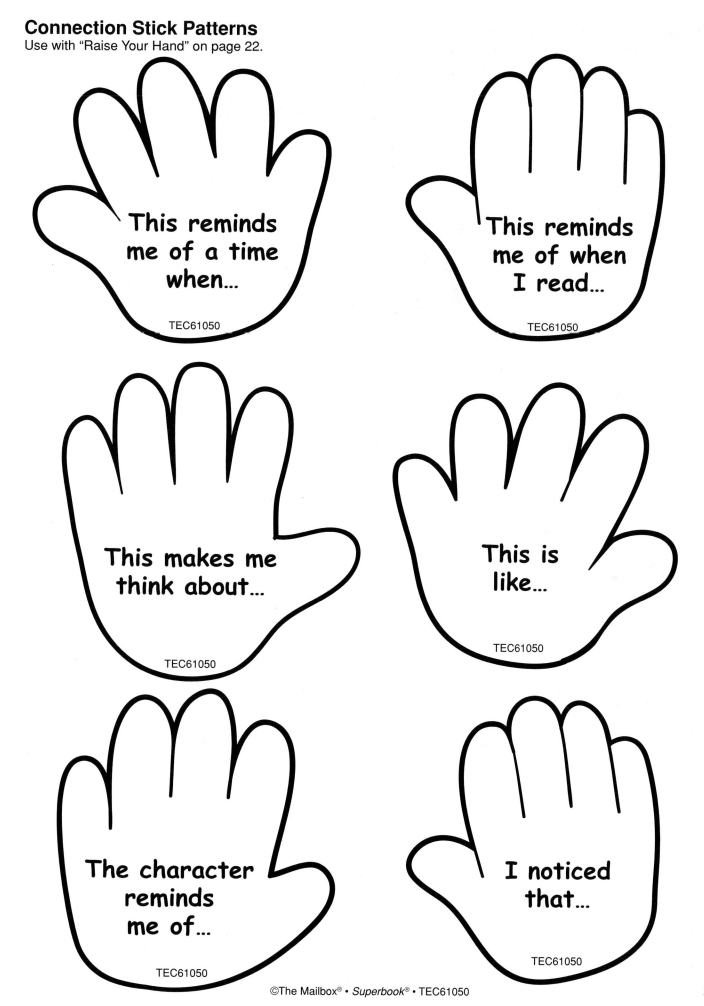

This reminds me of a time when...

TEC61050

This reminds me of when I read...

TEC61050

This makes me think about...

TEC61050

This is like...

TEC61050

The character reminds me of...

TEC61050

I noticed that...

TEC61050

I could

TEC61050

would not

TEC61050

what is that

TEC61050

if I ask

TEC61050

its name

TEC61050

right around

TEC61050

I know how

TEC61050

where can I

TEC61050

don't put any

TEC61050

it is about

TEC61050

let me see

TEC61050

open and find

TEC61050

pick it up

TEC61050

why is it

TEC61050

because it is

TEC61050

all together

TEC61050

to be there

TEC61050

there is

TEC61050

Riding the Wave

Color by the code.

The ocean is a large body of water.

The ocean is sometimes called the sea.

Oceans cover almost three-fourths of the earth.

It affects temperatures around the world.

The ocean affects the weather on the earth.

The moisture that brings rain comes from the ocean.

There are also deep valleys under the water.

There are long chains of mountains under the water.

Landforms in the ocean are much like landforms on land.

We get food and energy from the ocean.

We use the ocean to ship goods to other countries.

We use the ocean in many ways.

We swim, surf, and sail on the ocean.

The First Community

Read the passage.

Most of the settlers who first came to America did not plan to grow corn. Many did not even plan to work hard. They came to find gold and silver. They came to teach the native people about their church.

But the land where they settled was swampy. The water was not safe for drinking. They got sick. They went hungry. Many of those first settlers died. Then Captain John Smith took charge. He made people stop looking for treasure and start working. Smith helped the settlers survive their first winter.

Then the settlers tried to grow grapes, which did not do well in their climate. In time, the settlers learned to raise hogs and grow corn. They began to learn how to survive in the New World.

Find each pair of events in the passage.
Color the circle in front of the event that happened first.

1. ◯ Settlers came to America to find gold and silver.
   ◯ Settlers learned to raise hogs and grow corn.

2. ◯ The settlers chose swampy land.
   ◯ The settlers did not plan to farm corn.

3. ◯ The settlers tried to grow grapes.
   ◯ Many settlers got sick.

4. ◯ Captain John Smith took charge.
   ◯ John Smith helped the settlers survive their first winter.

5. ◯ The settlers began to learn how to survive in the New World.
   ◯ The settlers came to find gold and silver.

Find the Facts

If the statement is a fact, color the leaf green.
If the statement is an opinion, color the leaf orange.

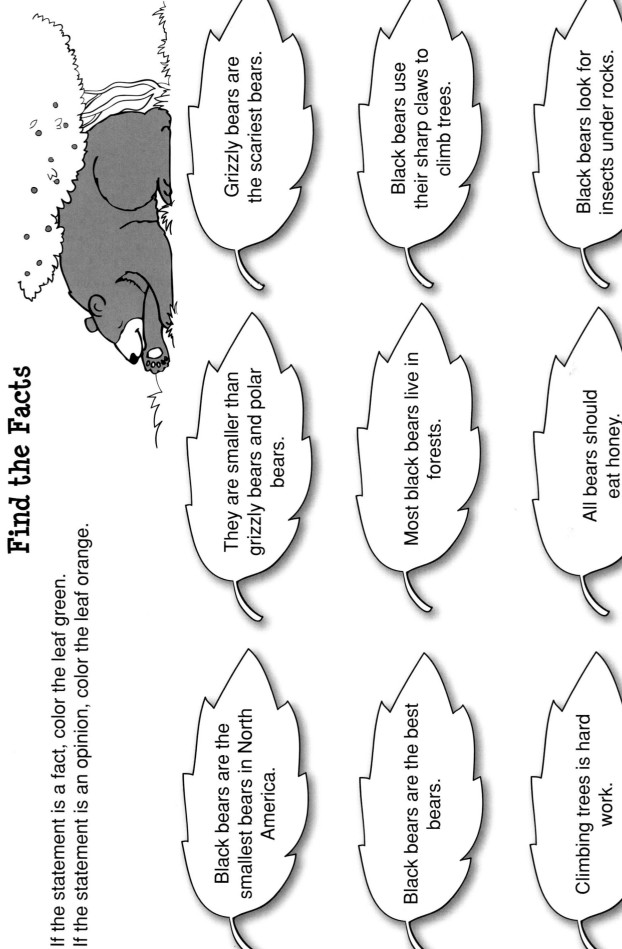

Grizzly bears are the scariest bears.

Black bears use their sharp claws to climb trees.

Black bears look for insects under rocks.

They are smaller than grizzly bears and polar bears.

Most black bears live in forests.

All bears should eat honey.

Black bears are the smallest bears in North America.

Black bears are the best bears.

Climbing trees is hard work.

ADD IT UP

Read the clues.
Cut out the boxes below.
Glue each box in place.

Dark clouds cover the blue sky.

It is Tim's birthday, and he does not think he is having a party.

Hope rolls the ball to Tim.

Tim makes his bed.

There is a bright flash of lightning and a loud clap of thunder.

Tim's dad takes him to the park.

Tim kicks the ball past Tina.

Tim digs all of the clothes out from under his bed.

The teachers clear the playground.

Tim's mom stays home and puts up streamers.

Tina chases the ball as Tim runs to first base.

Tim stacks his books and treasures on the bookshelf.

©The Mailbox® • Superbook® • TEC61050 • Key p. 309

Tim is cleaning his room.

Hope, Tim, and Tina are playing kickball.

There is a thunderstorm on the way.

Tim's mom and dad are planning a surprise party for him.

Story Elements

Story Collages

Challenge each student to design this book report by gathering a collection of pictures, words, and objects that tell about the setting, characters, and important events of a book. Also have him write the book's title, author, and illustrator on an index card. To make his collage, a student glues his collection and index card on construction paper and adds original writing and drawings as desired. Provide time for each student to share his collage with the class; then post it on a display. **Story elements**

Mr. Galloway,

Muggie Maggie
by
Beverly Cleary

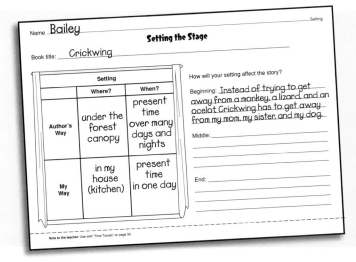

Name Bailey

Setting

Setting the Stage

Book title: Crickwing

Setting		
	Where?	**When?**
Author's Way	under the forest canopy	present time over many days and nights
My Way	in my house (kitchen)	present time in one day

How will your setting affect the story?

Beginning: Instead of trying to get away from a monkey, a lizard, and an ocelot Crickwing has to get away from my mom, my sister and my dog.

Middle: _____

End: _____

Note to the teacher: Use with "Time Travels" on page 39.

Time Travels

Students take a story to a new time and place during this setting activity. Read aloud a story and have students name its main events and settings. Give each child a copy of page 41. To complete the page, a student fills in the first row of the chart based on the read-aloud story. Then she describes a new setting for the story in the second row. Next, she considers how her new setting might affect the story's events and, on her paper, describes the changes. Finally, she reviews her information and uses it to write a new version of the story. **Setting**

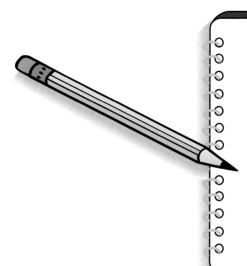

Character Journals

To help students understand the development of character, ask each student to pretend that he is the main character from a book. Have the student create three journal entries that the main character may have written during the course of the story. Remind students to select moments in the story that have important effects on the character. Then place students in small groups to share their entries and compare the events selected by each student. **Character**

In a Pickle

This center activity helps students identify problems and solutions. Copy the pickle patterns from page 42 onto green paper, making enough for each child to have one. Place the patterns at a center with a plastic jar, pencils, and scissors. Invite three to four students at a time to use the center. Each student cuts out a pickle and writes a problem he might have, such as losing a library book or forgetting his homework. Next, he shares the problem with the other students at the center and they discuss possible solutions. He describes his favorite solution on the back of his pickle cutout and places it in the jar. As time allows, choose pickles from the jar and share the problems and solutions with the class. After students have a good understanding of this skill, have them apply the process to problems and solutions in books they're reading. **Problem and solution**

Problem: I lost my library book, and it's due tomorrow.

Noah

Solution: I can retrace my steps with the help of my family.

Problem

Jack and Annie had to find the last clue to free Morgan from the spell.

Midnight on the Moon
by Mary Pope Osborne

Characters
Jack
Annie
Peanut
Morgan le Fay

Settings
Frog Creek, PA, in the present on the moon, in the future

Solution

Jack connected the stars on the map to make a mouse. That was the last clue, and Morgan was freed from the spell.

Buggy About Books

This project will have your students swarming to new titles as well as old favorites. Have each child bring in a favorite book from the library or from home. To share his book, he glues three three-inch paper circles in a row. Then he labels the circles with the book's title and author, characters, and settings. Next, he uses the wing pattern on page 42 as a template and cuts out two construction paper wings. After he glues the wings to the circles, he writes the story's problem on the left wing and its solution on the right wing. Showcase the students' favorite books, and post the completed butterflies nearby. Encourage students to flutter by for some good reading. **Story elements**

Name _____

Setting the Stage

Book title: _____

How will your setting affect the story?

Beginning: _____

Middle: _____

End: _____

Setting	Where?	When?
Author's Way		
My Way		

©The Mailbox® • Superbook® • TEC61050

Note to the teacher: Use with "Time Travels" on page 39.

Pickle Patterns
Use with "In a Pickle" on page 40.

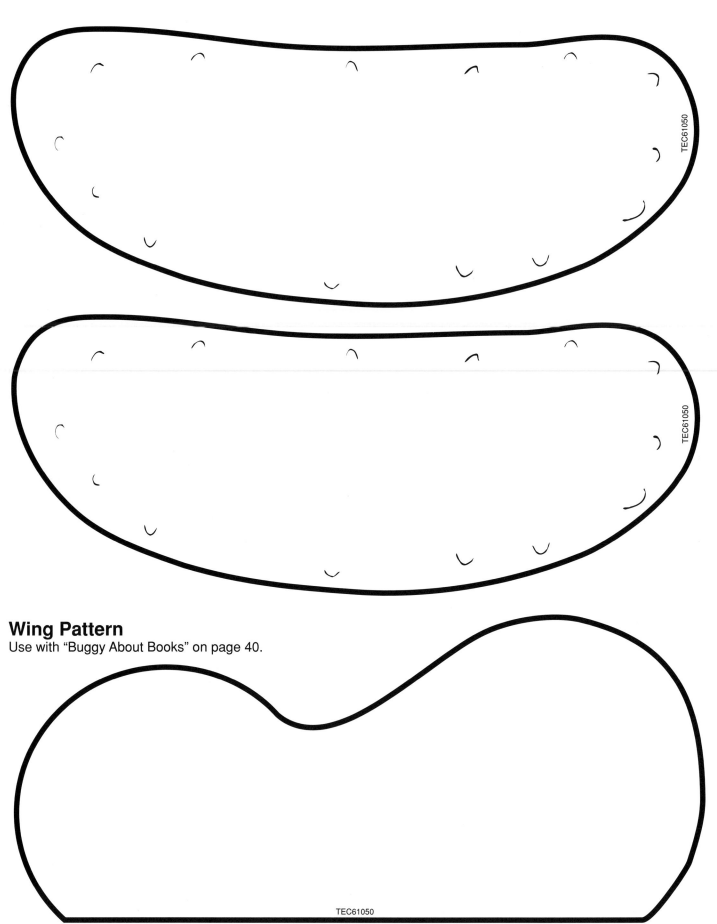

Wing Pattern
Use with "Buggy About Books" on page 40.

BOOK REPORTS & BEYOND

Five Ways to Share a Book

Book reports and literature sharing can be accomplished in a variety of ways. Encourage students to try some of the activities listed below.

- Invent a game that correlates with the plot of the book. Design a gameboard, write a list of instructions for playing the game, and add game pieces that relate to the story line.

- Make a map showing the setting of the story. Include a legend or map key to identify places on the map.

- Make a glossary of important words used in the story.

- Find another book by the same author or a book with a similar subject and compare the two stories.

- Create a character mobile from a wire hanger, string, and construction paper.

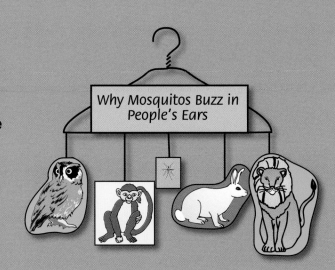

Why Mosquitos Buzz in People's Ears

Charlotte's Web
by
E. B. White

Illustrated by
Garth Williams

Story Sandwiches

Here's a tasty way for students to make a book report presentation! To complete his report, each student cuts out the patterns on page 45. He traces the bread pattern twice on a sheet of light brown construction paper and then cuts out the pieces to make two slices of bread. Next, the child programs each piece of his sandwich listed below, colors its contents, and stacks the pieces in the order shown. He uses a hole puncher and a brass fastener to assemble the pieces of his sandwich.

- top slice of bread: the title, author, and illustrator of the book
- lettuce: a list of the characters
- cheese: a description of the story's setting
- meat: a description of the story's plot
- bottom slice of bread: the student's reaction to the story

Scrapbook Reports

Create a class scrapbook with details from a chapter book. Purchase a blank scrapbook. Assign each student or group of students a chapter from the book and designate a page in the scrapbook for each chapter. Instruct the student or group to brainstorm important details from the chapter; then select items to represent the details on the list. Allow students to draw pictures or find actual items to glue on the designated pages of the scrapbook. To complete the page, the student writes a few sentences summarizing the chapter. Provide time for each student (or group) to present his scrapbook page to the class.

Character Conversations

This book report idea has students writing a dialogue between two story characters. Place students in pairs to represent two story characters; then challenge them to imagine what each character might say in a specific situation. What would Mary and Laura Ingalls discuss as they rode across the prairie in a covered wagon? How would Encyclopedia Brown confront a suspect in a case? Have students script the conversation, rehearse it, and then model the dialogue for the class. By the end of the assignment, the students will have reviewed several areas of the language arts curriculum!

Story Timelines

To help students gain an understanding of the story line, have them fashion a timeline showing the important events of a book. Give each student or group of students a length of bulletin board paper. Have students determine the overall structure of the book. Is it more logical to break it down into increments of time or by story events? Did the story take place over the span of a year or in a single day? Instruct students to determine the most appropriate way to outline the story; then mark chronological increments on the bulletin board paper. Label each increment with a sentence, a phrase, or an illustration of a story event and the time it took place. Have students compare the completed timelines to observe the similarities and differences in their classmates' interpretations.

bread

lettuce

meat

cheese

TEC61050

Grammar and Sentence Skills

A Proper Poem

Here's a poetic approach to helping students remember to capitalize proper nouns. Display the poem shown or give each student an individual copy (see page 57). Read each verse with students. Then revisit the first three verses and have volunteers name examples of the corresponding proper nouns. If desired, ask each student to keep a copy of the poem in his writing folder and encourage him to use it as a capitalization reference. **Capitalization**

Proper Noun Poem

Every **name** is a proper noun,
Whether it's for a person, a pet, or a town.

Months and **days** need capitals too.
So do **holidays**, it's true.

And don't forget that **states** and **streets**
Need capital letters to be complete.

Remember these tips and set proper nouns apart.
Use capital letters at the start!

Jan.	Marcus, Chloe
Feb.	
Mar.	Tanisha
Apr.	Scott, Ravi
May	
June	
July	Sami
Aug.	
Sept.	Joella, Nicky
Oct.	
Nov.	Miguel
Dec.	

The Short Way

These quick and easy ideas give students real-life practice using abbreviations. For reinforcement, instruct students to write the abbreviations with markers or colored pencils. **Capitalization**

Personal Titles: Divide students into small groups and give each group a blank booklet with construction paper covers and several white pages. Instruct each group to make a school staff directory that includes each staff member's title (Mr., Mrs., and Ms.). Give the directories to students who join your class midyear.

Days: Have each student list the abbreviations for the days of the week. Then encourage him to keep a log of his after-school activities throughout the week.

Months: Ask each youngster to list the months of the year, writing abbreviations for them as appropriate. Then invite each student, in turn, to announce his birthday month. Have each student write the names of his classmates beside the corresponding months or abbreviations. The completed lists are sure to help students keep track of upcoming birthdays!

"FLIP" for Titles

Begin this poster project with a nifty capitalization tip. Write "FLIP" vertically on the board. Tell students that the word will help them remember how to correctly capitalize titles. Then incorporate the words *first, last, important,* and *pronouns* as shown, explaining that they describe the words that should be capitalized in titles. Point out that small words such as *a, but,* and *of* should not be capitalized unless they are at the beginning or end of a title.

Next, give each student a large sheet of paper. Ask her to label it with a new title for her favorite book, movie, or television show. Encourage her to write a title that has at least three words. After she uses the acronym *FLIP* to check her work, invite her to illustrate her poster. **Capitalization**

First
Last
Important
Pronouns

Look in Books!

For this word scavenger hunt, divide students into small groups. Give each group a few grade-appropriate books, several small sticky notes, and one sheet of paper. Then ask each group to find in its books a designated number of words that demonstrate different capitalization rules. For added fun, challenge students to be the first group to accomplish the task. When a group finds an appropriate word, the students flag the page with a sticky note. Then a group member writes the word and the reason it is capitalized. At the conclusion of the search, ask each group to tell the class about its finds. **Capitalization**

Sentence Sensation

Whether you want to review just one capitalization rule or several of them, this activity has letter-perfect possibilities. Collect a class supply of letter manipulatives or cards, omitting less commonly used letters. Give each youngster a sentence strip and have him take a letter or card at random. Then instruct him to write a sentence with a capitalized word that begins with his chosen letter. For a greater challenge, ask students to write sentences that demonstrate certain capitalization rules. Post each student's sentence with his letter and use the display for an ongoing review of capitalization rules. **Capitalization**

B

We drove our car on Bradley Street.

Questions, Answers, and More

A handy end-mark reference is the result of this simple idea. Cut a picture from a magazine and glue it at the top of a sheet of chart paper. Below the picture, list three relevant, unpunctuated sentences: an exclamation, a question, and a statement. To begin, display the paper and have students read the sentences. Then invite them to tell what end mark is needed for each sentence and why. Once you confirm the correct punctuation, have students use different colors of markers to punctuate the sentences. Display the resulting poster in a prominent classroom location as a reminder of the correct use of exclamation marks, question marks, and periods. **End marks**

Wow, look at this chocolate cake!

Would you like a piece of cake?

I want a huge piece of cake.

Punctuation Fishbowl

Use this sentence-writing idea for either quick daily practice or as a unit review. Make several colorful copies of the fish cards on page 57 and then cut them out. Program each card with an end mark so that there are at least two cards for each of the three types of punctuation. Place the cards in an unbreakable fishbowl or a similar container.

To begin, have three or four students each remove a card from the container at random. Ask each cardholder to announce the type of punctuation on his card. Then post the cards in a row on the board. Next, instruct all of the students to write a sentence with each displayed end mark, using the end marks in the order they are posted. After the students complete their writing, direct their attention to each end mark, in turn. Have each of several volunteers read aloud his corresponding sentence and tell whether it is a statement, a command, an exclamation, or a question. **Writing sentences**

Sentence Drama

Invite students to practice the four types of sentences with this role-playing activity. Review the definitions of statements, questions, commands, and exclamations. Then place students in groups of four to create sentence dramas. Assign each group a situation to act out, such as Johnny trying to convince his mother to buy him a bike or three friends trying to equally share two apples. Have the students in each group work together to write a script for the situation. The script should consist of four sentences, one of each of the types mentioned above. After each group composes and rehearses a script, sit back and enjoy the shows! Hold the audience members accountable for identifying the types of sentences in each skit. **Types of sentences**

Fragment Alert

Increase students' awareness of sentence fragments by proposing a challenge. After a discussion on distinguishing a sentence fragment from a complete sentence, encourage students to speak only in complete sentences for a designated time period. During that time (can they make it an entire hour?), every utterance must have a subject and predicate and tell a complete thought. Have students keep track of how many times they hear an incomplete sentence (they will be listening to your sentences too!) and discuss the results at the end of the time period. **Complete sentences**

Would you like to drive this car?

statement   exclamation
question   command

Choose, Spin, and Write!

To prepare this small-group activity, have students cut out a variety of pictures from magazines. Collect the pictures and place them in a shallow box or a large manila envelope. Cut out a copy of the spinner pattern on page 58.

To begin, give each student a sheet of writing paper. Then ask one student to take a picture at random and show it to the group. Have her spin the spinner and name the corresponding type of sentence. Then instruct each student to write an original sentence of that type about the picture. After each student finishes his writing, have him read his sentence aloud. To continue, set the picture aside and have a different student take another picture and spin the spinner. **Types of sentences**

Super Shoppers

This bargain of an idea gives students practice using commas in a series. Write on the board a correctly punctuated sentence that lists three or more things that you might buy. Demonstrate how omitting commas or changing their placement can influence the clarity or meaning of the sentence.

Next, ask students to imagine that they can buy anything they would like for several different people. To write about their imagined purchases, have each student title a sheet of paper as shown. Ask her to list the names of several family members or friends. Beside each name, instruct her to use proper punctuation in a sentence that tells three or more things she would like to buy for the corresponding person. To check her work, have her highlight the commas and the word in each sentence that follows the last comma in the series. **Commas**

At the Store

Jack: I would buy a CD, roller skates, and a television.

Dad: I would buy a car, lawn mower, and motorcycle.

Mom: I would buy a boat, dishwasher, and necklace.

Carrie: I would buy a dollhouse, bike, and horse.

Wish You Were Here!

Once students are familiar with comma rules for letters, dates, and addresses, invite them to create picture postcards. To begin, write the school's address on the board for student reference. Next, have each student illustrate his dream vacation on the unlined side of a 5" x 8" index card. Then instruct him to draw a line down the center of the lined side of the card. To the left of the line, ask him to write a letter to the class about the vacation. After he checks his punctuation, have him write the school's address to the right of the line and add a sticker to resemble a postage stamp.

To showcase students' completed work, punch a hole in the top of each card and add a length of string for a hanger. Hang the cards on a titled board so that students may turn the cards and view both sides. **Commas**

Dear class,
   I went surfing today. It was really cool. The waves were huge!

Your friend,
   Alex

Ms. Brown's Class
Best Elementary
Small Town, PA 55555

"Why did you cross the road?" asked the dog.

"To get to the other side," said the chicken.

Showtime!

What better way to explore dialogue than with puppets? Place two puppets at a center stocked with writing paper. Post a two-sentence dialogue for students to use as a punctuation model. Arrange for three students to visit the center at a time. To introduce the center to students, explain that they will write puppet scripts. If desired, encourage students to write scripts that they can later present to children in a lower grade.

To prepare a script, two students perform a brief dialogue with the puppets as another student writes it. Once the exchange is written, the students write any additional information needed to clarify which puppet character spoke each sentence. Then they check their punctuation. **Quotation marks**

Whose Things?

This activity is packed with apostrophe practice! Place 12 familiar items in a small suitcase (or tote bag) and cut out a copy of the owner cards on page 58. To complete the activity, a student titles a half sheet of paper as shown. She pairs each card with an item. Then she lists the possessive forms of the words on the cards with the corresponding items. **Apostrophes**

Things I Packed
my brother's racecar
Uncle Max's key
Mom's book
Aunt Mary's recipe
a child's bear
my teacher's ruler

my teacher

Attracted to Sentences

Magnetic words make forming complete sentences hands-on fun! To prepare this center activity, bring to school a store-bought set of magnetic words or make a set of word manipulatives with magnetic paper. To designate an area for using the words, use bulletin board border to frame a section of a large magnetic board or the side of a filing cabinet. When a student visits the area, encourage him to use the words to form as many complete sentences as he can within a designated amount of time. Then have him write each sentence on a sheet of paper. **Complete sentences**

My mother planted carrots in our garden.

planted

mother

Take Two!

Use this class book project to remind students that a complete sentence has two parts. Give each student two blank cards: one white and one colorful. Instruct her to write a noun on the white card and a verb on the colorful card. Label a separate paper lunch bag for each of the two parts of speech. Then have each youngster deposit her cards in the appropriate bags.

Next, give each student a sheet of drawing paper. Ask her to take one card at random from each bag. Instruct her to write a sentence at the bottom of her paper, using the words in the subject and predicate. Then have her illustrate her sentence. Compile students' completed papers into a book titled "Simply Sentences." On each of several days, read a few pages from the book and have students identify the subject and predicate in each sentence. It's a quick way to warm up their language skills! **Subjects and predicates**

Time to Trade

Subjects and predicates are the focus of this simple class activity. Give each student a blank card. Also give him a copy of a blank two-column chart titled as shown. Then announce a kid-pleasing writing prompt, such as the day that aliens visited the school. Have each youngster write a relevant complete sentence on his card and sign his name. Next, instruct students to trade their cards with one another. After each student silently reads the sentence he received, have him write the subject and predicate in the appropriate columns on his paper. Instruct students to repeat the trading, reading, and writing process a designated number of times. Then ask them to return the cards to their owners. **Subjects and predicates**

Subjects	Predicates
All of the kids	watched the aliens land their spaceship.
The aliens	had long legs and lots of arms.
The spaceship	had flashing yellow lights.

Alicia is on the swim team.

The girls on her team think they will win the next meet.

Official Daily Subject

Daily Subject

Spark students' interest in writing sentences with some of their favorite topics: themselves and their classmates! Each day designate a different student as the Official Daily Subject. To learn more about the youngster and her interests, invite the class to ask her three questions. Then have each classmate write two positive sentences about the student, and ask the honored youngster to write two sentences about herself. Instruct each student to use a colored pencil to underline the complete subject in each of her sentences.

After you check students' work, place all of the papers in a construction paper folder and encourage the Official Daily Subject to take them home. Repeat the activity until each student has had a turn as the topic of the day. **Complete subjects**

Schoolwide Search

This school tour is a creative way to review nouns. Divide students into small groups. Give each group one copy of the recording sheet on page 59 and a clipboard or other portable writing surface. Assign each group a different location in the school, such as your classroom, the library, the office, or the cafeteria. Instruct one student in each group to write the names of her group members and their assigned location on the recording sheet. Then arrange for each group to visit its location for a designated amount of time.

During their visit, have group members record their observations by listing the corresponding nouns. Remind them to capitalize any proper nouns that they write. After all of the students return to the classroom, create a poster-size chart of each group's favorite listed nouns. **Nouns**

People	Places	Things
Ms. Roberts	office	fax machine
Mr. Hood	gym	telephone
parent	library	basketball
baby		mats
kids		shelves

Illustrated Grammar

Have students look through old magazines for pictures of people, places, and things. Ask them to work individually or in pairs to create lists of nouns and relevant verbs. Challenge students to write at least five nouns and five verbs for each picture. For a variation, reverse the lesson by giving your students a list of nouns and verbs and having them create pictures that illustrate the words. **Nouns**

A Busy Day

Invite students to recap the previous day's activities with this look at verbs. To begin, ask each youngster to write a paragraph about what he did the previous day. Encourage him to write about routine activities as well as any special things he did. After each student completes his writing, have him circle all of the verbs he used. Next, ask volunteers to name their verbs and challenge their classmates to tell whether each verb is an action verb or a form of the verb *be*. Then have each student determine how many action verbs he included in his writing. **Verbs**

Super Substitutions

How are pronouns helpful? That's what students find out with this editing activity. On an overhead transparency, write three or four sentences about one or more familiar staff members without using any pronouns. Display the sentences on an overhead projector. Read the sentences aloud and then invite students' feedback about how your writing sounds. Guide students to realize that using pronouns in place of some of the nouns would make the sentences sound better. Then invite volunteers to edit the sentences by replacing some of the nouns with pronouns. After the sentences are edited, read them again. Students are sure to agree that little words can make a big difference! **Pronouns**

Artful Descriptions

Promote art appreciation with this exploration of adjectives. Display a picture of a famous work of art. Ask students to silently study the artwork for a few moments. Then give each youngster a half sheet of paper and have her list ten adjectives to describe the artwork. After all students have finished their lists, have them, in turn, name one of their adjectives. (Encourage students not to repeat previously named adjectives.) Then discuss how the variety of words reflects different reactions to the art. **Adjectives**

From Cover to Cover

Picture book illustrations are the springboard for this adjective display. To prepare, back a small bulletin board with a light color of paper and title it "Picture-Perfect Words." Set a supply of colorful markers nearby. To begin, pair students. Then give each twosome one picture book and a supply of small sticky notes. As the students in each pair look through their book, have them write adjectives on sticky notes to describe chosen illustrations. Instruct them to flag the illustrations with the corresponding sticky notes. After each twosome has written at least five adjectives, invite the students in each pair to write their three favorite adjectives in large letters on the bulletin board. The result will be a valuable word-choice reference!
Adjectives

Lion Escapes!

A lion escaped from the zoo early today. Eyewitnesses said the lion ran everywhere. The police promise that the lion will be caught quickly.

How, When, and Where?

Try this newsworthy approach to adverbs. Divide a sheet of chart paper into three columns. Title the first column "How," the second column "When," and the third column "Where." Post the chart and guide students to brainstorm a list of corresponding adverbs for each column. Next, announce a made-up news event likely to interest students, such as a lion escaping from a zoo. Have each youngster write an appropriate headline on provided paper. Then instruct him to write a brief paragraph that includes adverbs that give information such as how, when, and where the event occurred. Encourage students to refer to the brainstormed lists as needed. After each reporter completes his writing, ask volunteers to read their news bulletins aloud and have their classmates identify the adverbs. **Adverbs**

Hot-Potato Grammar

Use this game to make the parts of speech a hot topic in your classroom. Label a separate beanbag for each part of speech you wish to reinforce. Program a class supply of paper strips with words that are examples of the parts of speech, writing one word per strip. Place the strips in a container. To begin, instruct students to sit in a circle and pass the beanbags around as you play some music. After a few moments, stop the music and remove a strip of paper from the container. Read the word aloud, use it in a sentence, and have students identify the part of speech. Then ask the youngster who has the corresponding beanbag to take your role during the next round of play. Resume the music to continue. **Parts of speech**

verb

noun

adjective

moon

shiny

dance

quiet

Under Investigation

The parts of speech are the topic of this word search. Divide a sheet of copy paper into as many columns as the number of parts of speech you want to reinforce. Then title each column with a different part of speech. Give each student a copy of the chart and a copy of a grade-appropriate passage. Next, ask each student to list words from the passage in the appropriate columns, challenging him to list as many as he can within a designated amount of time. At the end of the allotted time, confirm the correct words for each column. Then congratulate the student who correctly categorized the most words. **Parts of speech**

Nouns	Verbs	Adjectives	Adverbs
rabbit carrot pet hutch	hope jump nibble twitch	soft brown young	quickly early

Rolling Into Revision

With this small-group activity, a roll of the die leads to more interesting sentences. Cut out a copy of the die pattern on page 60. Fold the pattern on the thin lines to assemble the die and use tape to secure it. To begin, write on the board a simple sentence, such as "The dog ran." Have each student write the sentence on a sheet of paper. Then ask a student to roll the die and announce the corresponding part of speech. Next, instruct each group member to write the displayed sentence again, this time adding the designated part of speech. Once each youngster completes her sentence, ask a different student to roll the die. Continue as described until students have written a chosen number of sentences. Then invite students to compare their elaborated sentences with the sentence on the board. **Parts of speech**

Mix and Match

This colorful parts-of-speech idea doubles as a sentence-writing activity. Divide a bulletin board into five columns. Write each of these words on a different color of card: *nouns, pronouns, adjectives, verbs,* and *adverbs.* Post each card in a different column. Gather several blank cards of each featured color and distribute them to students. Have students program the cards with words that are the corresponding parts of speech, writing one word per card. Then post each card in the appropriate column.

On each of several days, invite students to write color-coded sentences with chosen words. For added fun, challenge students to write sentences that include designated parts of speech. **Parts of speech**

Check out the skill-building reproducibles on pages 61–64.

Proper Noun Poem

Every **name** is a proper noun,
Whether it's for a person, a pet, or a town.

Months and **days** need capitals too.
So do **holidays,** it's true.

And don't forget that **states** and **streets**
Need capital letters to be complete.

Remember these tips and set proper nouns apart.
Use capital letters at the start!

TEC61050

TEC61050

TEC61050

TEC61050

TEC61050

Owner Cards
Use with "Whose Things?" on page 50.

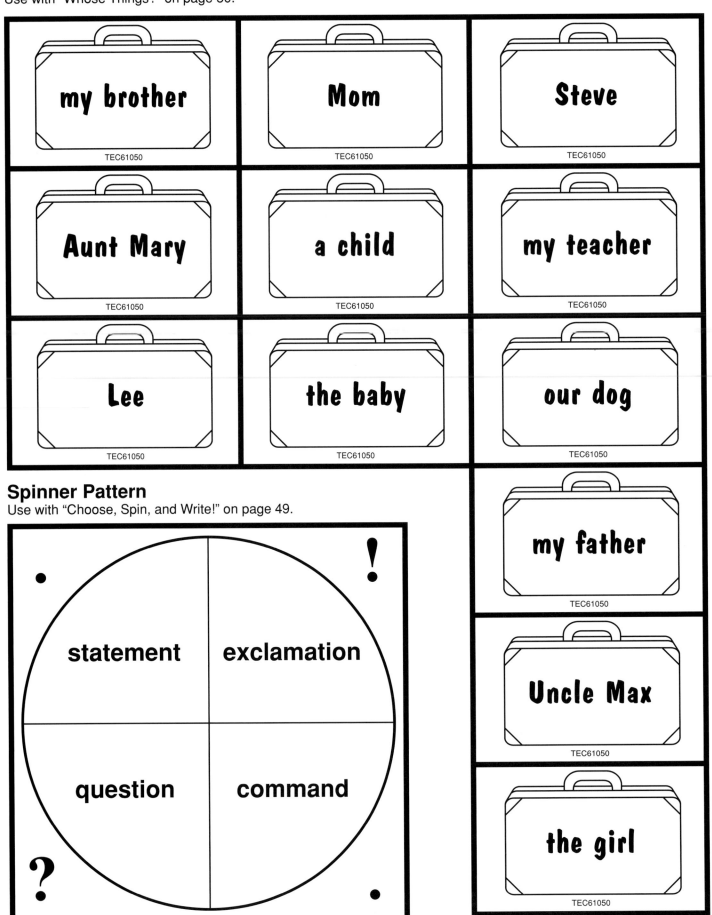

my brother

TEC61050

Mom

TEC61050

Steve

TEC61050

Aunt Mary

TEC61050

a child

TEC61050

my teacher

TEC61050

Lee

TEC61050

the baby

TEC61050

our dog

TEC61050

my father

TEC61050

Uncle Max

TEC61050

the girl

TEC61050

Spinner Pattern
Use with "Choose, Spin, and Write!" on page 49.

!

statement

exclamation

question

command

?

Name _____

Noun Search

Remember:
A proper noun begins with a capital letter.

Location: _____

People	Places	Things

Note to the teacher: Use with "Schoolwide Search" on page 53.

59

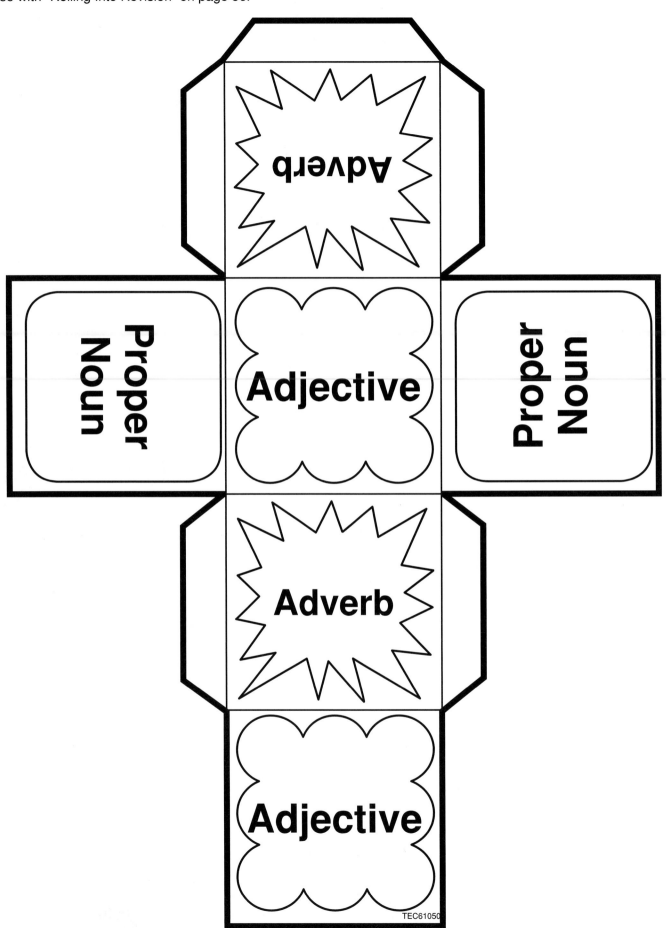

Adverb

Proper Noun

Adjective

Proper Noun

Adverb

Adjective

TEC61050

Ready to Race

Draw a circle around each letter that should be capitalized.

1. lily and lester will drive in a race on saturday.

2. The last time they raced was in march.

3. This is the biggest race in may.

4. The race is the day before mother's day.

5. lily trained for the race on mondays and wednesdays.

6. lester liked to train on tuesdays and thursdays.

7. Many people will drive to speedy city to see the race.

8. They may come from as far away as south town.

9. If lily wins, the two cats will race again in june.

10. If lester wins, the next race will be on the fourth of july.

To find out who won the race, color each letter you circled.
Unscramble the letters you did not color.
Then write the winner's name.

M	F	S	C	L	E	M
L	S	T	E	J	L	S
S	M	L	W	L	T	L
T	L	M	J	D	R	T

The winner: _____

Banana-Boat Float

Add the correct end mark to each sentence.
For each end mark, color a matching banana slice.

1. The Tasty Treat Shop has a great new dessert ___

2. Has anyone told you about it yet ___

3. Wow, that is a really big dessert ___

4. It is called a super banana-boat float ___

5. Boy, it will take a very long time to eat it ___

6. The dessert has five scoops of ice cream ___

7. What is your favorite flavor of ice cream ___

8. You can order an extra scoop ___

9. I always like the toppings the best ___

10. Do you like hot fudge or strawberries better ___

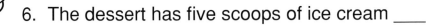

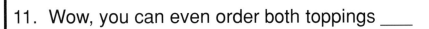

11. Wow, you can even order both toppings ___

12. Banana slices cover the top of the dessert ___

13. Many people want some cherries on top too ___

14. Would you like to order a banana-boat float ___

15. Hey, let's order one dessert and share it ___

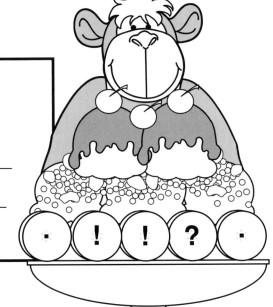

All Tied Up

If the punctuation is correct, color the circle in the *yes* column.
If the punctuation is incorrect, color the circle in the *no* column.
Then make the punctuation correct.

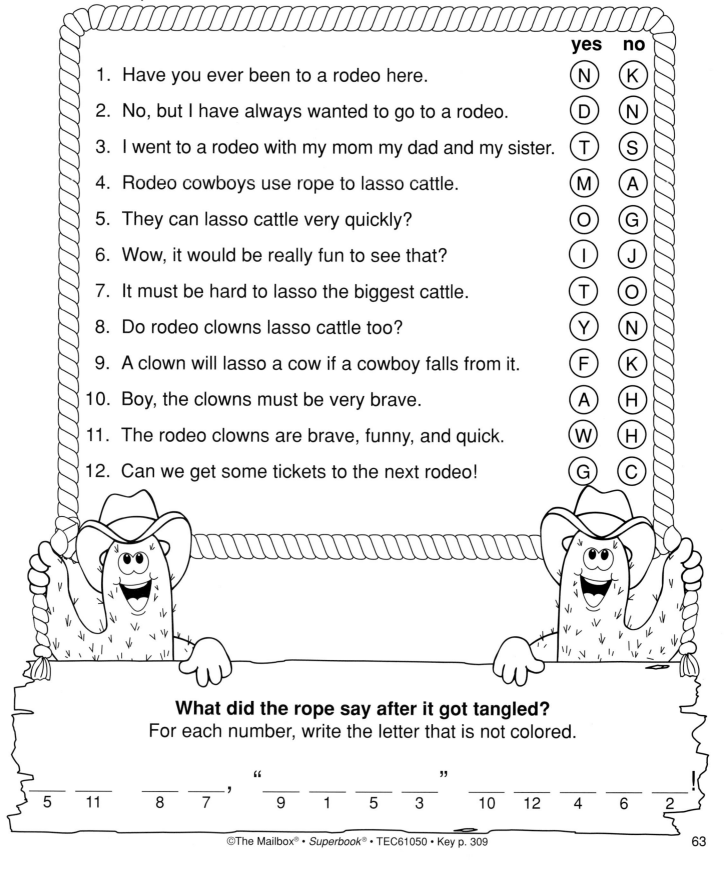

		yes	no
1.	Have you ever been to a rodeo here.	N	K
2.	No, but I have always wanted to go to a rodeo.	D	N
3.	I went to a rodeo with my mom my dad and my sister.	T	S
4.	Rodeo cowboys use rope to lasso cattle.	M	A
5.	They can lasso cattle very quickly?	O	G
6.	Wow, it would be really fun to see that?	I	J
7.	It must be hard to lasso the biggest cattle.	T	O
8.	Do rodeo clowns lasso cattle too?	Y	N
9.	A clown will lasso a cow if a cowboy falls from it.	F	K
10.	Boy, the clowns must be very brave.	A	H
11.	The rodeo clowns are brave, funny, and quick.	W	H
12.	Can we get some tickets to the next rodeo!	G	C

What did the rope say after it got tangled?
For each number, write the letter that is not colored.

___ ___ ___ ___ , " ___ ___ ___ ___ " ___ ___ ___ ___ !
5   11   8   7   9   1   5   3   10   12   4   6   2

Name_____

All About Us

Use the color code to underline the
  words in each series.
Then add commas to each sentence.

Color Code
red = the first item in a series
yellow = the second item in a series
blue = the third item in a series

1. My favorite colors are red yellow and blue.

2. I love to wear shirts pants and shoes that are these colors.

3. I wear these colors when I play go to school or stay home.

4. My bike coat and bedroom are yellow.

5. My hobby is making painting and fixing model cars.

6. I put my cars on shelves in cases and on my desk.

7. I win prizes ribbons and trophies at model-car shows.

8. My best cars are gifts from my dad mom and best friend.

9. My favorite subjects at school are math spelling and art.

10. I like to add subtract and spell at school.

11. I like books that are about dogs space and sports.

12. I am happy when I paint pictures draw posters or make
    things with clay.

Words in Season

Provide a vocabulary-building review of compound words with a learning center that changes with the seasons. Place a supply of index cards, scissors, colored pencils, and a dictionary in a center. To use the center, a student brainstorms a list of compound words related to the season, checks the spellings of the words in the dictionary, and then writes each word on an index card. The student illustrates each word on the back of the cutout. She then cuts apart the word in a puzzle-piece fashion, separating the individual words of the compound. Store each student's completed puzzle pieces in a decorated envelope at the center for other students to assemble.

Compound words

Alyssa

In this room, you will find good things to eat like grapefruit, oatmeal, peanuts, and pancakes. Many of these also have a dishwasher.

This is the kitchen.

Everyday Words

Give each small group of students a location—such as the classroom, the library, the playground, or the cafeteria—and have them brainstorm a list of compound words found there. Next, have a member of each group share the group's list aloud while you record the words on the board. Then have each student choose five words from one location and use them in a set of sentences. She writes the sentences on a piece of drawing paper without naming the location. Then she underlines each compound word and adds illustrations. On the back of her paper, she names the location where her compound words are found. Bind the completed pages in a book titled "Compounds All Around" and place it in your classroom library.
Compound words

Mix 'n' Match

To prepare this fun center, program white sentence strips with the first word of a common compound word. On each strip, cut two slits about five inches apart, as shown, and laminate them for durability. Trim about a half-inch off the width of a supply of colored sentence strips. Program each colored strip with three words, one or two of which will make a compound word when added to the initial word. Place the strip sets at a center with a dictionary, paper, and pencils. A child chooses one white strip and one colored strip. He feeds the colored strip through the slits and slides the strip to reveal each word. If the combined words make a compound, he records it on his paper. Encourage him to use the dictionary to confirm his answers. He continues until he has made ten compound words. If desired, also program white strips with the second word in a compound as shown. **Compound words**

sun flower

y foot

basket ball

light

Two of a Kind

Reinforce identifying synonyms each time you group students for partner work. In advance, label index cards with synonym pairs, one word per card. Be sure to make enough so each student has one. Randomly pass out one card to each child and have her find her classmate with the matching synonym card. As an alternative, organize small groups in the same manner, labeling sets of four cards with synonyms and allowing time for students to find classmates with matching synonym cards. **Synonyms**

Synonym Snakes

To prepare this small-group activity, cut a supply of construction paper circles for each group. Pass out the circles and assign each group a commonly used word. Have one group member write the word on a circle; then encourage the group members to brainstorm as many synonyms as they can for the word. Have the designated recorder write each synonym on a separate circle. Then have the other group members glue the circles together to resemble a snake, adding an additional circle for its head. If desired, have one student trace over the words with a black pen or marker. Have student groups share the synonyms on their snakes aloud; then post them as a visual reference.
Synonyms

happy   glad   pleased   delighted   chipper   sunny

Seven Up, Affix-Style

This twist on a classroom favorite helps students identify synonyms and antonyms. To start, give each child three sticky notes. Have him write his name and a pair of antonyms or synonyms on each one. Choose seven students to go to the front of the room with their sticky notes. The rest of the students lay their heads on their desks, cover their eyes, and put one of their thumbs in the air. Each of the seven students quietly moves around the room and places one of his sticky notes on a classmate's thumb. When all of the students have done so, they return to the front of the room and announce, "Heads up, seven up." Each student who received a sticky note stands up and, one at a time, reads the name and words on the note. He states whether the words are synonyms or antonyms. If correct, he takes his sticky notes to the front of the room while the student who chose him sits down. If incorrect, he sits down and the student who chose him stays up front. Once a player is out of sticky notes, he must sit out for the remainder of the game. Play continues in this manner until time is up.
Synonyms and antonyms

Match Point

Pair each student with a buddy to test his knowledge of antonyms. Prior to joining his partner, have each student secretly compose a list of ten antonym pairs. Keeping his list a secret, he joins his partner. Player 1 calls out a word from his list, and Player 2 names an antonym for the word. If her response matches what was written, she is awarded one point. Extra points are added for each additional antonym she names. Then the roles are reversed, and Player 2 calls out a word from her list. Play continues until both partners have called out each word on their lists. For an extra challenge, have the students play a second round using synonym pairs. **Antonyms**

Sing-Along Time

After a few rounds of this song, students are sure to remember the difference between antonyms and synonyms! **Antonyms**

Antonym Anthem
(sung to the tune of "Mary Had a Little Lamb")

Antonyms are opposites,
Opposites, opposites.
Antonyms are opposites,
Synonyms mean the same.

Antonyms are stop and go,
Fast and slow, yes and no.
Antonyms are opposites,
Synonyms mean the same.

Opposite Tales

Incorporate creative writing into this antonym activity. Have your students brainstorm a list of antonym pairs while you record their responses on the board. Instruct each student to select one word from a predetermined number of the pairs to use in a paragraph. After writing, each student underlines the words he chose from the list. The student then replaces each underlined word with its antonym. Provide time for students to share their "Opposite Tales" with the class. **Antonyms**

Word-Pair Dare

Place students in small groups to brainstorm as many pairs of homophones as possible. Compile the lists on a piece of chart paper and delete duplicate entries. When students have generated a list containing at least a class set of pairs, have each student select a different pair. On a piece of drawing paper, she writes a sentence using each homophone. Then she illustrates each sentence. Bind the completed pages in a book titled "How Many Homophones?" **Homophones**

A <u>hare</u> is an animal with long ears.
A buffalo is a large animal with <u>hair</u>.

Find the Treasure

To create this center, make several copies of the coin patterns on page 75 on yellow paper. Cut out the patterns; then program each coin with a homophone. To make the coins self-checking, label each homophone pair with a matching number on the backs of the coins. Next, cover an empty, rectangular baby wipe container with wood-grain contact paper (treasure chest). Place the coin cutouts in the treasure chest, and place it at a center. To complete the center, a student removes all of the coins from the chest and matches each homophone pair. He flips the cards over to check his work and then places the pair back in the treasure chest. **Homophones**

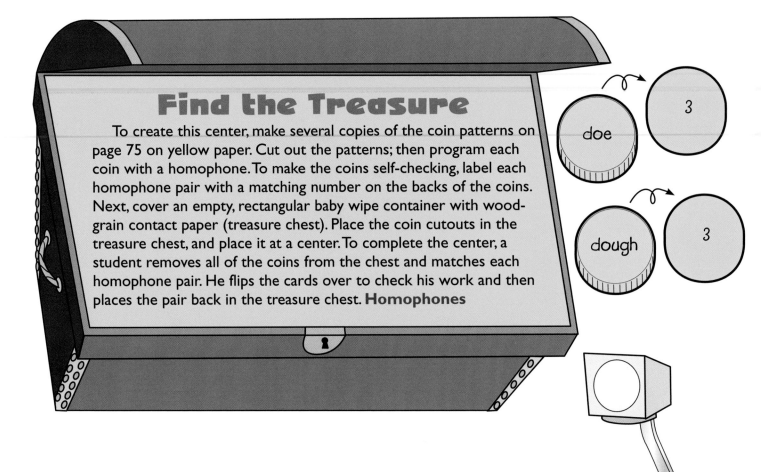

On the Hunt

Reinforce the correct meaning of each word in a homophone pair. Compose on an overhead transparency a paragraph that contains several homophones. Use the incorrect choice for several of the homophones. Display the paragraph for the class and have students identify which words were used incorrectly. Then have the class copy the paragraph, making the necessary corrections. **Homophones**

On the Hunt
Last knight, I went to a fancy party. At first I did knot no what to where, but then my made helped me pick out just the write outfit. Eye wore a blew dress and sum hi-heeled shoes. It was fun to get dressed up. I cannot weight to do it again!

Not Another "Bored" Game

To prepare this small-group game, give each student an index card. Have her write on the card a sentence using a homophone, and have her underline the homophone. Collect the cards and divide students into small groups. Give each group a small chalkboard or whiteboard and an appropriate writing tool. Choose a card and read the underlined word. Then read the sentence. Each group works together to correctly spell the homophone used in the sentence. Then they turn the board toward the teacher when completed. Award a point to each team that correctly spells the homophone. Choose a new card and continue play until all cards have been read. The team with the most points wins.
Homophones

I put my library book over <u>there</u>, but now I can't find it.

Polishing Up

Make use of your mismatched playing cards with this partner game. Cut pieces from an 8½" x 11" mailing label to fit your cards. Peel off the backing and secure a label to the face of each card. Write one word of a homophone pair on each card, making at least ten pairs. Shuffle the cards and place them at a center. A child places all of the cards facedown and turns over two cards. If he makes a homophone match, he removes the cards and takes another turn. If he does not make a match, he turns the cards facedown and his partner takes a turn. Play continues in this manner until all pairs have been matched.
Homophones

your

you're

whole

Attention, Please!

Spotlight homophones on your word wall with this simple idea. Before posting a word that has a homophone partner, place a sticker with it. Inform students that the sticker shows that the word sounds like another word but can be spelled another way and has a different meaning. Also encourage students to refer to a dictionary if they are unsure which form of the word to use. By drawing attention to the word, students become more aware of choosing—and spelling—the correct word in their work.
Homophones

Growing New Words

Give a copy of page 76 to each student pair; then have the students cut out the mat and word cards. A partner places a word card on the root word box and reads each prefix and suffix with the root word. He records the combinations that make new words on a separate sheet of paper and glues the root word at the end of the list. Then his partner chooses a new root word and records its words. The pair continues in this manner until all of the root words have been used. **Word parts**

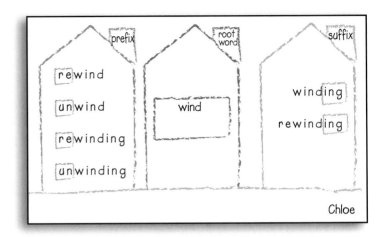

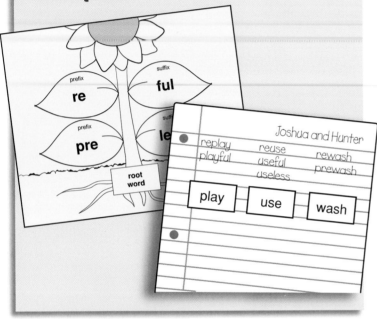

Simple Structures

Build understanding of word parts with this student-made graphic organizer. Post a root word on the board. Have each student list on a sheet of paper all the words she knows that use that word. After her list is complete, give each student a sheet of drawing paper and instruct her to draw three house shapes. Next, she outlines each house with a different color crayon. She draws a chimney on each house and labels it as shown. Then she writes the root word in the middle house and sorts the words from her list into the corresponding houses, placing any words that contain both prefixes and suffixes in both houses. Finally, she draws a box around each word part, using the corresponding-colored crayon. **Word parts**

Root Word "Eggs-change"

This center activity has students hunting for new words. Gather 12 plastic eggs and two baskets. Use a permanent marker to write a prefix on the left half of an egg and a matching root word on the right. Separate the egg and place each half in a basket. Continue with the remaining eggs. Then use an index card to label each basket to match its contents. Place the baskets, a supply of paper, and pencils at a center. A child chooses an egg half from the prefix basket and adds an egg half from the root word basket. If the halves make a word, he writes the word on his paper. Then he removes the root word and attaches another. He continues in this manner until all of the root words have been used. He then chooses a new prefix to build upon and continues in the same manner until he has used a dozen prefixes. **Word parts**

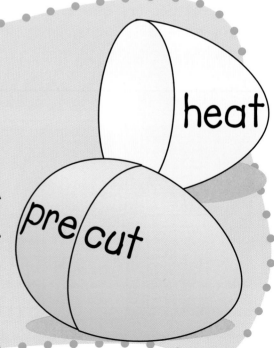

Word Trains

Put students on the right track to identify word parts with this locomotive word display. Duplicate several sets of the train patterns on page 75 on heavy tagboard. To make a word train, each student will need colored construction paper, crayons or markers, glue, and access to a dictionary. Have each student use the train patterns to trace each car on his construction paper. Then the student peruses the dictionary for a word containing both a prefix and a suffix. Ask him to write the prefix on the engine, the root word on the boxcar, and the suffix on the caboose. After cutting out each piece, the student glues the cars together. Mount the completed word trains on a bulletin board titled "All Aboard the Word Express!" **Word parts**

re   view   ing   use   ness

Partner Patrol

Send your students on a scavenger hunt for examples of prefixed words. Distribute a dictionary and assign a prefix to each pair of students. Have partners work together to find five words with the designated prefix. In addition, ask each pair to find two words that begin with the same prefixed letters but are not a prefixed word. Instruct the pair to write each word on a notecard. When the class is ready, call on the pairs to share their findings. Have them display their cards for the class to observe. After announcing the letters of the prefix and its meaning, the partners call on volunteers to identify the two "outlaw" words in the set. Then have each pair code its word cards for self-checking. Store the cards in a center for students to use during free time. **Prefixes**

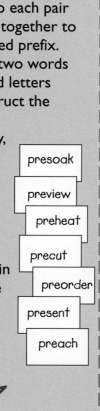

presoak
preview
preheat
precut
preorder
present
preach

Our outlaw words are present and preach.

1. almost
2. burst
3. least
4. stroke

Shopping for Words

Looking for a way to spice up students' spelling work? Notepads designed for grocery lists are the answer! Have students use the decorative paper to record the week's words, to alphabetize their words, or to show syllabication. Put a notepad at a spelling center for students to record their center work as well. Spelling

Personal Dictionaries

Spelling lists will always be on hand when your students have their own personal spelling dictionaries. To make a spelling journal, bind 26 pieces of lined notebook paper inside a letter-size manila folder. Provide markers or crayons for each student to decorate his covers. Then have him label each page with a letter of the alphabet. After a student is given a new list of words, have him copy each word on the corresponding page in his dictionary. The dictionary should be kept in the student's desk as a reference during writing time, spelling games, and independent studying. **Spelling**

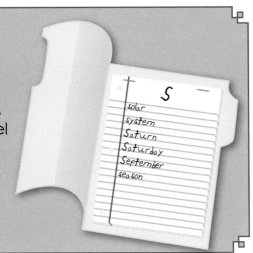

Word Examinations

Help your students learn their spelling lists by identifying familiar parts of each word. Model the process for the students the first time the activity is used; then allow students to complete the process on their own in the following weeks. Review the spelling list with the class. Ask a volunteer to select a word and identify letter combinations, prefixes, suffixes, or mnemonic devices that make the word easier to spell. Use a different color marker to write the identified part of the word on an overhead projector transparency. Fill in the remaining letters with black marker. Demonstrate a few examples; then have students try it on their own. Discuss the results with the class. Each student will find a way to remember the spelling of each word and can compare his method with those of his classmates. Making each word more familiar will help students recall its correct spelling. **Spelling**

basket   piece

design   hear

Stuck on Words

Students will be more likely to study their spelling lists at home when they have a special place to keep the word list. Prior to sending home the first spelling list of the year, have each student make a special magnet for attaching the list to the refrigerator at home. Provide students with squares of poster board and an assortment of markers. Have each student decorate a poster board square with brightly colored designs. Cover the square with clear Con-Tact covering for durability; then attach a strip of magnetic tape to the back of the square. Send the magnets home with the first spelling list, reminding students to study the list every time they walk by the refrigerator. **Spelling**

please

plate

player

plane

plain

Weekly Broadcaster

At the beginning of each week, choose one student to serve as the spelling broadcaster of the week. Have the student record himself saying and spelling each word while speaking into a cassette recorder. If desired, have him include the word in a sentence as well. Place the completed tape at a listening center for students to visit during the week. As an alternative, play the tape as a time-filling activity. Not only will students enjoy hearing their peers on tape but they will also get extra review of their spelling words! **Spelling**

whistle:
w–h–i–s–t–l–e.

Movin' and Groovin'

Help your kinesthetic learners identify the letters of their spelling words. Post the spelling list where everyone can see it. Then assign consonants and vowels their own movements, such as clapping for consonants and snapping for vowels. Call out a word from the list and have students say each letter while performing the related movement. Spell each word three times, increasing the speed each time. Correct spelling will be a snap! **Spelling**

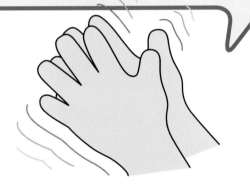

I (snap) – *s* (clap) – *l* (clap) – *a* (snap) – *n* (clap) – *d* (clap).

Whole-Class Word Sort

Label each of five sentences strips with a set of guide words, such as animal–free, friend–mail, main–powder, pour–snail, and snake–zebra. Tape the sentence strips to the board. Give each child a 3" x 5" sticky note, and have her choose a spelling or vocabulary word to write on it. One by one, have each child come to the board and place her word under the correct set of guide words. Encourage students to monitor the accuracy of each entry placement with a thumbs-up or thumbs-down response. Repeat the process at a later date when spelling and vocabulary words have changed. **Reference skills**

animal-free

butterfly

community

Look What's Cooking!

Gather two stew pots (or cut construction paper pots) and a paper plate. Then write two different sets of guide words on index cards and tape each card to a pot. Cut simple vegetable shapes, such as circles or ovals, from colored construction paper. Label each shape with a word that belongs with either set of guide words. To make the center self-checking, write each set of words on a small piece of paper and tape each list to the bottom of the matching pot. Put the shapes on the plate, and place the plate at a center with the pots. A child chooses a word card from the plate and puts it in the pot with the matching guide words. When all of the word cards have been placed, he removes one set of cards from the pot and turns over the pot to check his work. **Reference skills**

Blooming Vocabulary

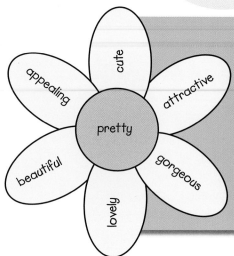

Help students replace overused words with fresh, new ones. Use the petal pattern below to copy six colorful petals for each child. Give each student a four-inch construction paper circle, the petals, and access to a thesaurus. First, she writes an adjective or a verb in the middle of the circle and then cuts out the petals. Then she glues each petal to the back of the circle. With the help of the thesaurus, she labels each petal with a synonym for the center word. Post the completed flowers on a display, and encourage students to use the resulting flower garden to add some freshness to their writing. **Reference skills**

Check out the skill-building reproducibles on pages 77–81.

Flower Petal Pattern
Use with "Blooming Vocabulary" on this page.

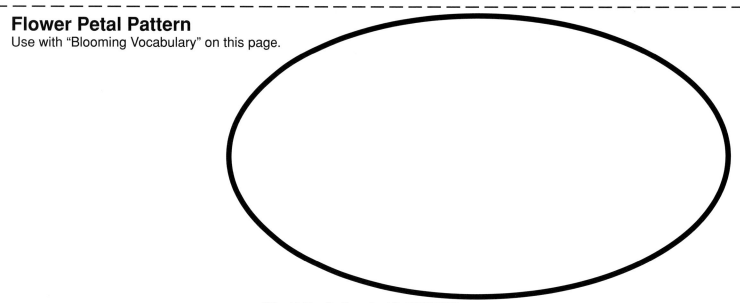

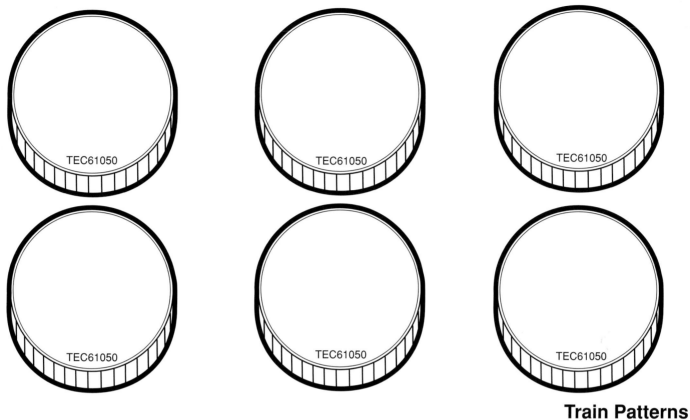

TEC61050
TEC61050
TEC61050
TEC61050
TEC61050
TEC61050

Train Patterns
Use with "Word Trains" on page 71.

boxcar

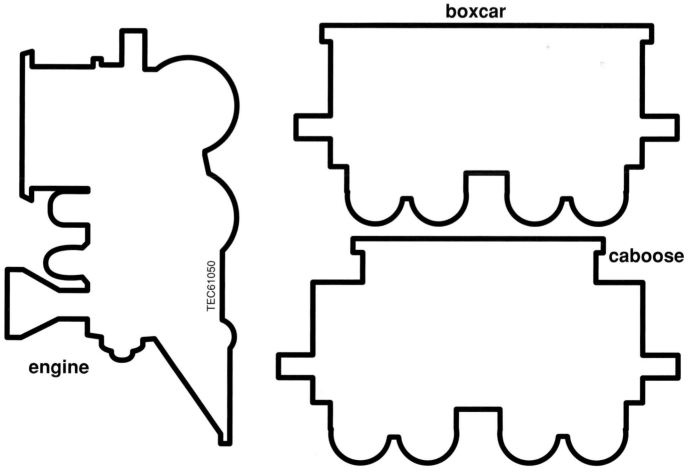

caboose

engine

TEC61050

TEC61050

Sorting Mat and Cards
Use with "Growing New Words" on page 70.

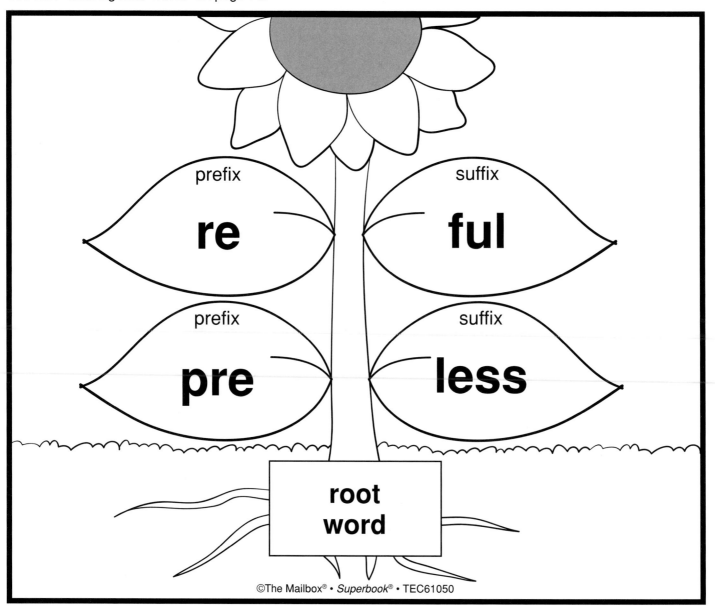

prefix
re

suffix
ful

prefix
pre

suffix
less

root word

©The Mailbox® • *Superbook*® • TEC61050

view	teach	heat	pay
TEC61050	TEC61050	TEC61050	TEC61050
care	play	harm	use
TEC61050	TEC61050	TEC61050	TEC61050
help	power	place	wash
TEC61050	TEC61050	TEC61050	TEC61050

Hike to the Top!

Write a synonym for each bold word or phrase on the lines below.

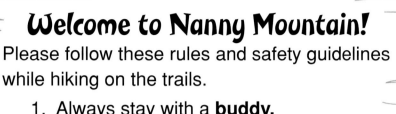

Welcome to Nanny Mountain!

Please follow these rules and safety guidelines
while hiking on the trails.

1. Always stay with a **buddy.**
2. **Sip** plenty of water.
3. Wear comfortable **footwear.**
4. Stay on the marked **paths.**
5. **Watch out for** wild **animals**.
6. **Throw** your **trash** in the marked bins.
7. Keep your dog **close** to you.
8. Trails open at **dawn** and close at **dusk.**

"Sssssome" Collection

Write the homophone that correctly completes each sentence.

1. _____ you know Stuart?
   (Do, Due)

2. He has been collecting stamps _____
   years. (for, four)

3. Stuart does not have many _____
   stamps. (plane, plain)

4. He likes to _____ pretty ones.
   (chews, choose)

5. _____ of his stamps have bright colors.
   (Some, Sum)

6. His favorite stamp is royal _____.
   (blew, blue)

7. Sometimes his _____, Stan, helps
   him sort the stamps. (sun, son)

8. Stan cannot _____ until he has his
   own collection. (wait, weight)

Name _____

In Tune

Add a prefix to each root word to make a new word.
Write the new word on the line.
Color each prefix after you use it.

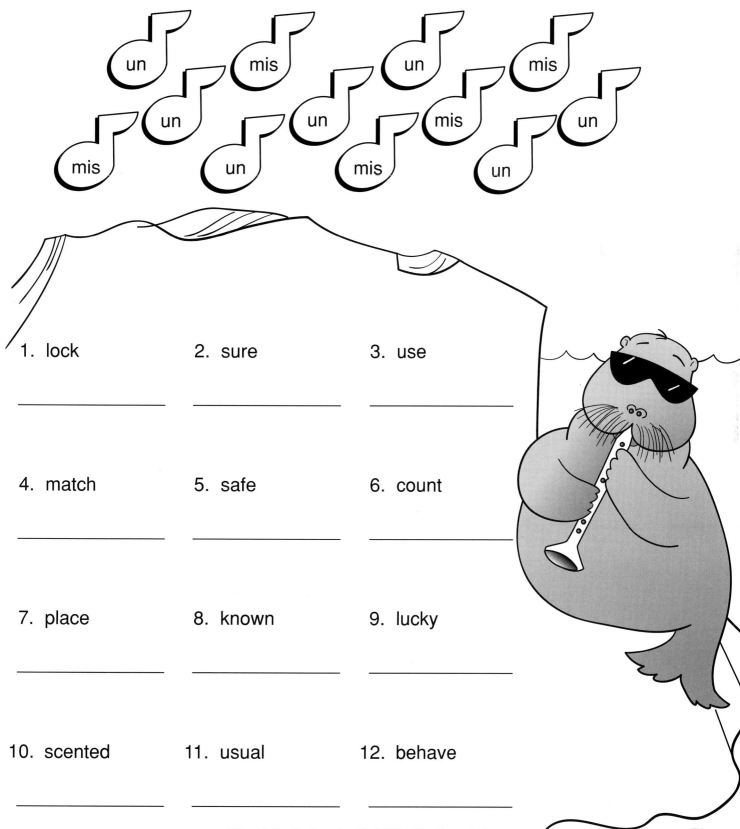

1. lock

_____

2. sure

_____

3. use

_____

4. match

_____

5. safe

_____

6. count

_____

7. place

_____

8. known

_____

9. lucky

_____

10. scented

_____

11. usual

_____

12. behave

_____

Related Rabbits

Choose the suffix to correctly complete each word.
Write the new word on the line.
Color the suffix and follow the path to learn where
   the rabbit family lives.

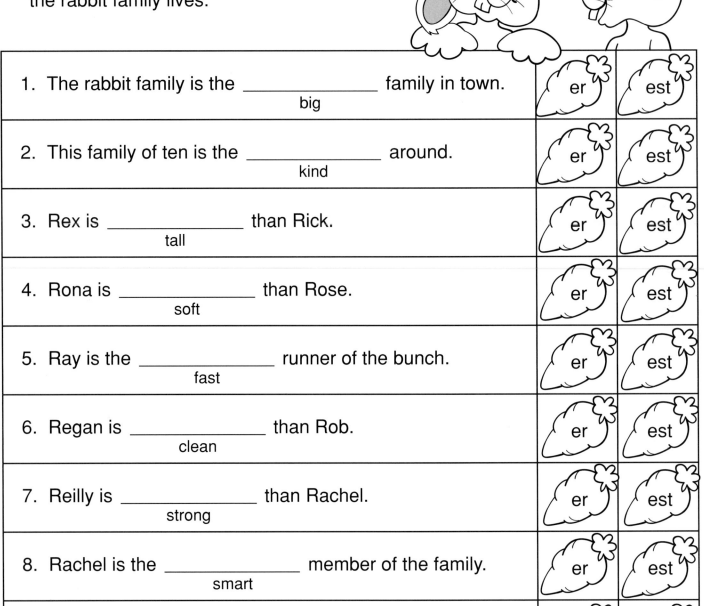

1. The rabbit family is the _____ family in town. big	er	est
2. This family of ten is the _____ around. kind	er	est
3. Rex is _____ than Rick. tall	er	est
4. Rona is _____ than Rose. soft	er	est
5. Ray is the _____ runner of the bunch. fast	er	est
6. Regan is _____ than Rob. clean	er	est
7. Reilly is _____ than Rachel. strong	er	est
8. Rachel is the _____ member of the family. smart	er	est
9. Reed has the _____ smile of them all. bright	er	est
10. Do you know a _____ family? cool	er	est

Circle the place where the rabbits live.　　　　**Rabbit City, SD**　　**Albunny, NY**

　　　　©The Mailbox® • Superbook® • TEC61050 • Key p. 310

Name_____

Exploring Space

Look at the word bank.
Write the word that goes between each set of guide words.

1. air
_____
astronaut

2. Earth
_____
explore

3. land
_____
lift

4. Mars
_____
moon

5. phases
_____
Pluto

6. revolve
_____
rotate

7. Saturn
_____
space

8. star
_____
sun

9. Uranus
_____
year

Word Bank
Venus
launch
rocket
planet
eclipse
asteroid
Mercury
shuttle
star map

Paragraph Modeling

Students often need a model or formula to help them organize their thoughts into paragraph form. Provide students with a recipe like the one below for writing different types of paragraphs. **Writing process**

Descriptive Paragraph Recipe

1 topic sentence that includes important information about the subject

2 sentences that describe the way the subject looks, sounds, smells, tastes, or feels

2 sentences that tell what the subject does or how it is used

1 sentence that tells your opinion about the subject

yield: one well-written paragraph

Personal Word Banks

Have each student compile personal word lists to refer to when working on a writing assignment. Instruct each student to designate several pages in her journal for word banks. Post a suggested list of word bank topics, such as emotion words, shape words, weather words, ways to move, ways to speak, and ways to describe time. Then provide time for students to brainstorm words for each category. Remind students to add to the lists whenever a new term comes to mind. **Writing process**

Ways to Move

walk   fly
run   gallop
skip   shuffle
drive

Young Authors' Station

Set up a Young Authors' Station with all the materials students need to complete a story from start to finish. Provide lined paper for rough drafts, pencils, pens, markers, good quality paper (both lined and unlined) for final copies of text and illustrations, manila folders, and a stapler. Remind students to leave a wide left margin on the final copies so that the binding will not interfere with the text. When a student completes a story, she staples it in a manila-folder cover. She decorates the cover with the title, her name, and an illustration. For a finishing touch, she composes a paragraph titled "About the Author" for the back cover of her book. **Writing process**

Primary Books

Encourage students to produce their best efforts with a writing assignment designed to be shared with younger audiences. Have your students produce texts such as ABC booklets, counting books, or simple stories. For an extended project, the students could compose question-and-answer booklets. Have a younger class provide questions such as "How do fish breathe underwater?" or "Why does it lightning?" Then your students can use research skills to find the answers to these questions for their booklets. **Writing process**

Why does it lightning?

How do fish breathe underwater?

Rough Draft Guidelines

Instead of using their erasers, have students cross out unwanted portions of text with a single line or edit their text using the proofreading marks at the top of page 96. This will prevent smudges on and tears in the paper and will allow each student to have a visual record of the progress on his written work. He may also want to refer to his original text to retrieve an idea or a turn of phrase that would be lost with erasing. This way, the student learns that the rough draft is not intended to look like a finished piece of work but rather a work in progress. For proofreading practice, have the child complete the worksheet at the bottom of page 96. **Writing process**

Selecting a Topic

The following methods make choosing a topic easy and fun:

- **Go Fish**
  Program a supply of fish-shaped cutouts with topics or story starters. Place the cutouts in a fishbowl. A student can "fish" for an idea by selecting a cutout from the bowl.

- **Story Spinner**
  Number a spinner, as shown, and post a list of topics to correspond with the numbers. A student spins to determine a topic for her story. Post a new topic list periodically to supply students with fresh ideas.

Topics
1. Lost in the woods
2. Shipwrecked
3. Found $1,000
4. Plan a
5. Late
6. Stu
7. Ap
8. Fou

- **Think Thematic**
  At the beginning of a unit or theme-based study, have students brainstorm a list of related topics. Record the responses on chart paper. Keep the list on display for students to refer to when selecting a writing topic.

Ocean
squid
coral
whales
shark
beach
shells

- **Class-Created Topics**
  Keep a file box and a supply of index cards handy for students to jot down interesting topic ideas. After a student records an idea on an index card, have her file it alphabetically or by subject. Allow students to refer to the box when selecting a topic.
  Writing process

Topic Box

Tell about a trip to the grocery store with your mom.

What is your favorite toy? Explain.
Avery

If you could meet anyone in the world, who would you choose to meet? Explain.   Mario

What do you like to do with your friends?
Kara

That's My Idea!

Keep students' journal-writing motivation high by having them create their own prompts. Direct the child to think of a topic or question that the entire class would be able to write about. Have him write his idea, along with his name, on an index card. Collect the cards and store them in your desk. Once a week, select a card to feature at journal time. Invite the card's author to present his journal topic to the class. Students are sure to enjoy exploring each other's topics! **Journal writing**

Compare a Pair

Use your journal time to increase students' comparing and contrasting skills. Cover the outside of a shoebox with construction paper. Decorate the covered box with shoe cutouts and the title "Pick a Pair!" Cut apart a copy of the strips at the top of page 97 and then put them in the box. Also make enough copies of the writing paper at the bottom of page 97 for each child to make a mini journal. Periodically select a topic from the box to feature during journal time. Each child responds to the prompt in his special journal. After several of the prompts have been used, invite students to add some new suggestions to the box. Journal writing

Journals for All Seasons

Store journal prompts in festive seasonal containers to inspire students year round! For added fun, write the prompts on appropriate paper cutouts. For example, in the fall, write prompts on candy corn-shaped cutouts and put them in a plastic pumpkin. Or, during winter, program different vegetable-shaped cutouts with prompts and then place the prompts in a soup pot. See the list for more suggestions. **Journal writing**

Seasonal Prompts
- apple cutouts in pie tins
- cookie cutouts in a holiday tin
- snowflake cutouts in a top hat
- heart cutouts in a candy box
- gold coin cutouts in a plastic pot
- egg cutouts in an egg carton or basket
- flower cutouts in a flowerpot
- seashell cutouts in a sand pail

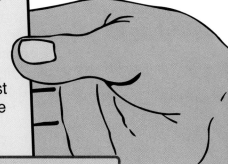

Journal Buddies

For a change-of-pace journal activity, pair students with a journal buddy for the week. After each student has completed a journal entry, have him trade journals with his buddy. On the following day, the buddies respond to the entries written the day before and then return the journals to the original owners. Repeat the routine for the remainder of the week. Challenge the buddies to learn at least three new things about each other during the course of their dialogue. **Journal writing**

Special-Interest Journals

Revitalize the process of journal writing with special-interest journals. Allow each student to choose a subject or special interest, such as a sports figure, an animal, or a hobby. Each day, have students record information about the subjects in their journals. Encourage each child to write about the subject for a designated length of time, such as a two-week period, before switching to a new topic. This challenges the student to investigate a topic with some thoroughness. Journal writing

Literature-Response Journals

Reinforce a variety of language-arts skills by culminating each story with small-group discussions and individual journal entries. As the class begins a new literature selection, post a list of questions that will apply to the story. Leave the list in view for students to refer to for the duration of the book. When the class has finished reading the book, provide time for students to silently reflect on the questions. Then place students into small groups to discuss the questions aloud. Complete the activity by having each student return to his desk and write about each question in his literature-response journal. **Journal writing**

The following questions can be used with any story:

1. Did you like this story? Tell why or why not.

2. How did the story make you feel?

3. What was the most interesting part of the story?

4. If you could be one of the story characters, who would you be? Tell why.

5. What will you remember most about this book?

Figuratively Speaking

Spark creative writing by challenging students to use a variety of literary techniques to describe an object. After selecting a topic, each student must describe it by using a simile, an example of personification, and a metaphor. Extend the activity by having each student paint or draw a picture to accompany the description. **Descriptive**

September 12

warm and spicy nugget-size chicken fried to a crispy crunch

hot yellow corn topped with warm melted butter

cold juicy peaches sliced just right

toasty soft rolls

chilled white milk

Menu Redo

At the beginning of the month, assign each day of the school lunch calendar to a different student or pair of students. Direct each student to rewrite the day's menu, adding descriptive details that will make the food even more appealing to readers. Encourage the writer to add words that describe the taste, smell, texture, and appearance of each food item. Collect the rewritten menus and, on the appropriate day, invite the author or authors to present the menu to the class. **Descriptive**

Who's There?

These descriptive writings will result in a fun guessing game for students. On a copy of one of the door patterns on page 98, have each student write a paragraph that describes herself. Remind her to include details about her looks—including her eye color, hair color, and whether she is a boy or a girl—along with descriptive clues to her identity. Next, have her write her name and draw a picture of herself on a sheet of drawing paper trimmed to the size of the door. Then have her place the door atop her drawing and staple along the left side so that it can be opened to reveal her picture. Display the projects where students can visit and attempt to guess who's behind each door. **Descriptive**

KNOCK! KNOCK! KNOCK! KNOCK! KNOCK! KNOCK! KNOCK! KNOCK! KNOCK! KNOCK!

Who's There?
I am a tall girl with black hair and brown eyes. My hair is short and curly. I like to wear a head-band. My favorite thing to do at recess is to jump rope with my friends. In school, I like to learn my spelling words.

Jasmine

Brown Bag It!

Place a small item—such as a pencil, puzzle, or bookmark—inside a brown paper lunch sack. Give a sack to every student. Instruct each student to peek at the item inside his bag. Challenge the student to write a description of the item without mentioning it by name. Provide time for each student to read his description to the class; then have him call on three classmates to try to identify the object. The classmate who successfully identifies the object gets to read his description next.
Descriptive

Descriptive Sentences

Encourage students to use description in their writing with this write-and-draw project. Give a 12" x 18" sheet of drawing paper to each student. Tell students to make a crease down the middle of their papers. On the left side of the papers, have students copy and illustrate a simple sentence such as "The bear sat." Provide time for students to show their completed illustrations to the class. After everyone has had a chance to share, ask students why there was a wide variety in the pictures drawn for the same sentence. Discuss ways to improve the sentence by adding detail and description. Instruct each student to add to the sentence so that it tells more about the picture he has drawn. Encourage the student to use adjectives, prepositions, and adverbs to compose a descriptive sentence and write it on the right side of the paper. Share the illustrations once more, having each student read his new sentence to the class. Descriptive

Food for Thought

Make writing a special occasion by giving students a treat to reinforce the topic. Let students chew on a piece of sugarless gum while they think about the sticky subject. Instruct students to either write a descriptive paragraph about gum, list different ways to use chewing gum, or give directions for blowing a bubble. Set aside one day a week to give your students a treat as a springboard for creative-writing ideas. There's no telling what a piece of candy, a pretzel stick, or an apple slice might inspire! Descriptive, expository

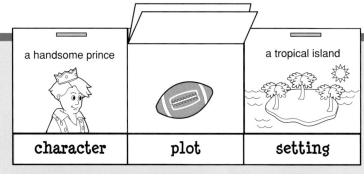

a handsome prince		a tropical island
character	plot	setting

Flip Book Story Starters

To make his flip book, each student cuts apart the strips on page 99 along the bold lines. Then he cuts along each dotted line, taking care not to cut all the way to the top. He staples, as shown, the three narrow strips atop the wider strip that has character, setting, and plot labels.

To select a story topic, the student simply flips through the pages and selects one element from each section. He then uses the elements to craft a story. After writing, have students store the flip books in their writing folders to be used again. **Narrative**

Noteworthy News

Set the stage for a creative-writing assignment with a handful of headlines! Cut out a class supply of interesting headlines from a newspaper. (Or to save time, cut out several different headlines and make copies of each one to create one per student.) Place the headlines in a container. Pass the container around the room and have each student remove one headline. Instruct each student to write a story and draw an illustration to match his headline. Then have the student glue the headline, story, and picture to a sheet of construction paper. Display the completed projects on a bulletin board for students to enjoy. Narrative

City to Put Leash Law Into Effect

25th Annual County Fair Opens

Fire Damage Closes Mall

Getting Started

Encourage students to turn to their favorite books when they're looking for a way to start their own stories! Read aloud the first sentence of a favorite book, and guide the class to alter the sentence. For example, the sentence "In the deep, dark forest lived a bear and her bear cubs..." could be changed to "In the deep, dark ocean lived a shark and ten fish..." Write the altered sentence on chart paper and repeat the procedure with two more books. Post the chart at the writing center, and encourage students to add altered sentences to it. During writing time or a visit to the center, a child can use one of the sentences to get her story started. **Narrative**

Story Sequels

Have each student select a story she has read. Instruct the student to write a paragraph describing what's happening to the characters at the end of the book. Direct her to pick up from that point and write about what will happen next. Remind students to include several of the story characters in the sequel as well as to describe any changes in the setting. Encourage the children to illustrate their sequels. If desired, bind the stories for your classroom bookshelf so students can enjoy reading their classmates' creations.
Narrative

Comic Strip Stories

Turn to the funny papers for narrative-writing ideas. Cut out several comic strips from the newspaper. White-out the words in the speech bubbles. Have students use the pictures of the comic strip as clues in determining the sequence of events. Then have students write a story based on the illustrated events.
Narrative

I'll never forget the time my mom surprised me for my birthday. I woke up, and my mom told me to get dressed. I had no idea where we were going. I fell asleep in the car on the way. When I woke up, we were at the zoo!

Memory Quilt

Piece together students' favorite memories with this paper patchwork quilt project. To make a quilt square, a student frames off a one-inch border on a nine-inch construction paper square. He uses various craft supplies to decorate the frame. Next, he writes a paragraph telling about a delightful or funny memory or another favorite memory. After editing, he publishes the writing on an eight-inch square cut from lined notebook paper. Finally, he glues the smaller square in the middle of the decorated square. Collect the writings and display them side by side on a board titled "Memory Quilt."
Narrative

Serving Up Sundaes

In advance, write on the board a list of ice-cream flavors, sauces, and toppings. Give each child a copy of page 100. In the box at the top of the page, have the child draw a diagram of his favorite ice-cream sundae. Direct the child to label each part of the sundae, including the flavor of each ice-cream scoop, sauce, and topping. Next, have the child refer to his diagram as he writes on the bottom of the page the directions for making the sundae. For added fun, provide the listed materials and allow each child to follow his directions to make his own sweet treat. **Expository**

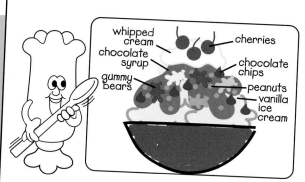

Here is how to make Savan's super sundae. First, scoop lots of vanilla ice cream into the dish. Then squirt chocolate syrup on top of the ice cream. Next, sprinkle peanuts, chocolate chips, and gummy bears on top of the syrup. Finally, plop some whipped cream all over the top and add a few cherries.

Caring for a Horse

The horse will eat grass and hay. It may also like fruits, berries, nuts, and other plants.

Animal Visitors

Display on the board a picture of an animal. Ask students to imagine that the pictured creature is coming to the classroom to visit for a week. Explain that the animal must be kept as comfortable as possible during its visit. Guide students in a discussion of the types of things they need to know about the animal before it arrives, and list each suggestion on the board. Encourage students to consider topics such as what the animal eats, what type of shelter it needs, and what temperature it prefers. Next, give each small group of students access to several nonfiction books about the animal, as well as white construction paper, crayons, and a stapler. Instruct group members to refer to the listed topics as they create an instruction manual for caring for the animal. Once all of the groups have completed their manuals, place the manuals in the classroom library for everyone to enjoy. If desired, repeat the activity using a picture of a different animal. **Expository**

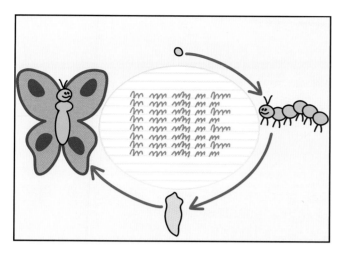

Experiencing Life Cycles

These expository paragraphs double as an assessment tool for an animal life cycle study. First, each student writes the stages of the life cycle of an animal you are studying, consulting reference materials as necessary. Then she imagines that she is that animal and writes a paragraph explaining the changes she will undergo throughout her life. To publish her writing, the child cuts out the paragraph and glues it on a sheet of construction paper. Then she adds illustrations, as shown, of each stage in the animal's life cycle. Provide time for each child to share her work with the class. **Expository**

Welcome Classmates

Help new students find their way around the school with a student-created welcome manual! Assign each small group of students a location within the school. Include each destination a new student may need to know, such as the cafeteria, office, and gym. Instruct the group to write a list of directions from the classroom to its assigned location. Challenge group members to include directional words as well as sequential words, such as *next, then,* and *last.* Next, have each group edit its directions and copy them on the bottom half of a sheet of white copy paper. Then have group members draw a map on the top half of the paper to illustrate their directions. Collect the completed pages, photocopy them, and bind the copies together. When a new student joins the class, present him with a copy of the welcome manual. **Expository**

Help Wanted

For a real-life writing lesson, have students write help-wanted ads. To begin, give each small group of students several examples of want ads. The groups take turns reading their ads aloud, noting details such as the title of the job, the skills and experience required, and the salary. Once students are familiar with want ads, each child writes her own ad for an imaginary job. She publishes her ad by using a black pen or fine-tip marker to write it on newsprint.

Post the ads on a board titled "Help Wanted."
Expository

Love animals?

A local pet store is looking for someone to play with the animals after the store closes. You must not be afraid of snakes or frogs. You have to work every night. Experience with pets of your own is a must. Call for salary details.

Special Deliveries

Practice letter-writing skills while building positive attitudes and self-esteem. Review the parts of a friendly letter with your students. Then write each student's name on an individual slip of paper. Place the names in a decorated container; then have each student select one. Instruct the student to write a letter to the classmate named on the paper. The letter should include positive remarks and encouraging statements directed to the student. Collect the completed letters; then present each letter to its recipient. If desired, repeat the activity throughout the year to promote a positive classroom environment. **Letter writing**

Character Letters

Use a story that the class has been reading as a springboard for this activity. Have each student write a letter as one of the characters in the story, using details from the story as a purpose for writing. For example, the character Fern in *Charlotte's Web* could write a letter to her father convincing him to spare Wilbur's life. A student from The Magic School Bus series could write a letter to a friend describing one of her unusual field trips. Provide time for students to share their letters with their classmates, or bind the letters into a class booklet. Letter writing

Keeping in Touch

Supply each student with a pocket folder with brads and several sheets of notebook paper. On a designated day of the week, each student writes a letter to her parents telling them about school happenings. The student secures the completed letter in the folder using the brads. Before the child takes the folder home, place school notes, memos, or handouts in the pockets. Encourage parents to write a note back to their child and place it (as well as any necessary correspondence to you) in the folder before the student brings it back to school. Then provide a time for student volunteers to share with the class the messages their parents have written. **Letter writing**

March 3, 2007

Dear Mom and Dad,
We are studying the layers of the earth. We live on a layer called the crust, just like the crust on a piece of bread!

people

crust

not bread

Love,
Shay

Dear Mr. Goodbar,...

Have each child bring in a wrapper from his favorite candy bar for real-world writing practice. Help the child use the information on the wrapper or possibly from the Internet to locate the address of the manufacturer. The child writes a business letter to the company describing why the candy is his favorite. Make a copy of his final letter and return it to him. Then he addresses an envelope, tucks his letter inside, and drops it in the mail. Staple any responses that the students receive along with copies of the students' original letters on a board titled "Sweet Correspondence." Letter writing

My Mailbox

For weekly authentic writing practice, have each student label a spiral notebook with her name and the title shown. Once a week, direct the child to draft a letter to you in her notebook. Explain that she should use the letter-writing opportunity to ask questions, talk about problems, or share experiences, such as successes or adventures. Collect the notebooks and write a response letter to each child, commenting on her thoughts and answering any questions she had. **Letter writing**

Classroom Correspondence

When it's time to send home a school notice—such as a class picture schedule, field trip information, or holiday party news—have your students do the writing. Direct each child to write a letter to his parents including the information you provide or information from the original notice. Review each child's letter for accuracy before sending it home. Letter writing

Don't Forget the Third-Grade Field Trip

Where: City Zoo

When: Friday, April 20

What to bring: a sack lunch,

$2 for admission fee

April 13, 2007

Dear Mom,
    Please remember that my class is going on a field trip. On Friday, April 20, we are going to the city zoo. I need to bring a sack lunch and $2 for the admission fee. I think we will have a great time!

Love,
Tony

Check out the skill-building reproducible on page 102.

soft
furry
purr
climb
chase
jump
sleep

Kittens
by Lindsey
Kittens purr.
They have soft fur.
They chase their tails
And climb in pails.
They like to leap
And then they sleep.

Catalog Poems

Students begin writing a catalog poem with a brainstorming session. After selecting a topic, each student generates a list of words and phrases that relate to the topic. After the list is complete, the student arranges the items into a rhythmic pattern. Rhyming words are not essential but can add to the fun and challenge. **Poetry**

Sunny days
Purple flowers
Rainbows galore
Insects buzzing
Nests in trees
Gardens blooming

Seasonal Acrostic Poems

At the beginning of a season, have each student write the name of the season on his paper vertically. Each letter in the word becomes the initial letter in a line of the poem. **Poetry**

Syllable Cinquains

In a syllable cinquain, the student creates a five-line poem in which there are a certain number of syllables in each line. Model the format of the syllable cinquain below. **Poetry**

Line 1:	Title	
Line 2:	Description of title	2 syllables
Line 3:	Action about the title	4 syllables
Line 4:	Feeling about the title	6 syllables
Line 5:	Synonym for the title	8 syllables
		2 syllables

Tadpoles
Amphibians
From egg to fish to frog
I like to watch them change
their looks.
Froggies

CONCRETE POEMS

In a concrete poem, the shape or design helps express the meaning or feeling of the poem. The words may define, describe, or analyze the subject. Provide unlined paper, stencils, and an assortment of writing instruments for students to use when composing a concrete poem. **Poetry**

The leaf drifted down to the ground.

Haiku

Introduce your students to haiku, a traditional Japanese form of poetry. These poems are very simple, but rich in imagery; students may wish to illustrate their completed works. The poem consists of three unrhyming lines with the syllable pattern shown below. Poetry

Line 1: 5 syllables
Line 2: 7 syllables
Line 3: 5 syllables

The tiny, gray bird
Sits quietly in the tree
As the daylight fades.

Diamante Poems

Students will have to use their knowledge of the parts of speech to write this seven-line, diamond-shaped poem. Give each child a copy of the poem form on page 101. Guide him through the following directions to complete his poem. Poetry

Line 1:   topic (noun)
Line 2:   two adjectives
Line 3:   three action words
Line 4:   a four-word phrase
Line 5:   three action words
Line 6:   two adjectives
Line 7:   rename the topic

Football
Fast, exciting
Run, catch, throw
What a great game!
Tackle, block, kick
Rough, tough
Pigskin

Clerihew Verses

Once students become familiar with rhyming couplets, challenge them to write a clerihew. This four-line verse consists of two couplets and tells about a person. The first line of the poem should end in the person's name. Poetry

My name is Matt Carter,
And I like to barter.
I'll trade you this pickle
For only a nickel.

Limericks

Tickle your students' funny bones with a look at limericks. These humorous poems contain five lines. The first, second, and fifth lines rhyme, as do lines three and four. Get your students started with the phrase "There once was a..." Poetry

There once was a bright red rose
With a smell that would tickle your nose.
Since it has a big thorn
That is sharp like a horn,
No one picks it; it just grows and grows.

Proofreading Marks

Delete a word or sentence.	The dog ran ~~very~~ quickly.
Capitalize a lowercase letter.	<u>m</u>r. Jones
Change a captial letter to lowercase.	the Ðog
Correct a spelling mistake.	quickly ~~quikly~~
Add ending punctuation.	The dog ran quickly.
Add a comma.	The dog ran, jumped, and barked.
Indent a new paragraph.	¶

TEC61050

Name _____ Proofreading

What a Great Day!

Use proofreading marks to correct the passage.

   Today i woke up early. My mom Made pancakes

for me Pancaiks are my favorite breakfast food! I

put on my coat and went outside. My friends and I

playeed at the park all day. We jumped skipped, and

ran. We threw a footBall to each other.

Later, it was time to go home My favorite show

was on television. on the show, they tell say

funny stories, do magic tricks and sing songs.

It was a grate day!

©The Mailbox® • Superbook® • TEC61050 • Key p. 310

Compare and contrast a pair of family members.

TEC61050

Compare and contrast two states.

TEC61050

Compare and contrast two of your favorite foods.

TEC61050

Compare and contrast two jobs you would like to have.

TEC61050

Compare and contrast two places you like to visit.

TEC61050

Compare and contrast two things you are good at.

TEC61050

Compare and contrast two types of pets.

TEC61050

Compare and contrast two of your favorite books.

TEC61050

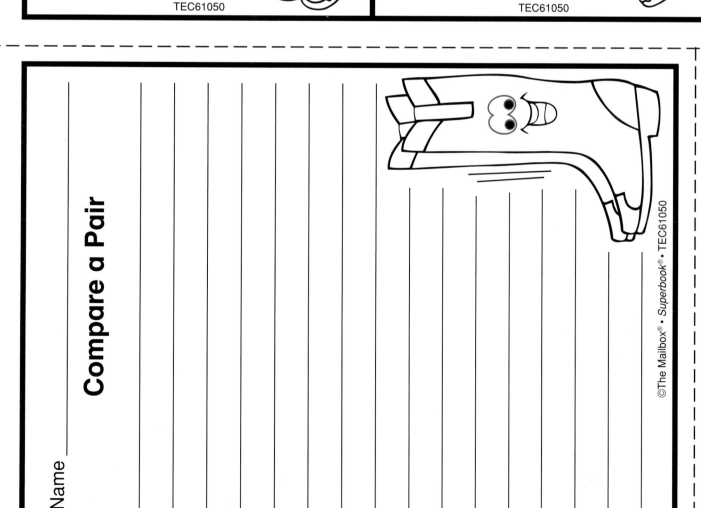

Compare a Pair

Name

©The Mailbox® • Superbook® • TEC61050

Note to the teacher: Use alone or with "Compare a Pair" on page 84.

97

Door Pattern
Use with "Who's There?" on page 86.

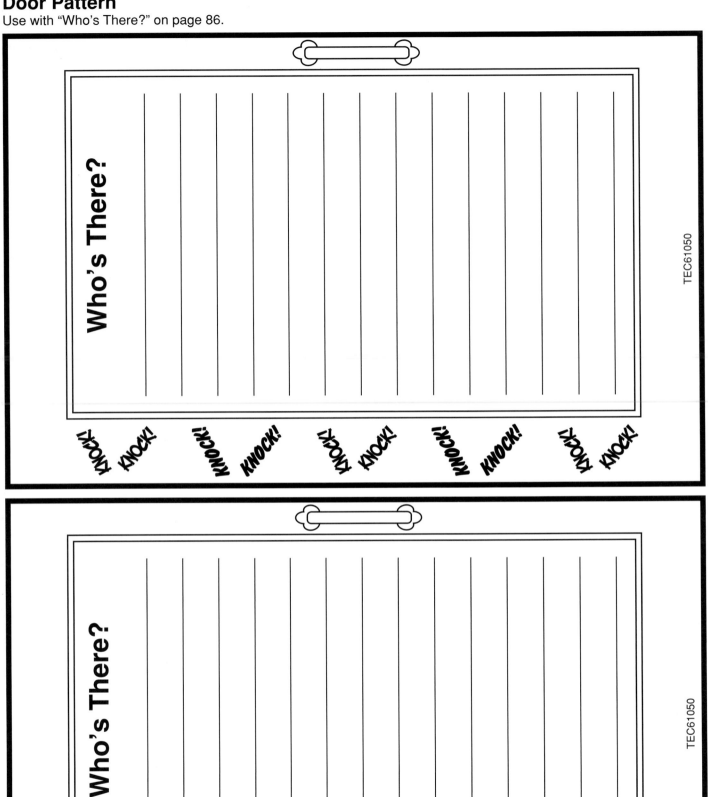

a handsome prince	tries to run away from home	a tropical island
a clever fox	is baking cookies	the top of a mountain
a friendly mouse	is playing football	under the sea
a busy mail carrier	is having a birthday party	in a cave
character	**plot**	**setting**

Note to the teacher: Use with "Serving Up Sundaes" on page 90.

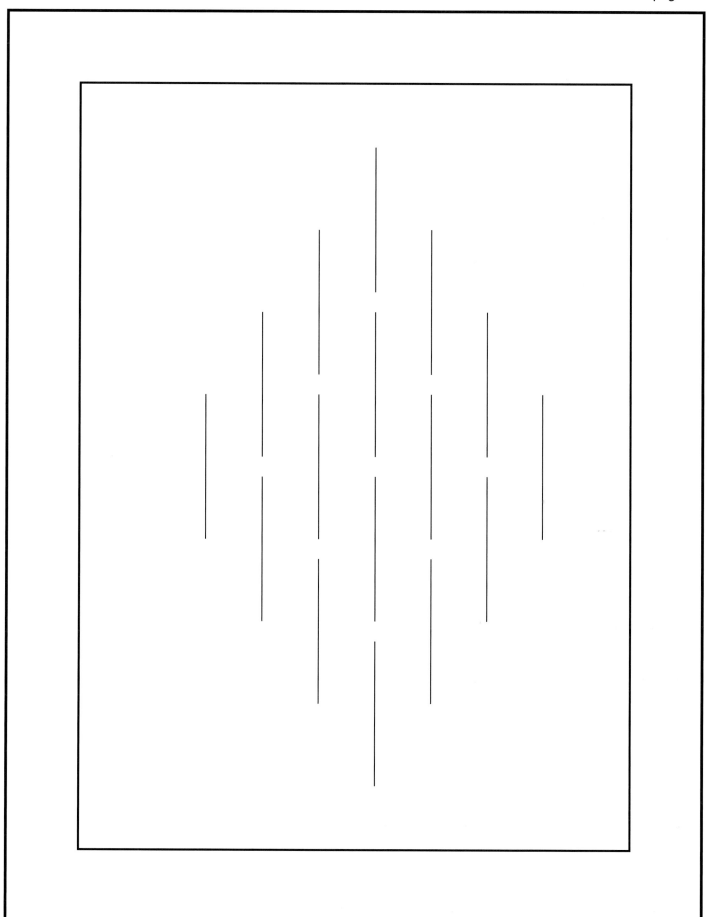

A Letter From Camp

Label each part of the letter.
Use the word bank to help you.

Word Bank
date   closing   signature
body   greeting

June 10, 2007 ← _____

Dear Mom and Dad, ← _____

    I am having a good time at camp. We

are learning how to swim. We are also

riding horses. Next Tuesday, we are

going to hike to the top of Mount Blue. _____

I can't wait!

    How are you? How is my dog? I miss

you all very much.

        Love, ← _____

        Kia ← _____

Complete each sentence.
Use the word bank to help you.

1. The _____ tells to whom the letter is written.

2. The _____ tells the name of the person who wrote the letter.

3. The _____ tells when the letter was written.

4. The _____ is the main part of the letter. It tells the reader what the writer wanted to say.

5. The _____ is before the signature.

Number Concepts

FREEZE FRAME

Program a class supply of 5" x 7" index cards, each with a different numeral from zero to nine. Give one card to each student. Call on four volunteers to come to the front of the room with their cards. Give them five seconds to arrange themselves and freeze to make the largest numeral possible. Then give the rest of the students a chance to join in. Allow ten seconds for students to arrange themselves in groups of four to make a numeral larger (or smaller) than the one created by the volunteers. Remind students to pay close attention to the place value of each number before they freeze into position. Repeat the activity until each student has had an opportunity to be at the front of the room. **Comparing numbers**

9

8

5

3

Place-Value Shuffle

Give each student ten index cards. Instruct each student to program each of his cards with a different numeral from zero to nine. Also give the student a sheet of paper to fold into thirds. Have the student label the sections as shown. To play the game, each student places his shuffled index cards face-down. As you say, "Flip," each student removes the top card from his stack and places it on a section of his paper. After the card is placed, it cannot be moved. After three cards have been flipped, determine who has made the largest numeral. **Place value**

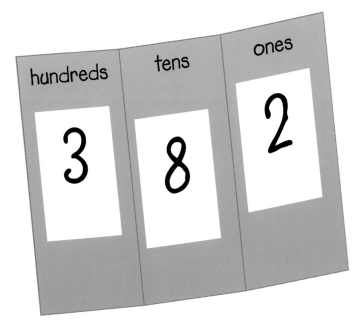

For variations on the game, try the following:

* Have each student play as described above, but try to make the lowest numeral possible with three cards.

* Write a numeral on the chalkboard. Have students play as directed above, trying to create a numeral as close to yours as possible.

* Pair students to play the game as described above. Instruct partners to add their numerals together to try to make the highest or lowest score in the class.

* After students have placed their cards on the paper, announce a place value. The student with the highest (or lowest) numeral in that place earns a point. The first student to earn ten points wins the round.

* Add a fourth section to the paper to include the thousands place. Then play as described above.

ESTIMATION CELEBRATION

Designate an Estimation Celebration Day. Include throughout the day activities such as estimating by threes or fives the number of steps it takes to cross the classroom, the length of a desktop, the height of five math books in a stack, the number of times a student can write her name in one minute, and the number of crackers in a package. Have each student make her estimate, record it on paper, and then find the actual measurement. Compare the estimates to the actual results. **Estimation**

Daily Math Drill

Incorporate an ongoing number-concept review as part of a daily routine. Cut apart the numerals from a hundred chart and place them in a cup. At the start of each math lesson, pull out six numerals from the cup. Have your students answer the following questions about each numeral:

1. Is the numeral odd or even?
2. Is this numeral a double or a triple?

Then have the students determine which is the least/greatest numeral in the group and have them arrange the numerals from smallest to largest. **Number concepts**

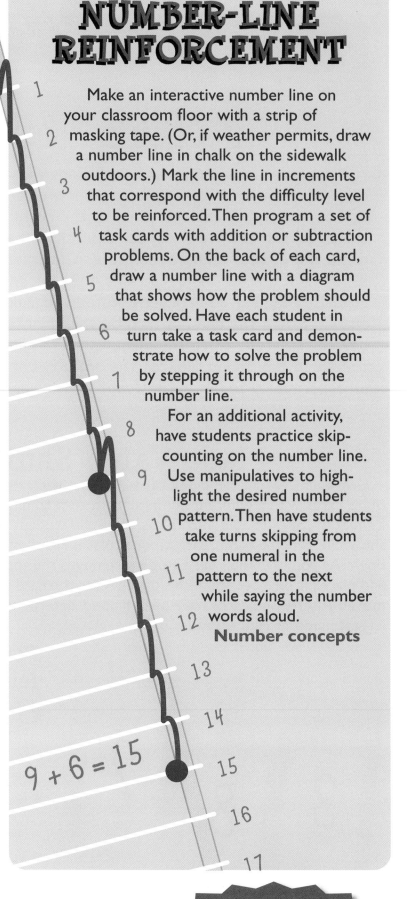

NUMBER-LINE REINFORCEMENT

Make an interactive number line on your classroom floor with a strip of masking tape. (Or, if weather permits, draw a number line in chalk on the sidewalk outdoors.) Mark the line in increments that correspond with the difficulty level to be reinforced. Then program a set of task cards with addition or subtraction problems. On the back of each card, draw a number line with a diagram that shows how the problem should be solved. Have each student in turn take a task card and demonstrate how to solve the problem by stepping it through on the number line.

For an additional activity, have students practice skip-counting on the number line. Use manipulatives to highlight the desired number pattern. Then have students take turns skipping from one numeral in the pattern to the next while saying the number words aloud. **Number concepts**

$$9 + 6 = 15$$

Check out the skill-building reproducibles on pages 105–108.

Jumbled Hundreds

Fill in the missing numbers.
The first one has been done for you.

A.
	54	
63	64	65
	74	

B.
	36		
			48

C.
	6	
	16	

D.
75	
	86

E.
	40
59	

F.
19	
	30

G.
12		
		24

H.
87		89	

I.
91		93

J.
	43		46

K.
58	
	79

L.
	2	
11		

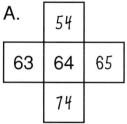

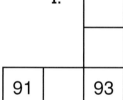

5	6

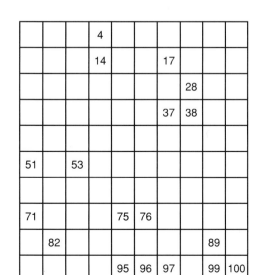

		4				
	14		17			
				28		
			37	38		
51	53					
71		75	76			
82				89		
	95	96	97		99	100

Name _____

Taking Tickets

Cut apart the tickets at the left.
Decide which tickets go with each roll.
Glue the tickets in order from least to greatest.

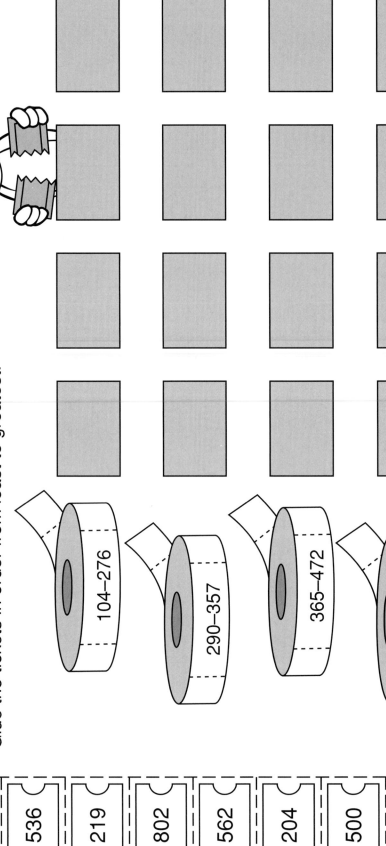

104–276

290–357

365–472

496–654

672–812

422	330
246	536
573	219
356	802
299	562
801	204
394	500
112	380
704	698
467	293

Recess Riddles

Write each three-digit number.
Cut apart the numeral cards below and use them to help you.

A. Use the numerals 7, 3, and 0. Form the largest number you can make. ___ ___ ___	B. This number is between 306 and 314. The sum of its digits is 6. ___ ___ ___	C. Put a 4 in the ones place and a 7 in the hundreds place. Make the largest number possible. ___ ___ ___
D. Use the numerals 1, 8, and 2. Put the 2 in the tens place. Form the smallest number you can. ___ ___ ___	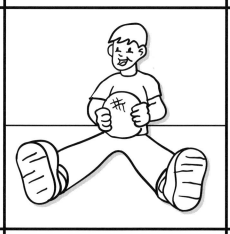	E. The sum of its digits is 8. The number is between 221 and 226. ___ ___ ___
F. Put a 0 in the tens place and a 3 in the ones place. Make the largest number you can. ___ ___ ___	G. Use the numerals 3, 5, and 6. Make the smallest number you can. ___ ___ ___	H. Use the numerals 7, 3, and 0. Put the 0 in the tens place. Make the largest number you can. ___ ___ ___

0	1	2	3	4	5	6	7	8	9

Name_____

Computation Station

Round each number to the nearest hundred.
Color the key with the matching number.

A. 323 _____   B. 675 _____   C. 452 _____

D. 99 _____   E. 804 _____   F. 247 _____

G. 530 _____   H. 761 _____   I. 386 _____

J. 111 _____   K. 692 _____   L. 909 _____

M. 372 _____   N. 182 _____   O. 589 _____

P. 617 _____   Q. 926 _____   R. 338 _____

100	400	500	600	300	700
200	700	900	200	100	400
800	900	800	300	500	600

ADDITION & SUBTRACTION

Fast Facts

For this partner center, prepare a tagboard spinner similar to the one shown. Attach a paper clip to the center with a brad. Also label each of nine blank cards with a different number from 1 to 9. Place the cards and spinner at a center stocked with blank paper. When a twosome visits the center, one child spins the spinner and the other child chooses a card. Then each player writes and solves the corresponding addition problem on a sheet of paper. After comparing their answers to check for accuracy, students switch roles and play again. **Basic facts**

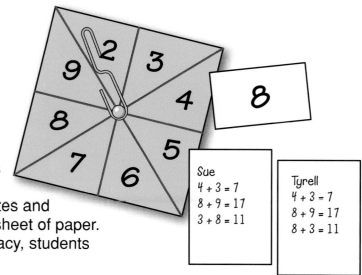

Sue
4 + 3 = 7
8 + 9 = 17
3 + 8 = 11

Tyrell
4 + 3 = 7
8 + 9 = 17
8 + 3 = 11

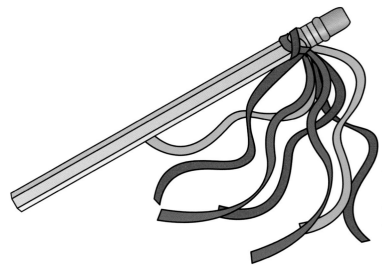

Math Wizard

Encourage students to memorize basic math facts with this rewarding idea! Each day, invite a different child to orally answer a desired number of math facts. If he answers them correctly in a given amount of time, title him the daily math wizard and reward him with a wizard wand—an unsharpened pencil with curling ribbon attached to it. No doubt, students are sure to be motivated to practice math facts! Basic facts

Around the Room

Gather a set of addition and subtraction flash cards (with the answers on the backs) so there is one card for each child in your class. Write each featured math problem on a sheet of paper and make a class supply. Then place a card faceup on each child's desk, and give each student a copy of the prepared sheet.

To begin, each student silently solves the problem she was given and flips the card to check her answer. Then she locates the corresponding problem on her paper and draws a check by the problem if she answered it correctly or draws an X if she answered it incorrectly. On your signal, each student rotates along a predetermined route to a different desk. Continue in this manner until each child has solved each problem. At the conclusion of the activity, each child will have a record of the facts she knows and the ones she needs to practice. **Basic facts**

Name Sarah

| 9 ✓ | 7 x | 10 x |
| − 3 | + 8 | − 4 |

| 6 ✓ | 5 ✓ | 12 ✓ |
| + 4 | + 9 | − 6 |

| 8 ✓ | 3 ✓ | 9 ✓ |
| + 8 | + 8 | − 7 |

| 9 x | 6 ✓ | 9 x |
| + 7 | − 2 | + 6 |

9
− 7

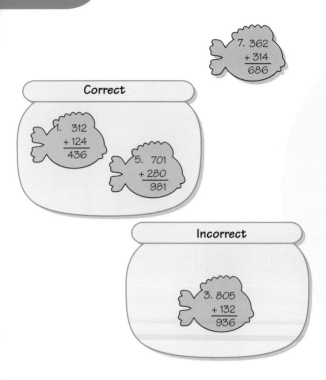

Fish Frenzy!

For this center, label a supply of construction paper fish cutouts with different two- or three-digit addition or subtraction problems. Program half of the problems with correct answers and the other half with incorrect answers. Then number the fish and prepare an answer key. Also trim two sheets of bulletin board paper into two fishbowl shapes; then label one bowl "Correct" and the other "Incorrect." Place the fishbowls, fish, answer key, and a supply of paper at a center. When a child visits the center, she chooses a fish, solves the problem on her paper, and places the fish on the corresponding bowl. After she sorts all of the fish in this manner, she uses the answer key to check her work. **Larger numbers**

Pick Three

All you need for this quick small-group game is a deck of cards! Remove the jokers and face cards and then randomly choose three cards from the deck. Place the three cards faceup and encourage the group members to mentally add the three numbers together. Ask the first child who raises his hand to announce the sum. If he is correct, he takes the cards. If he is incorrect, another group member may answer. Continue in the same manner until all of the cards have been used. The student with the greatest number of cards is declared the winner! **Three addends**

Pile On the Points

Here's a fun way for your class to practice a variety of addition and subtraction skills! Cut out enough copies of the game cards on page 112 to make a class supply. Program the indicated cards with different addition and subtraction problems. Divide your class into two teams and designate one side of the board for each team.

To play, write "200" on each team's side of the board to represent the starting score. Invite a child from Team 1 to take a card, read it aloud, and perform the corresponding operation(s) on the board. After verifying her answer, have her erase the problem (leaving the answer). Then have a member of Team 2 repeat the process on his side of the board. Continue in this manner until each child has had a turn. The team with the highest score wins! **Larger numbers**

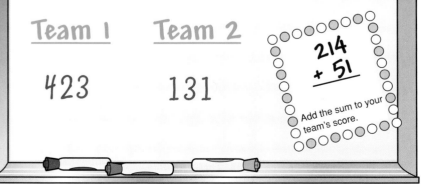

$$124 + 275$$

$$312 + 133$$

400

Quick Sums

Here's a simple way for students to practice estimating sums. Program a class supply of cards with different three-digit addition problems. Choose problems so that when the sums are rounded to the nearest hundred, there are a variety of answers from 100 to 1,000. To begin, give each child a card and announce a rounded number. Each child whose estimated sum matches the announced number holds up her card. Scan for accuracy, and then have students trade cards to play again. **Estimating sums**

Toss It!

Grab a muffin tin to help students practice adding three-digit numbers! To prepare, program both sides of a supply of counters with different one-digit numerals; then store them in a container. Place the container and a six-cup muffin tin in an open area of the classroom. In turn, invite each of six students to toss a counter into the muffin tin. If a counter lands in an occupied section, the child tosses again. When all six sections are full, ask a volunteer to read the two resulting three-digit numbers. Then have each student write and solve the corresponding addition problem on a sheet of paper. After verifying youngsters' answers, have a different group of students toss the counters to play again. **Larger numbers**

Super Shoppers

Display several classroom items on a table within students' view. Write the name of each item on a chart and assign each one a different price. For addition practice, have each child write on a sheet of paper the names and prices of two items she would like to "buy." Then instruct her to add the prices together. Invite students to share their shopping lists and total prices. For subtraction practice, announce a starting amount of money for students to write on their papers. Then have each child choose one item and subtract its price from the amount on his paper. Continue in the same manner as time allows. **Money**

pencil = $1.20
markers = $3.43
math book = $5.68
joke book = $6.80

Andrea

$$\$10.50 - \$3.43 \over \$7.07$$

markers

Ethan

$$463 + 458 \over 921$$

Check out the skill-building reproducibles on pages 113–118.

Game Cards

Use with "Pile On the Points" on page 110.

Add the sum to your team's score.

TEC61050

Add the difference to your team's score.

TEC61050

Add the sum to the other team's score.

TEC61050

Add the difference to the other team's score.

TEC61050

Add 100 to your team's score.

TEC61050

Add 100 to the other team's score.

TEC61050

Subtract 100 from your team's score.

TEC61050

Subtract 100 from the other team's score.

TEC61050

Double your team's points.

TEC61050

Triple your team's points.

TEC61050

Double the other team's points.

TEC61050

Triple the other team's points.

TEC61050

Name _____

A "Paw-fect" Catch

Add.

D 26
+ 43 ●

H 11
+ 17 ●

O 43
+ 54 ●

S 40
+ 39 ●

S 57
+ 32 ●

N 61
+ 32 ●

R 44
+ 52 ●

A 10
+ 23 ●

W 24
+ 21 ●

F 20
+ 75 ●

L 16
+ 30 ●

I 12
+ 66 ●

Which types of fish make the best security guards?

To solve the riddle, write the letters from above on the matching numbered lines below.

___ ___ ___ ___ ___ ___ ___ ___ ___   ___ ___ ___   ___ ___ ___ ___ ___ ___ ___ ___
89 45 97 96 69 95 78 79 28   33 93 69   46 78 97 93 95 78 89 28

Shop 'til You Drop!

Add.
Show your work.
Color the tag with
  the matching answer.

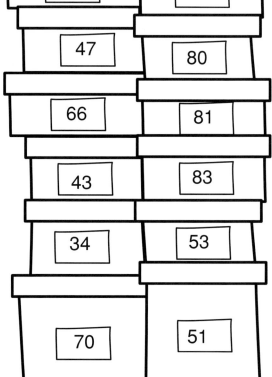

82	94
72	65
71	50
47	80
66	81
43	83
34	53
70	51

```
  28        32        46        25
+ 19      + 18      + 37      + 45


  13        37        56        18
+ 58      + 14      + 25      + 16


  39        25        37        24
+ 27      + 28      + 45      + 19


  43        29
+ 37      + 36


  34        57
+ 38      + 37
```

Name _____

Ladybugs on a Leaf

Add.
Color by the code.

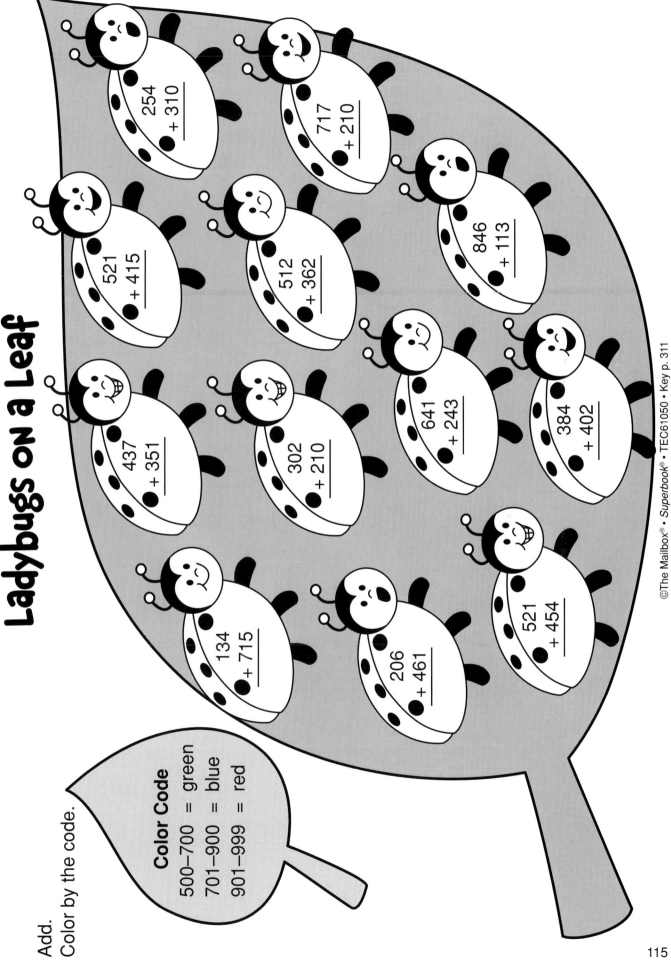

$$254 \atop + 310$$

$$717 \atop + 210$$

$$521 \atop + 415$$

$$512 \atop + 362$$

$$846 \atop + 113$$

$$437 \atop + 351$$

$$302 \atop + 210$$

$$641 \atop + 243$$

$$384 \atop + 402$$

$$134 \atop + 715$$

$$206 \atop + 461$$

$$521 \atop + 454$$

Color Code
500–700 = green
701–900 = blue
901–999 = red

©The Mailbox® • Superbook® • TEC61050 • Key p. 311

115

Wake Up!

Subtract.
Circle if correct.
Help Gus find Greg by drawing a line to connect
   the circled problems.

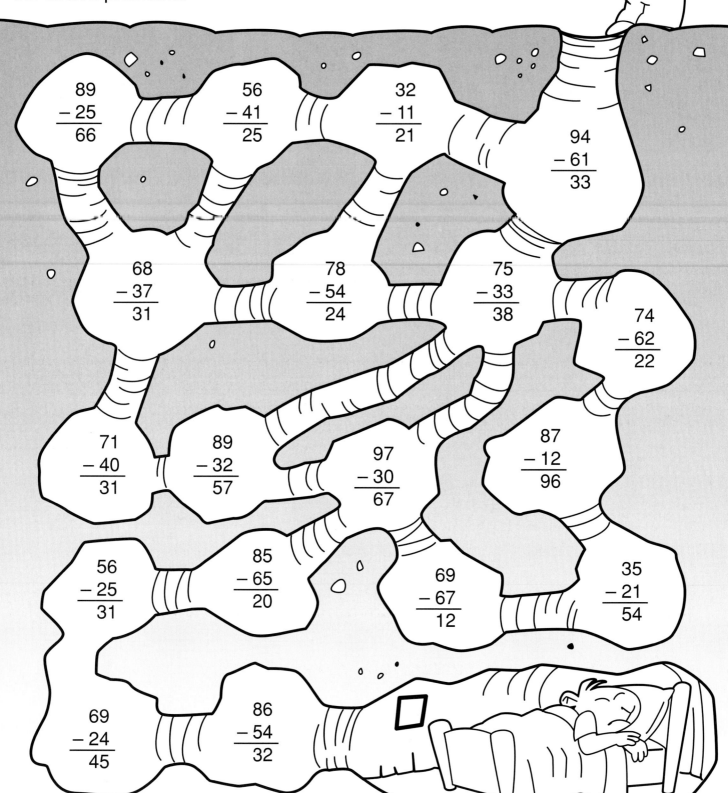

$$\begin{array}{r} 89 \\ -\ 25 \\ \hline 66 \end{array}$$

$$\begin{array}{r} 56 \\ -\ 41 \\ \hline 25 \end{array}$$

$$\begin{array}{r} 32 \\ -\ 11 \\ \hline 21 \end{array}$$

$$\begin{array}{r} 94 \\ -\ 61 \\ \hline 33 \end{array}$$

$$\begin{array}{r} 68 \\ -\ 37 \\ \hline 31 \end{array}$$

$$\begin{array}{r} 78 \\ -\ 54 \\ \hline 24 \end{array}$$

$$\begin{array}{r} 75 \\ -\ 33 \\ \hline 38 \end{array}$$

$$\begin{array}{r} 74 \\ -\ 62 \\ \hline 22 \end{array}$$

$$\begin{array}{r} 71 \\ -\ 40 \\ \hline 31 \end{array}$$

$$\begin{array}{r} 89 \\ -\ 32 \\ \hline 57 \end{array}$$

$$\begin{array}{r} 97 \\ -\ 30 \\ \hline 67 \end{array}$$

$$\begin{array}{r} 87 \\ -\ 12 \\ \hline 96 \end{array}$$

$$\begin{array}{r} 56 \\ -\ 25 \\ \hline 31 \end{array}$$

$$\begin{array}{r} 85 \\ -\ 65 \\ \hline 20 \end{array}$$

$$\begin{array}{r} 69 \\ -\ 67 \\ \hline 12 \end{array}$$

$$\begin{array}{r} 35 \\ -\ 21 \\ \hline 54 \end{array}$$

$$\begin{array}{r} 69 \\ -\ 24 \\ \hline 45 \end{array}$$

$$\begin{array}{r} 86 \\ -\ 54 \\ \hline 32 \end{array}$$

No Rush!

Subtract.
Show your work.

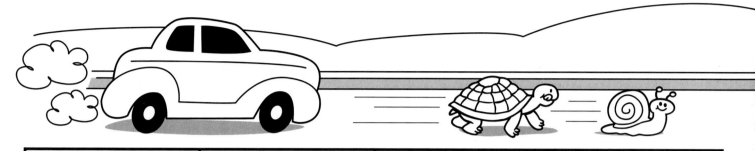

32 − 19 D	64 − 28 S	81 − 37 R	50 − 32 R
74 − 35 E	87 − 59 E	76 − 18 W	93 − 28 A
68 − 49 R	71 − 68 C	83 − 26 V	92 − 67 I

Which driver never speeds?

To solve the riddle, write the letters from above on the
matching numbered lines below.

$\overline{65}$ $\overline{36}$ $\overline{3}$ $\overline{44}$ $\overline{28}$ $\overline{58}$ $\overline{13}$ $\overline{18}$ $\overline{25}$ $\overline{57}$ $\overline{39}$ $\overline{19}$!

Off-Road Adventure

Subtract.
Show your work.
Color a rock with a matching answer.

(A) 955
− 673

(B) 747
− 128

(C) 650
− 304

(D) 763
− 482

(E) 819
− 258

(F) 663
− 406

(G) 982
− 455

(H) 857
− 763

(I) 536
− 441

(J) 412
− 108

(K) 279
− 192

(L) 638
− 209

(M) 485
− 348

(N) 984
− 165

(O) 790
− 578

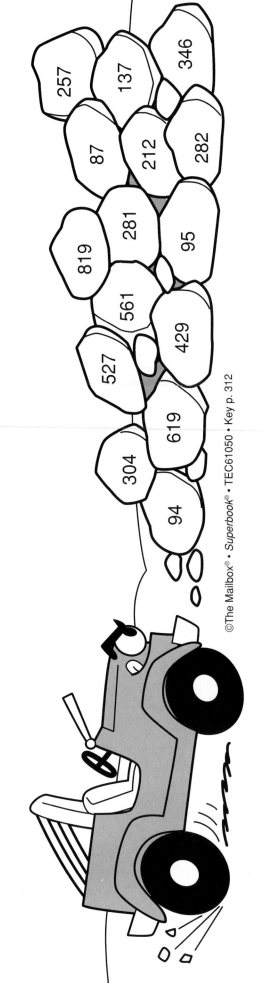

257
137
346
87
212
282
819
281
95
561
429
527
619
304
94

✖ Multiplication & Division ➗

Hands-on Helpers

Introduce multiplication facts with a special type of manipulative for each set of facts. Students will use the manipulatives to make a visual diagram to help them understand the concept of counting in groups. Multiplication

- When learning the multiplication facts of two, use carnival tickets as manipulatives. Separate the tickets from a double roll, leaving each ticket pair connected together. Give each student ten sets of tickets. Call out appropriate fact problems and have each student diagram the problem with the tickets on his desktop, showing that groups of two are counted to arrive at the answer. Then have each student make a set of flash cards for the facts of two.

- When learning the multiplication facts of three, distribute pattern-block triangles to each student. (Make sure each student has ten triangles.) Students will count the sides of each triangle to help them understand that the facts are solved using groups of three. After using the triangles to determine the facts of three, have each student make a set of flash cards for the facts.

- To help students learn the facts of four, distribute ten plastic forks with four tines apiece to each student. Students count the tines on each fork to make one group of four.

- The facts of five can be introduced with disposable plastic gloves. The students count the fingers on each glove to make a group of five. After fives have been introduced, manipulatives are optional since students will have a good understanding of the concept of multiples.

Getting Ready

Prior to having students learn their multiplication facts, initiate a daily skip-counting drill. For the first week, have students count by twos to 18 (which will review multiplication facts to nine). Start and end the counting with a different number each day to increase the students' understanding and awareness. The second week, begin skip-counting by threes to 27. Advance to the next number every week until you reach skip-counting by nines to 81. (Remember to keep reviewing the previous skip-counting patterns periodically.) By the time you introduce multiplication facts, students will already be familiar with the multiples of each number. **Multiplication**

3, 6, 9, 12, 15, 18, 21, 24, 27

This pan has three rows and four columns. That would make 3 x 4, which equals 12. This pan can also have four rows and three columns, which makes 4 x 3. That answer also is 12.

Show-and-Tell

After reminding students that arrays are made of rows and columns, give them time to search for arrays in their daily lives. Encourage each child to bring in an example or a picture of an item organized into arrays, such as a muffin pan, an ice cube tray, or juice box sets. On a designated day, have her share her chosen item and demonstrate how to use it to make a repeated addition or multiplication sentence. **Multiplication**

3 x 2 = 6

Keeping Count

Relate skip-counting to multiplication with this group project. Assign each group of two or three students a number to skip-count by; then give each group a supply of drawing paper. As students skip-count by their assigned amount, they write each number on the bottom of a page. Next, they draw a picture to match the number shown, organizing the picture into sets by their assigned number. Finally, they number the sets and write a multiplication sentence that matches the picture. Bind the completed books and place them in your math center or class library for a quick review. **Multiplication**

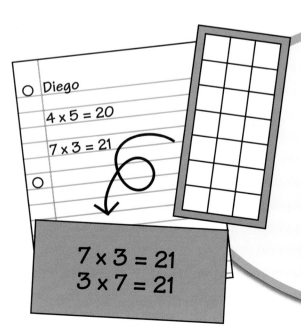

Diego
4 x 5 = 20
7 x 3 = 21

7 x 3 = 21
3 x 7 = 21

Flash Cards

Provide extra practice with arrays and multiplication facts. Cut out rectangular arrays from one-inch graph paper and mount each on construction paper. Then write each array's multiplication facts on the back. A child chooses a card and uses the rows and columns to determine one of its multiplication facts. He writes the multiplication sentence on a sheet of notebook paper and, if desired, also writes the product. Then he flips the card over to check his work. He continues in this manner until he has recorded ten facts. Multiplication

Less Is More

A little goes a long way when you help your students memorize facts. To start, assign every student the same two multiplication facts to practice. Use flash cards with the same facts to drill the class for about five minutes. The next day, give the students two new facts to practice. Again take five minutes to drill the facts with flash cards, this time using all four facts. Continue each day in this manner and, before too long, students will be multiplication experts. Multiplication

Today's Facts

$3 \times 8 = 24$

$2 \times 5 = 10$

Sets of Store Items

For this partner project, gather a large supply of grocery store circulars. Give each student duo several circulars from the same store and week. The students locate pictures of items that are packaged in sets—such as toilet paper, juice boxes, or soap—and cut them out. Next, they glue down matching sets in a row; then they write a repeated addition sentence and a multiplication sentence under it. Post the completed projects on a display titled "Good Times at the Store." **Multiplication**

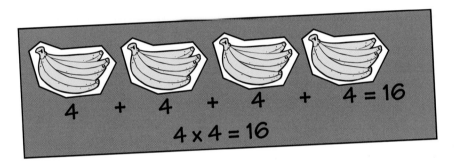

$4 + 4 + 4 + 4 = 16$

$4 \times 4 = 16$

Beach-Towel Toss

Apply fabric paint to a gently used beach towel, dividing the towel into ten sections. Label each section with a number from one to ten. Once dry, lay the towel on a flat surface. Divide the class into teams. A child tosses two beanbags on the towel, uses the numbers they land on in a multiplication sentence, and names the product. If correct, award his team a point. Play continues until each child has a turn. The team with the most points wins. **Multiplication**

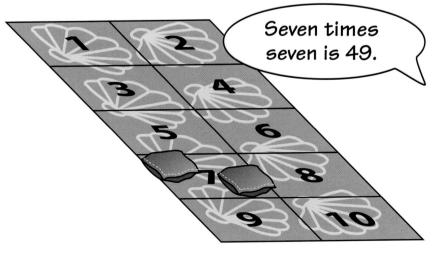

Seven times seven is 49.

6 × 7

Fact-Finding Mission

To prepare this partner game, remove the face cards and "10" cards from a deck of playing cards. Place the remaining cards at a center with a calculator. To play the game, Player 1 turns over two cards and names a multiplication fact that equals the resulting two-digit number. Then Player 2 uses the calculator to check the answer and, if it's correct, Player 1 receives a point. Player 2 repeats the process, and play continues in this manner for as long as desired. The player with more points wins. **Multiplication**

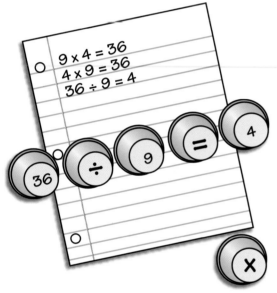

Stacks-of-Facts Center

Use a permanent marker to label the bottoms of three small paper cups with the numbers of a fact family, and stack them together. Also label a cup with a multiplication sign, another one with a division sign, and another with an equal sign. Place the cup sets at a center with paper and pencils. A child chooses a set of cups and manipulates them to create a multiplication sentence. He records the sentence on his paper. Then he repeats the process three more times, making and recording another multiplication sentence and two division sentences. When finished, he restacks the cups, chooses a new set, and repeats. Relating multiplication and division

$12 \div 3 = 4$

Clear-Cut Answers

Give each child a sheet of half-inch graph paper and have her cut out a rectangle. She counts the total number of grid squares in the rectangle and records the number on her paper. Then she cuts the shape into rows or columns and records the number cut. Finally, she counts the number of squares in one of the resulting pieces and records that as her answer. She glues the resulting strips on her paper and repeats the process with a new rectangle. **Division**

Check out the skill-building reproducibles on pages 123–127.

Name

Sweet Reward!

Multiply.

0 x 3 = ☐

2 x 1 = ☐

5 x 3 = ☐

1 x 4 = ☐

1 x 1 = ☐

3 x 3 = ☐

2 x 2 = ☐

1 x 5 = ☐

2 x 3 = ☐

5 x 5 = ☐

4 x 0 = ☐

5 x 2 = ☐

4 x 3 = ☐

0 x 1 = ☐

2 x 0 = ☐

4 x 5 = ☐

4 x 4 = ☐

3 x 1 = ☐

5 x 4 = ☐

3 x 2 = ☐

Noisy Neighborhood

Multiply.

(I) 7 x 6 = _____

(M) 9 x 3 = _____

(E) 7 x 5 = _____

(Y) 8 x 7 = _____

(K) 8 x 9 = _____

(U) 6 x 8 = _____

(D) 6 x 5 = _____

(N) 6 x 4 = _____

(R) 7 x 7 = _____

(H) 8 x 8 = _____

(P) 8 x 0 = _____

(C) 9 x 6 = _____

(T) 7 x 9 = _____

(A) 7 x 3 = _____

(I) 6 x 6 = _____

(B) 8 x 2 = _____

(H) 9 x 9 = _____

(T) 8 x 5 = _____

How do you keep a dog from barking in your front yard?

To solve the riddle, match the letters above to the numbered lines below.

___ ___ ___ ___ ___ ___ ___ ___ ___ ___ ___ ___ ___ ___ ___ ___ ___ !
0 48 40   81 36 27   42 24   63 64 35   16 21 54 72 56 21 49 30

Name

Rush Hour

Divide.
Color by the code.

Color Code
1, 2, 3 = green
4, 5, 6 = yellow
7, 8, 9 = blue

63 ÷ 7 = ___

12 ÷ 3 = ___

8 ÷ 8 = ___

36 ÷ 9 = ___

24 ÷ 8 = ___

54 ÷ 9 = ___

28 ÷ 4 = ___

72 ÷ 8 = ___

9 ÷ 3 = ___

45 ÷ 9 = ___

16 ÷ 8 = ___

36 ÷ 6 = ___

42 ÷ 6 = ___

20 ÷ 4 = ___

40 ÷ 5 = ___

64 ÷ 8 = ___

125

Lunch to Go!

Use the numbers on each set of cherries to make a fact family.

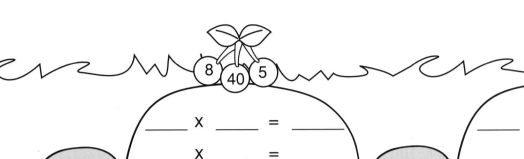

___ × ___ = ___
___ × ___ = ___
___ ÷ ___ = ___
___ ÷ ___ = ___

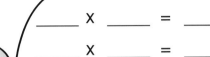

___ × ___ = ___
___ × ___ = ___
___ ÷ ___ = ___
___ ÷ ___ = ___

___ × ___ = ___
___ × ___ = ___
___ ÷ ___ = ___
___ ÷ ___ = ___

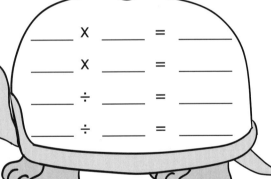

___ × ___ = ___
___ × ___ = ___
___ ÷ ___ = ___
___ ÷ ___ = ___

___ × ___ = ___
___ × ___ = ___
___ ÷ ___ = ___
___ ÷ ___ = ___

___ × ___ = ___
___ × ___ = ___
___ ÷ ___ = ___
___ ÷ ___ = ___

Name _____

Musical Multiplication

Solve.

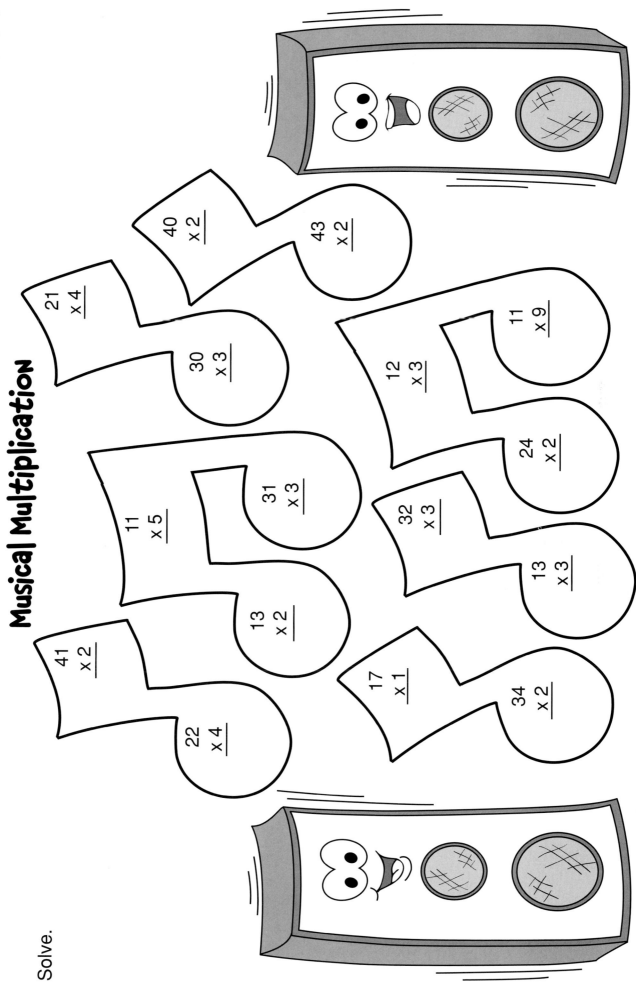

21
x 4
_____

40
x 2
_____

43
x 2
_____

30
x 3
_____

12
x 3
_____

11
x 9
_____

24
x 2
_____

11
x 5
_____

31
x 3
_____

32
x 3
_____

13
x 2
_____

13
x 3
_____

41
x 2
_____

17
x 1
_____

34
x 2
_____

22
x 4
_____

FRACTIONS

Fruity Fraction Introductions

Write the fractions ½, ⅓, and ⅙ on the board. Give a slip of paper to each student and have her write her name and what she considers the largest of the three fractions on her paper. Collect the papers and then cut pieces of fruit into halves, thirds, and sixths. Call out each name from the slips of paper and give each student the fractional amount written on her paper. Students will quickly recognize that one-half is the largest of the three fractions, especially if they received only one-sixth of a treat! **Comparing**

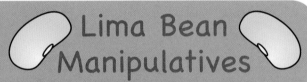

Lima Bean Manipulatives

Make an inexpensive set of fraction manipulatives with a bag of dried lima beans and a can of spray paint. Working outside, lay the beans in a single layer on a sheet of newspaper. Spray one side of the beans with a coat of spray paint; then allow them to dry. To use the manipulatives, hand each student four beans. Have the student shake the beans in his hand and drop them on his desk. Show each student how to write a fraction by recording the amount of colored sides facing up (the numerator) over the total number of beans (the denominator). Have the student repeat the activity ten times, recording the fractional amount each time. Repeat the activity as needed when introducing other denominators.
Parts of a set

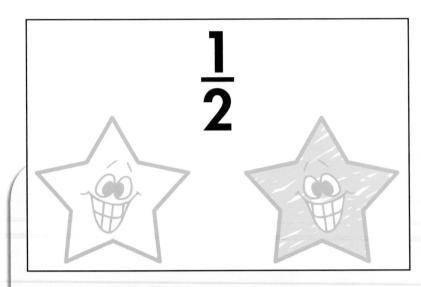

Group Posters

Students demonstrate their understanding of fractions with this group project. Divide students into groups of four and provide each group with a piece of construction paper and four index cards. Also assign each group a common fraction. Instruct each student to illustrate his group's fraction on an index card and then glue it to the construction paper. After each group shares its poster with the class, display the posters on the classroom wall as a visual reminder. **Sets of objects**

Terminology Tip

Help students remember which part of the fraction is called the numerator and which is called the denominator. Point out that the **d**enominator is the number **d**own south, and the **n**umerator is the number up **n**orth! **Vocabulary**

$$\frac{\textbf{N}\text{umerator (Up }\textbf{N}\text{orth)}}{\textbf{D}\text{enominator (}\textbf{D}\text{own South)}}$$

Fishy Fun

Give each student 12 gummy fish or fish-shaped crackers. Instruct him to manipulate the fish into two equal groups and to name the number of fish in each group. Use the information to explain to students that one-half of 12 is six. Next, have him reorganize his fish into three equal groups, naming the number in each. Have him draw the model on a piece of paper and write the number of fish equal to one-third. Continue in this manner, having students show four equal groups, six equal groups, and 12 equal groups. When finished, allow students to nibble on their catch! **Sets of objects**

$\frac{1}{3}$ of 12 = 4

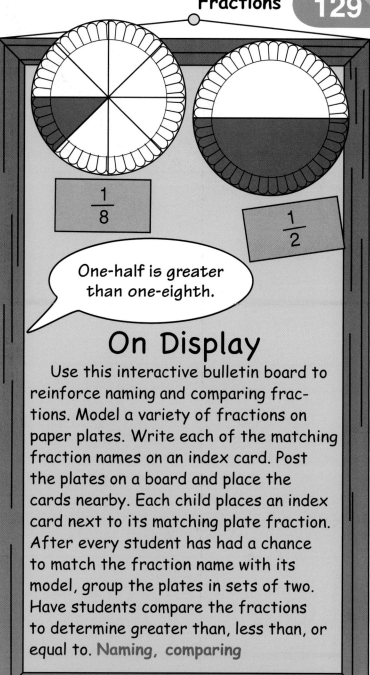

$\frac{1}{8}$

$\frac{1}{2}$

One-half is greater than one-eighth.

On Display

Use this interactive bulletin board to reinforce naming and comparing fractions. Model a variety of fractions on paper plates. Write each of the matching fraction names on an index card. Post the plates on a board and place the cards nearby. Each child places an index card next to its matching plate fraction. After every student has had a chance to match the fraction name with its model, group the plates in sets of two. Have students compare the fractions to determine greater than, less than, or equal to. **Naming, comparing**

They're the Same

Model equivalent fractions by first instructing each child to fold a sheet of drawing paper in half. Then have her unfold the paper and color one of the two equal parts. Point out that one-half is colored. Next, have each student refold the paper in half and in half again. Direct her to unfold the paper to see that there are now four equal sections, two of which are colored. Share with students that the shading has not changed but now there are four equal sections, or two-fourths, colored. Bring students to the conclusion that one-half is equivalent to two-fourths. Continue folding several more times to discover other fractions equivalent to one-half. **Equivalent fractions**

Check out the skill-building reproducibles on pages 130 and 131.

Fetch!

Name each fraction set in two ways.

A.

$$\frac{}{4} = \frac{}{2}$$

B.

$$\frac{}{6} = \frac{}{3}$$

C.

$$\frac{}{8} = \frac{}{4}$$

D.

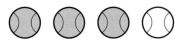
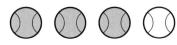

$$\frac{}{8} = \frac{}{4}$$

E.

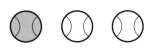

$$\frac{}{9} = \frac{}{3}$$

F.

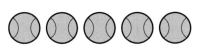

$$\frac{}{10} = \frac{}{2}$$

G.

$$\frac{}{12} = \frac{}{4}$$

H.

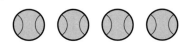

$$\frac{}{12} = \frac{}{3}$$

Name_____

Polly Want a Cracker?

Compare the fractions in each pair.
Write >, <, or = in each circle.

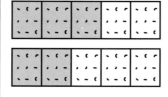

$\dfrac{1}{4}$ ◯ $\dfrac{3}{4}$

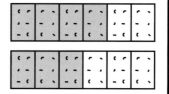

$\dfrac{3}{5}$ ◯ $\dfrac{2}{5}$

$\dfrac{4}{6}$ ◯ $\dfrac{3}{6}$

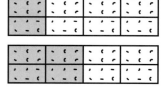

$\dfrac{2}{8}$ ◯ $\dfrac{4}{8}$

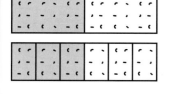

$\dfrac{1}{2}$ ◯ $\dfrac{3}{6}$

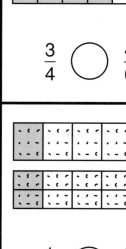

$\dfrac{3}{4}$ ◯ $\dfrac{4}{6}$

$\dfrac{6}{12}$ ◯ $\dfrac{4}{6}$

$\dfrac{1}{5}$ ◯ $\dfrac{2}{10}$

$\dfrac{2}{3}$ ◯ $\dfrac{3}{6}$

$\dfrac{3}{7}$ ◯ $\dfrac{4}{7}$

$\dfrac{6}{10}$ ◯ $\dfrac{4}{10}$

$\dfrac{6}{8}$ ◯ $\dfrac{6}{10}$

Shadow Chasers

To prepare this partner activity, gather a piece of chalk and a measuring stick for each student pair. Early in the day, take students to a sunny spot on the playground or sidewalk and have each duo find a place where they can easily see their shadows. One student in each pair stands still while his partner traces around his feet with chalk and writes the student's name under the tracing. Then the partner measures the length of the student's shadow and records the time and length on a sheet of paper. The students switch roles and repeat the process. Every hour or two, allow the pairs to return to the same location to remeasure their shadows. At the end of the day, have students discuss their findings. If desired, have each pair graph their results or use the data to write word problems.
Length

MEASURING ME

Have each student visually divide a sheet of construction paper into eight equal sections. Then have the student find the measurements of his hand, thumb, pinkie, index finger, foot, leg from knee to ankle, shoulder to shoulder, and arm from elbow to shoulder. Each student records a measurement in one section of his poster. If desired, have the students label and illustrate each section.
Length

Hand	Foot
5 inches	8 inches
Thumb	Knee to Ankle
$1\frac{1}{2}$ inches	$10\frac{1}{2}$ inches
Pinkie	Shoulder to Shoulder
$1\frac{1}{2}$ inches	1 Foot
Index Finger	Elbow to Shoulder
$2\frac{1}{2}$ inches	$10\frac{1}{2}$ inches

Inching Along

This student-made inchworm really measures up! To make one, a student cuts a six-inch length of half-inch-wide ribbon or elastic. Then she uses craft glue to secure six pom-poms side by side on the ribbon and draws two simple eyes as shown. After the glue dries, she can use the six-inch worm to estimate the lengths of classroom items, such as a pencil or the side of her desktop. For an added challenge, pair students and have them combine their inchworms to estimate the perimeter of objects around the classroom.
Estimating, perimeter

Sticky Square Units

To introduce the concept of area, gather a few rectangular objects—such as a book, a file folder, and a poster—and a supply of sticky notes. Post the objects on the board or along the board's ledge. Demonstrate how to find the area of the first object by covering it with sticky notes as shown. Count the number of sticky notes used and write the area in square units. Repeat the steps with each of the remaining objects. Afterward, place the sticky notes and a few new rectangular objects at a center for individual student practice. **Area**

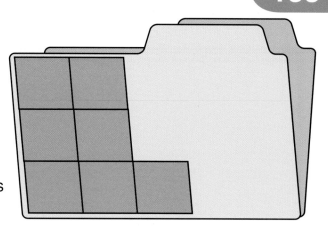

Over or Under?

Display five common items, such as a globe, stapler, or textbook. Have each student write on a sheet of paper an estimate for each item's weight. Next, weigh each object to reveal its actual weight. Ask students to raise their hands to show whether their own estimates were over or under the actual weight. Then determine which student had the closest estimate. If desired, repeat the activity, having students estimate the height or volume of each object. **Weight**

Liquid-Measurement Equivalences

Use this handy reference chart to show students how liquid measurements compare. To make a chart, each student will need a copy of the patterns on page 134. Instruct each student to color the patterns as follows: gallon—orange, half-gallons—purple, quarts—green, pints—yellow, cups—blue. After coloring each piece, have the student cut out each shape and cut along the dotted lines indicated on the piece. Have each child stack the pieces as shown and staple at the top. Students can readily see the equivalences of each standard measurement by lifting a section of the chart. For example, by lifting a half-gallon section, the student will see that a half-gallon is equal to two quarts, four pints, or eight cups. This pattern can also be adapted to show equivalent fractions. Capacity

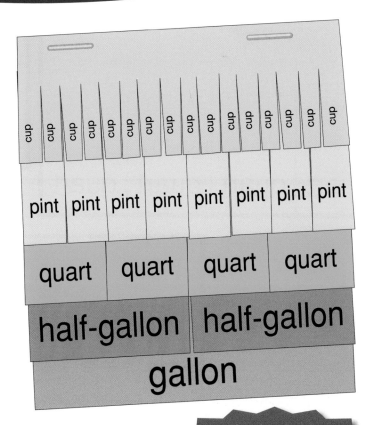

Check out the skill-building reproducibles on pages 135 and 136.

Liquid-Measurement Patterns

Use with "Liquid-Measurement Equivalences" on page 133.

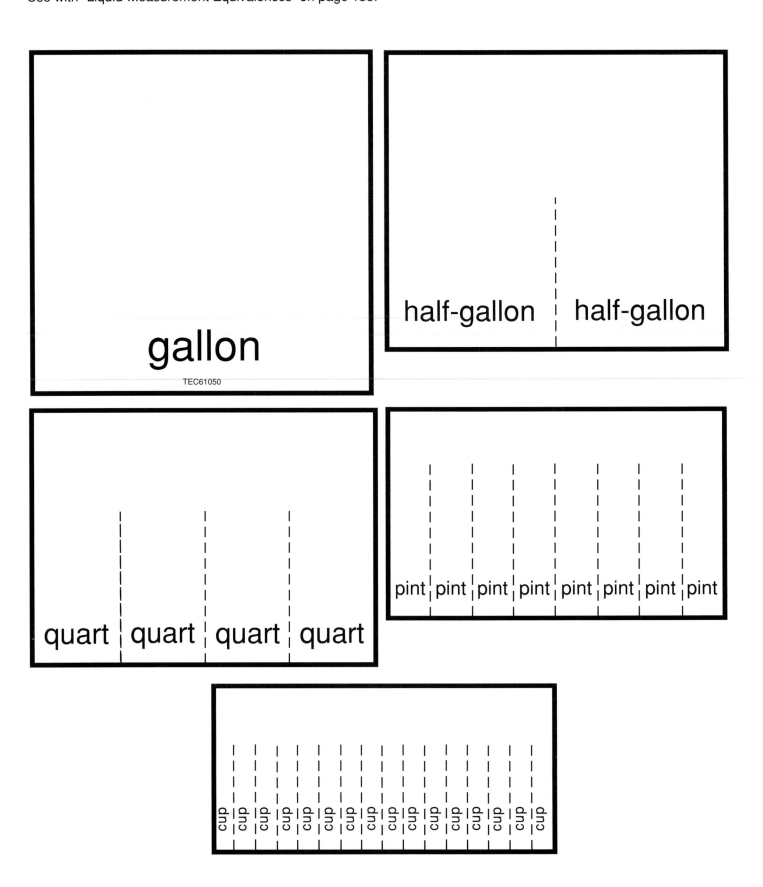

gallon

TEC61050

half-gallon | half-gallon

quart | quart | quart | quart

pint | pint | pint | pint | pint | pint | pint | pint

cup cup cup cup cup cup cup cup cup cup cup cup cup cup cup cup

Works of Art

Use a centimeter ruler to measure each side to the closest centimeter.
Add to find the perimeter of each painting.

A. The Tree

___ + ___ + ___ + ___ = ___ cm

B. Mice

___ + ___ + ___ + ___ = ___ cm

C. Fishy Fish

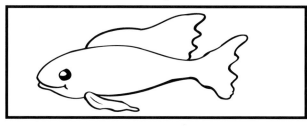

___ + ___ + ___ + ___ = ___ cm

D. Scratching Post

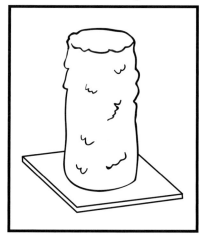

___ + ___ + ___ + ___ = ___ cm

E. Here, Birdy!

___ + ___ + ___ + ___ = ___ cm

Piggy Banks

Name _____

Cut out the coin cards on the left.
Use exactly three coins to match each amount.
Glue the cards in place.

55¢
16¢
25¢
40¢
12¢
31¢

Geometry

Alphabet Symmetry

Demonstrate the concept of symmetry with this small-group activity. Give each small group a set of newspaper headlines. Instruct each group to choose ten different letters from their headlines and cut them out. Have them arrange the letters in a row and ask them which letters can be cut in half to create identical shapes. Tell the students to check their choices by drawing a line of symmetry on each selected letter and then cutting the letter in half. If the pieces match, the line of symmetry is correct. **Symmetry**

SYMMETRICAL DRAWINGS

Provide a supply of magazines for students to look through to find a picture of a symmetrical object (such as a face, a sandwich, or a couch). Instruct the student to cut the picture on its line of symmetry and then glue one of the halves to a sheet of drawing paper. Have the student finish the picture by drawing the missing half to create a symmetrical image. **Symmetry**

Congruent Shapes

Reinforce the concept of congruent figures with a set of attribute blocks and a supply of drawing paper. Distribute a sheet of paper to each student and instruct him to fold it to create four sections. The student selects four attribute blocks and traces one block in each section of his paper. After everyone has filled in all four sections, instruct students to compare papers. When a student finds a paper featuring a shape that is congruent to one on his own paper, he has the classmate sign that section of his paper. Remind students that both the shape and size of the drawings must match in order for them to be congruent. Congruency

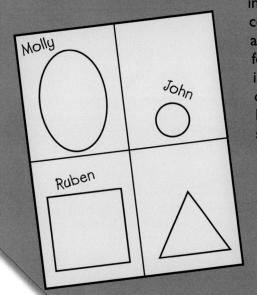

Teesha's Parrot
circles: head, eyes, body
ovals: wings
triangle: beak

Geometric Animals

This review of plane figures will have your students roaring for geometry! Provide a supply of colorful, construction paper scraps. Each student uses the paper scraps to cut out at least three different polygons and then glues them together to form a jungle animal of her choice. When she finishes, she lists on an index card her animal's name, the shapes used to make the animal, and on which body parts the shapes were used. Post the animals and cards on a display titled "It's a Geometry Jungle Out There!" **Plane Figures**

Solid-Figure Mobiles

Provide each group of four students with an enlarged tagboard copy of each pattern on pages 139 and 140, scissors, glue, markers, construction paper scraps, yarn, and a wire coat hanger. Direct each group to decorate the patterns before assembling them into solid figures. The group attaches a length of yarn to each assembled figure and then ties it to a wire coat hanger. Have the students discuss the name and attributes of each figure and use construction paper scraps to make labels. Then they tape the name and attribute labels to the yarn above each matching figure. Suspend the completed projects from the ceiling for a visual reference to solid figures. **Solid Figures**

Show-and-Tell

Present students with a homework challenge that reinforces solid geometric shapes. Ask each student to bring items from home that represent these solid shapes: a pyramid, a cone, a cylinder, a cube, a rectangular prism, and a sphere. Provide time the following day for students to share the objects they brought from home. After sharing the items, have each student place his objects on a table set up for the display. Have students group all like figures together to emphasize the name and property of each figure. Solid Figures

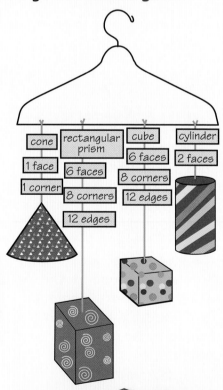

Check out the skill-building reproducible on page 141.

cylinder

rectangular prism

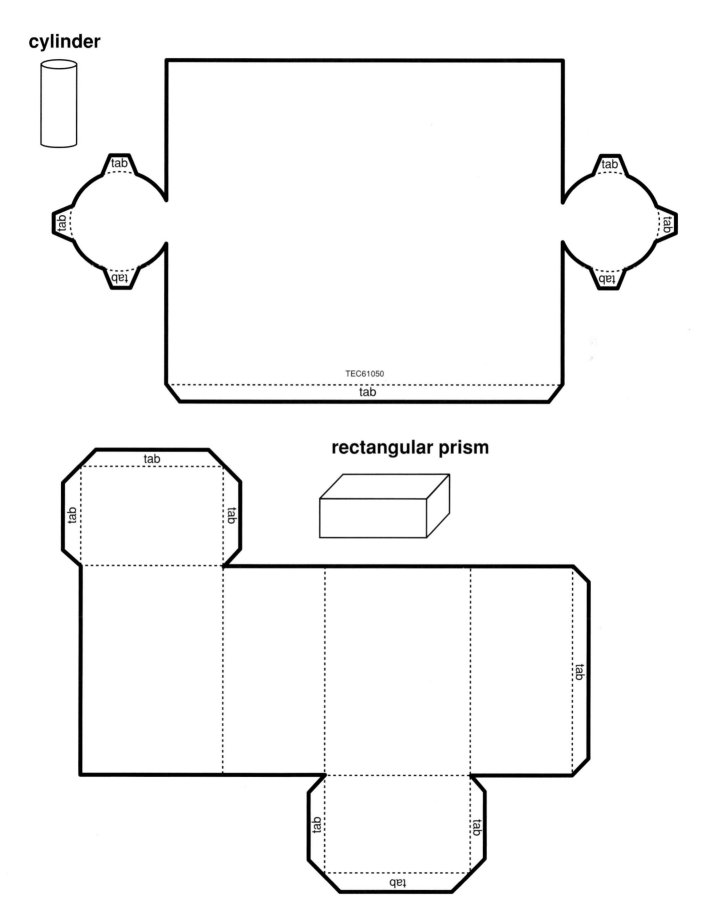

TEC61050

Solid-Figure Patterns

Enlarge and use with "Solid-Figure Mobiles" on page 138.

cone

cube

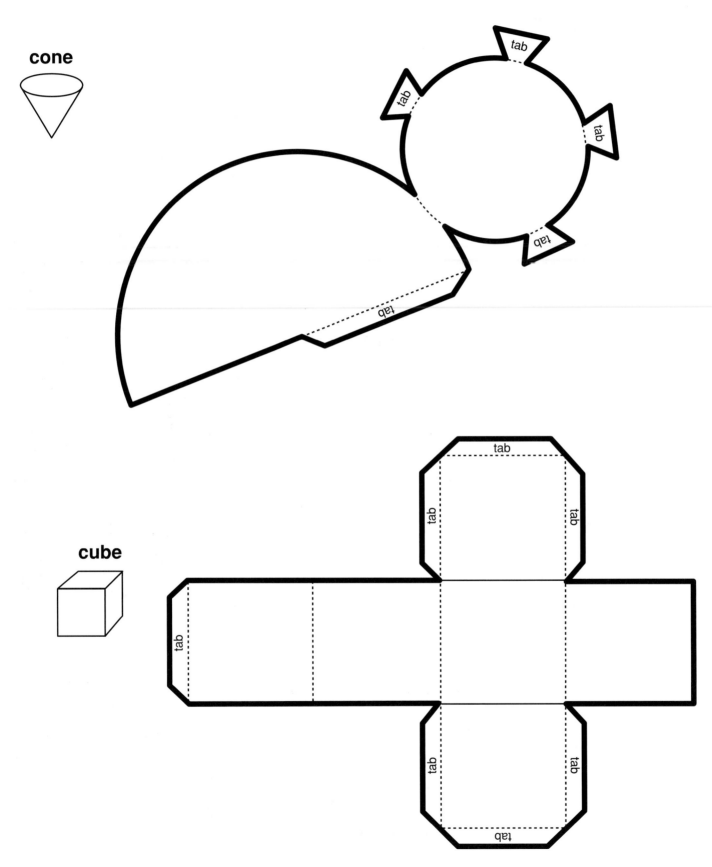

School Supplies

Cut out the cards.
Look at the bold angles.
Glue each card on the matching door.

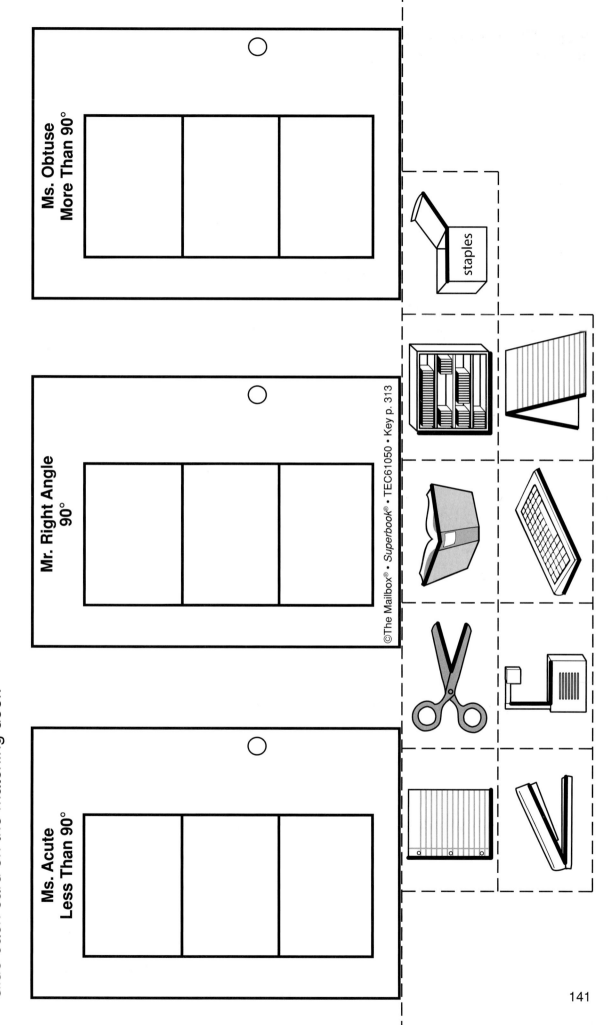

**Ms. Obtuse
More Than 90°**

**Mr. Right Angle
90°**

**Ms. Acute
Less Than 90°**

©The Mailbox® • *Superbook*® • TEC61050 • Key p. 313

staples

GRAPHING AND PROBABILITY

Book It!

Provide students with graphing practice as they record the number of books that they read each month. Divide the class into four or five groups, and assign each group a color. Post a class-size bar graph programmed with the colors representing each group. When a student finishes reading a book, give him a sticky note in his group's color. Instruct him to attach it to the appropriate column on the graph. At the end of the month, compare the results. Then have each student write five questions about the data shown on the graph. Provide time for students to read their questions to the class and call on volunteers to answer. **Bar graphs**

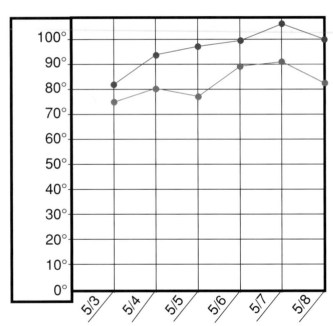

Temperature Tracking

Keep track of your city's high temperatures for one week and use the data to have students construct line graphs. At the end of the week, distribute a copy of the graph on page 144 to each student. Instruct the student to number the left side of the graph paper by ten-degree increments and to write the date for each day on the diagonal lines at the bottom of the graph. Show students how to place a dot on the graph above each date to record the temperature.

Extend the activity by recording the high and the low temperatures for a week. Have each student use a different color to record each type of temperature on the graph.

Line graphs

Eye-Catching Circle Graphs

Introduce the concept of circle graphs with a group activity. Divide the class into groups of eight students. Give a copy of the circle graph on page 145 and a supply of crayons to each group. Inform students with like eye color to each color a connecting section of the circle graph with a crayon of the same color. Tell each group to complete the graph's key by placing a color dot for each color represented on the graph and writing the name of the eye color beside it. If desired, compile each group's data on a larger circle graph with a section for each student. Or use the data to show fractional amounts.

Circle graphs

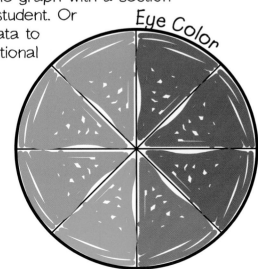

Eye Color

Pictographs Made Easy

Help students with reading pictographs whose pictures represent more than one. Draw attention to the key and the value of the picture. Then, as each child reviews each row of data, have him skip-count and write the number represented beside each picture. He not only practices reading the graph correctly, but he also creates an easy reference for answering graph-related questions.
Pictographs

Favorite Pizza Toppings

Pepperoni	◯3	◯6	◯9	
Sausage	◯3			
Extra Cheese	◯3	◯6	◯9	◯12

Each ◯ = 3 students

upon
kept
around
present
above

What Are the Chances?

Challenge students to show off their spelling and probability knowledge with this integrated activity. Prior to the lesson, write five spelling words on the board. To begin, review with your students the meanings of the words *certain, likely, unlikely,* and *impossible*. Next, ask each student to number a piece of paper to five. Using the spelling word list as a reference, ask a series of five questions about the words whose answers will be *certain, likely, unlikely,* or *impossible* (see the examples). Review the answers with the class and repeat the activity another day with another set of words. *Likelihood of events*

What are the chances you will spell a one-syllable word? (unlikely)
What are the chances you will spell a two-syllable word? (likely)
What are the chances you will spell a word with at least one vowel? (certain)
What are the chances you will spell a word that is a proper noun? (impossible)
What are the chances you will spell a word that ends with a consonant? (likely)

I Predict That...

To prepare this partner center, place five red cubes and five blue cubes in a paper bag. Also, make a class supply of the recording sheet on page 145. Place the copies and the bag at a center. To play, each partner examines the number and color of cubes in the bag and then writes his name on a recording sheet. Partner 1 records his prediction for the first color that he thinks he will pick and then draws a cube. He records the actual color picked and then awards himself a point if his prediction was correct. Leaving the cube out of the bag, Partner 2 takes a turn. Round 1 continues until all ten cubes have been drawn. Players should discover that the likelihood of choosing a particular color changes with each pick and, if necessary, change how they make their predictions. Players return the cubes to the bag and repeat for two more rounds. The player with more points at the end of the game is the winner. **Predicting outcomes**

Check out the skill-building reproducible on page 146.

Line Graph

Use with "Temperature Tracking" on page 142.

_____
title of graph

TEC61050

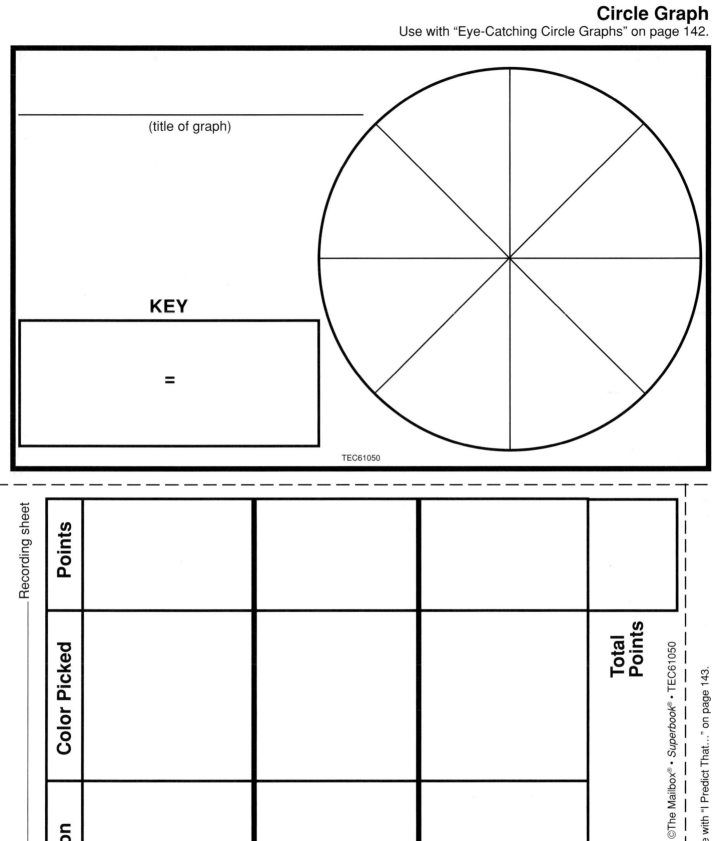

_____
(title of graph)

KEY

=

TEC61050

Player _____

Recording sheet

	Prediction	Color Picked	Points
Round 1	1.		
	2.		
	3.		
	4.		
	5.		
Round 2	1.		
	2.		
	3.		
	4.		
	5.		
Round 3	1.		
	2.		
	3.		
	4.		
	5.		
		Total Points	

©The Mailbox® • Superbook® • TEC61050

Note to the teacher: Use with "I Predict That..." on page 143.

145

Ready for Recess

Look at the spinner.

1. Which game will you most likely spin? _____

2. Which game will you least likely spin? _____

Use a paper clip and a pencil to make a spinner.
Spin the spinner and color a box to match each game spun.
Keep spinning and coloring until you have 20 boxes colored in all.

Basketball																			
Kickball																			
Tetherball																			
Wall Ball																			

3. How do your results compare to your predictions?_____

_____

Why do you think that happened? _____

_____

4. If you spun the spinner 20 more times, which game do you think you would spin the most?

_____

Why? _____

_____

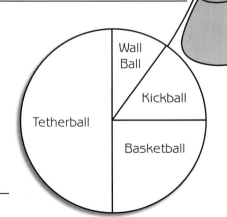

ALGEBRA

Button, Button

Send a note home with students requesting that they bring in any unwanted buttons. Assign students to small groups and give each group a handful of buttons and access to resealable plastic bags. Direct each group to explore various ways to sort its buttons. Next, have each group select one sorting method, sort its buttons, and place each group of buttons in a different bag. Invite each student group to present its work to the class and explain its sorting method. Later, open the bags, display all of the buttons in a center, and challenge students to investigate all of the sorting possibilities! **Sorting**

1	2	3	4	5	6	7	8	9	10
11	12	13	14	15	16	17	18	19	20
21	22	23	24	25	26	27	28	29	30
31	32	33	34	35	36	37	38	39	40
41	42	43	44	45	46	47	48	49	50
51	52	53	54	55	56	57	58	59	60
61	62	63	64	65	66	67	68	69	70
71	72	73	74	75	76	77	78	79	80
81	82	83	84	85	86	87	88	89	90
91	92	93	94	95	96	97	98	99	100

Jumping Beans

To begin this skip-counting activity, give each child a hundred chart, a handful of beans, and crayons. Assign a number from 1 through 10 and explain that this is the number that students will use as their skip-counting pattern. Next, direct each student to place a bean on each number in the pattern. For example, place a bean on 2 and each of its multiples. When he finishes, have him color each number in the pattern as he removes each bean. Then assign a different number and have students repeat the steps, using a different-colored crayon. Once they have finished, lead students in a discussion about the differences and similarities in the numbers in each pattern. For an added twist, divide the class into groups and assign two different numbers to each group. When all groups have finished, discuss similarities and differences between the finished charts. *Skip-counting*

From Produce to Patterns

To prepare this center, purchase several green bell peppers, onions, and carrots. Cut one of each vegetable in half as shown. Show students how to dip the halves into paint and use them to stamp a pattern onto a 4" x 18" construction paper strip. Store the cut vegetables in a center, along with paint and a supply of construction paper strips. Invite each student who visits the center to use the vegetables to stamp a pattern onto a strip. The next day, cut a new set of vegetables in half, and the center is ready to go again! **Patterns**

What's Missing?

A balance scale and a set of matching manipulatives will help you give your students a visual understanding of missing addends. Display the scale in front of the class and place six manipulatives on one side of the scale and two manipulatives on the other. On the board, write 2 + __ = 6. Next, ask students how many pieces you should add to the side with two pieces to make it balance with the side with six pieces. To confirm their predictions, add one piece to the scale at a time as students count the pieces out loud. When the scale is balanced, add the resulting number (4) to the problem on the board. Repeat the activity with other problems. To assess individual understanding, have each child complete the reproducible on page 150. **Missing addends**

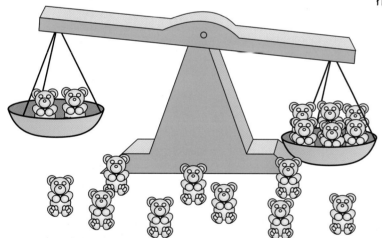

Thoughtful Math

Have students complete a copy of page 149 and then take the learning a step further with this quick activity. Direct the student to select one of the tables from the page. Next, on the back of the page, have her write to explain the strategy she used to find the function for the table. Provide time for each student to share her explanation with the class before she turns in her completed page. **Function tables**

Home, Tweet Home

Follow the rule to complete the table.

Rule: Add 3.

3	
5	
8	
9	

Rule: Subtract 0.

8	
7	
6	
4	

Rule: Add 4.

2	
5	
7	
9	

Rule: Add 8.

5	
7	
8	
9	

Rule: Subtract 2.

9	
5	
3	
2	

Rule: Add 4.

0	
4	
6	
8	

Rule: Subtract 5.

8	
7	
6	
5	

Rule: Subtract 4.

9	
7	
6	
4	

Note to the teacher: Use alone or with "Thoughtful Math" on page 148.

Name _____

Beautiful Balloons

Write each missing addend.
Color a balloon with the matching addend.

8 + _____ = 13

4 + _____ = 11

5 + _____ = 9

6 + _____ = 12

2 + _____ = 10

8 + _____ = 14

7 + _____ = 12

3 + _____ = 8

7 + _____ = 15

3 + _____ = 12

4 + _____ = 8

6 + _____ = 6

9 + _____ = 13

5 + _____ = 7

1 + _____ = 8

9 + _____ = 18

Balloons: 4, 6, 7, 5, 9, 2, 7, 5, 5, 4, 8, 6, 9, 4, 0, 8

Note to the teacher: Use alone or with "What's Missing?" on page 148.

On the Map

Key words are easy to find with this mathematical display. Use black paper to make two roads. Then cut two rectangular road signs and label each as shown. Also make several color copies of the car pattern on page 153 and cut them out. Have students name words and phrases that indicate when to multiply or divide. Write each on a car and post the car on the matching road. Encourage students to reference the display when they solve word problems. As an added review, include two more roads and cars to your map, "Addition Avenue" and "Subtraction Street."

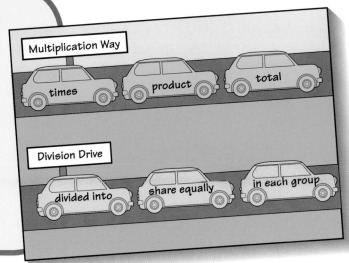

Multiplication Way: times, product, total

Division Drive: divided into, share equally, in each group

C

8 miles a day
for 5 days
total number of miles

U

at practice

P

Day 1	Day 2	Day 3	Day 4	Day 5

S

40 miles

At practice, Rita Rabbit ran 8 miles a day for 5 days. What was her total number of miles?

CUPS

Help students break down the problem-solving process with this easy-to-remember organizer. Have each student fold a sheet of drawing paper into fourths and label each section as shown. Then challenge him to solve an assigned word problem in order by sections. He lists crucial information needed to solve the problem in the C section, writes unneeded information in the U section, draws any necessary picture or other graphic representation in the P section, and shows his solution in the S section.

Problem Jar

Here's a simple way to slip more problem-solving practice into the school day. Label two plastic jars as shown. Cut word problems from old workbooks or reproducibles and place them in the problem jar. When a student has a few extra minutes, she pulls a question from the problem jar and writes her name on the back. She solves the problem, showing her work right on the paper. Then she places it in the solution jar. Every few days, select a few slips from the solution jar. Award the students with correct answers a small prize.

Problems

Solutions

8. Harry eats 2 snacks every hour he works. One day he ate 12 snacks. How many hours did he work?

_____6_____ hours

To get ready for Thanksgiving, Tom Turkey gained two pounds each day. How much weight did he gain after one week?

Holiday Helpers

Enlist the help of your students with this seasonal idea. At the beginning of each month, have each student write a word problem based on a monthly theme, such as Thanksgiving or Valentine's Day. Have each student solve his problem; then collect the problems. Then, each day, choose one to serve as the problem of the day. Have the author display his problem on the overhead and have the rest of the class solve it. Allow the student author to show the class his strategy for solving the problem and to call on two others to share their strategies.

Flower Arrangements

To set up this partner center, make two copies of the flower pattern on page 153 in each of the following colors: red, orange, and blue. Make three copies of the pattern in yellow. Also make five copies of the pot pattern. If desired, use plastic pots and silk flowers instead. Place the pots and flowers at a center, along with a class set of page 154. Students work together to read and solve each problem, using the manipulatives to help them.

Market Value

Make the guess-and-check strategy a daily special, and students will be loyal customers. Post a chart like the one shown. Explain to students that the cost of the items in your make-believe store equals the sum of its letters. For example, a cat costs $24.00 because $3.00 (c) + $1.00 (a) + $20.00 (t) equals $24.00. Challenge students to use the guess-and-check strategy to find each of the following: a pet that costs more than a cat, a pet that costs less than a cat, and an item that costs more than $100.00. Compare answers and encourage students to explain their strategies for solving. If desired, post a new challenge each day, such as finding the lowest-priced vegetable or highest-priced toy.

a = $1.00	n = $14.00
b = $2.00	o = $15.00
c = $3.00	p = $16.00
d = $4.00	q = $17.00
e = $5.00	r = $18.00
f = $6.00	s = $19.00
g = $7.00	t = $20.00
h = $8.00	u = $21.00
i = $9.00	v = $22.00
j = $10.00	w = $23.00
k = $11.00	x = $24.00
l = $12.00	y = $25.00
m = $13.00	z = $26.00

Car Pattern
Use with "On the Map" on page 151.

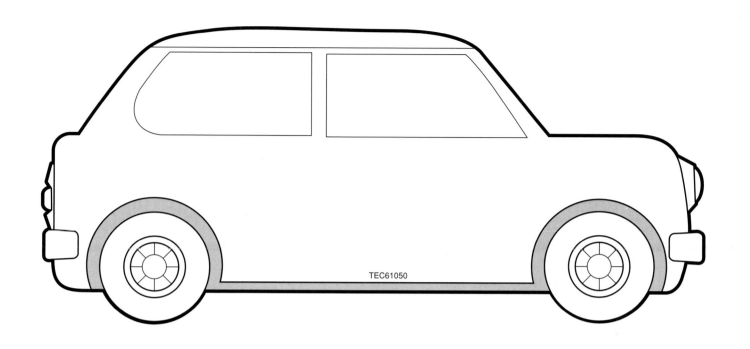

Flower and Pot Patterns
Use with "Flower Arrangements" on page 152.

Pocketful of Posies

Color the flowers to match the clues.

Problem A

Flowers needed: 2 red, 2 blue, 1 yellow

Clue: The red flowers are in the end pots.
Clue: The yellow flower is not next to any red flowers.

Problem B

Flowers needed:
2 orange, 3 yellow

Clue: One orange flower is on the end.
Clue: The other orange flower is next to it.

Problem C

Flowers needed: 2 yellow, 2 blue, 1 orange

Clue: The yellow flowers are next to each other.
Clue: The blue flowers are next to each other.
Clue: The orange flower is between a yellow and a blue flower.

Problem D

Flowers needed: 2 red, 2 orange, 1 yellow

Clue: The red flowers are between the orange flowers.
Clue: The yellow flower is next to just one red flower.

Problem E

Flowers needed: 2 yellow flowers, 2 blue flowers, 1 orange flower

Clue: The orange flower is not next to a yellow flower.
Clue: A yellow flower is between two blue flowers.

©The Mailbox® • Superbook® • TEC61050 • Key p. 314

PLANTS

Begin your unit on plants with a brainstorming session. Ask your students to think of all the products we get from plants. Record the responses on the board. Then have students demonstrate their understanding with a group activity. Provide a supply of old magazines for students to use to cut out examples of plant products. Place students in small groups to sort their pictures into different categories, such as food, building materials, paper products, clothing, and decoration. Give a piece of chart paper, glue, and a marker to each group. Instruct each group to list the categories and glue the pictures under the appropriate headings. Display the completed posters during your study of plants.

It Starts With a Seed

Most students know that many plants start out as small seeds—now you can show them how the transformation takes place! Ask each student to bring in a clear glass jar from home. Instruct the student to line the inside of the jar with two folded, wet paper towels. (To keep the towels in place, crumple a third towel and stuff it in the center of the jar.) Give each student several bean seeds, and have her place them between the paper towels and the side of her jar. Find a warm, dark place to store the jars. Have students check their jars daily to keep the towels moist and observe the changes from seeds to plants.

Seed Sort

Ask students to bring examples of seeds to class. Remind them to look for seeds in fruit, on plants in their yards, in seed packages, and on trees. If desired, bring in a few seeds that students may have not considered, such as a coconut, an avocado pit, poppy seeds, a raw peanut, and kernels of popcorn. Place the seeds in a center. Then ask groups of students to visit the center and determine ways to group the seeds. Provide time for students to discuss their grouping ideas with the class. Then use the seeds for the following activity.

How Does Your Garden Grow?

After students have observed the seeds in the sorting activity above, have them further their investigations by studying the different types of seeds as they grow. Fill the cups of empty, clean egg cartons with potting soil. Have students plant different seeds in each cup, making sure to label which type of seed is in each cup. Then place the "gardens" in a sunny location and help students water and care for them. Have students record observations about which seeds sprout first, which produce leaves the fastest, which grow tallest, and the differences in leaves and stems. If possible, transplant the seedlings to an outdoor location for further study.

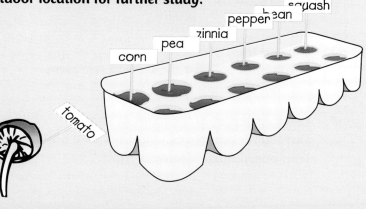

Eat Your Vegetables!

After students become familiar with the different parts of a plant, challenge them to bring edible plant parts for show-and-tell. Encourage your students to find edible roots (such as turnips, carrots, and radishes), leaves (such as spinach, lettuce, and cabbage), seeds (such as peas, corn, and kidney beans), stems (such as celery and asparagus), and flower clusters (such as cauliflower and broccoli). After each student shares his plants and identifies their parts, assist students in washing the vegetables. Then hold a plant-tasting party!

Portrait of a Plant

Reinforce the names of the parts of a plant by having your students create colorful diagrams. Each student needs a sheet of white construction paper, a green pipe cleaner, a piece of string, glitter, crayons, scissors, and glue. Instruct each student to make the model as follows:

1. Use a brown crayon to draw a horizontal line about two inches from the bottom of the paper. Color the bottom portion of the paper brown to represent the soil.

2. Glue the green pipe cleaner perpendicular to the soil to represent the stem.

3. Draw and color simple petals and leaves as shown.

4. Apply a small amount of glue in the center of the petal. Sprinkle with glitter to represent the pollen.

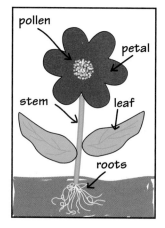

5. Unravel the string. Glue it under the stem to represent the root system.

6. Label each part of the plant as shown. Display the completed diagrams on a bulletin board titled "Plant Portraits."

More Plant Pizzazz

Incorporate the following activities into your study of plants:

- Have each student grow an edible sprout garden. Instruct the students to each wet a paper towel and place it in a shallow tray. Sprinkle each paper towel with mustard, celery, radish, wheat, cress, and alfalfa seeds. After the seeds sprout, allow the students to taste the sprouts. Discuss the different flavor of each type of sprout.

- Have students bring in a collection of leaves from home. (Remind students to have an adult identify any unfamiliar leaves, as some plants are poisonous to the touch.) Place the leaves and a magnifying glass in a learning center. During free time have students observe the leaves using the magnifying glass.

- Have students research plants from different habitats. Assign groups of students to find out about desert, forest, polar, jungle, ocean, or rain forest plants. Provide time for each group to share its findings with the class.

Check out the skill-building reproducibles on pages 157 and 158.

A Place for a Plant

Help the plant choose a pot.
Color the box that has the word that completes each sentence.
Color the pot.

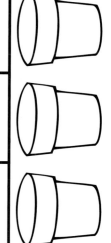

cooked	living	paper
colors	water	places
leaves	needs	roots
petals	water	trees
soil	stores	boxes
light	green	sound
air	fire	covering
kitchens	rain	doors
sun	matches	towels
vines	light	moons

1. Plants are _____ things.

2. They can live in many types of _____.

3. All plants have the same _____.

4. Plants need _____.

5. Plants get minerals from _____.

6. Plants need _____.

7. Plants also need _____.

8. Plants get water from _____.

9. They get light from the _____.

10. Plants need water, air, soil, and _____.

©The Mailbox® • Superbook® • TEC61050 • Key p. 314

157

Name _____

Plant Parts

Label each part of the plant.
Use the word bank to help you.

_____

_____

Word Bank
stem
leaf
roots
flower

Complete each sentence.
Use the word bank to help you.

Word Bank
sunlight
flower
stem
minerals
leaves
roots

1. The __ __ __ __ holds up the plant.

2. The __ __ __ __ __ hold the plant in the ground.

3. The __ __ __ __ __ __ makes seeds that grow new plants.

4. The __ __ __ __ __ __ take in carbon dioxide and release oxygen.

5. The roots take in water and

   __ __ __ __ __ __ __ __ from the soil.

6. The leaves use __ __ __ __ __ __ __ __ to make food for the plant.

Animals

Take Your Pick

Provide time for students to share their prior knowledge about animals with this activity. Label each of six plastic milk lids with a different animal group: insect, amphibian, mammal, reptile, fish, bird. Share the labels with the class; then place the lids in an empty animal cracker box. Invite a child to draw a lid from the box and share something he knows about that group of animals. Record the student's response on a sheet of chart paper, return the lid to the box, and repeat the process with another child. After each child has shared a fact, use the chart to record what students learn throughout your animal study.

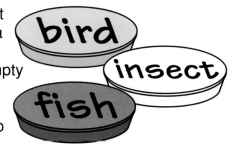

Research Safari

Encourage cooperation as students go on a scavenger hunt. To begin, put reference materials in various places in your room. Give each student a copy of page 161 and have him choose a partner. Set a timer for a pre-determined amount of time and have student pairs visit the various reference materials to list as many animal names as they can for each group. When time has expired, pairs take turns sharing their lists. Record responses on the board with the corresponding group. If desired, reward student pairs who work well together with animal stickers or animal crackers.

From A to Z

Help students classify their animal facts with this simple organizer. Give each child a copy of page 162 and access to a variety of reference materials. She chooses an animal to research and writes its name across the top of the sheet. Then, as she finds words or brief facts related to her animal, she writes it with the corresponding letter. When she fills as much of the chart as possible, she glues it to a large sheet of construction paper and adds an illustration of her animal on the back. Bind the completed projects in a class book and place it in your class library. As an alternative, have each student use the completed chart to write a report on her chosen animal.

Name _Sam_

Research Safari

Classifying animals

Amphibians	Birds	Fish
frog	ostrich	
salamander		

Please remember to spell correctly!

Insects	Mammals	Reptiles

Animal: _snake_

A	B	C	D
Anaconda	eats birds	coils	lives in deserts
E most lay eggs	F forked tongue	G may live on the ground	H hisses
I do not often live	J Jamaican boa	K King snake	L legless

Wild Kingdom Want Ads

Advertise students' knowledge of animal needs with this creative-writing project. To begin, review with students the basic needs of animals (food, shelter, water). Then provide each student with access to research materials and have her gather information about how those needs are met for a chosen animal. Next, share an example of a newspaper want ad. Then have each student create an ad of basic needs, taking the perspective of her researched animal. Post completed projects on a display titled "Want Ads From the Wild Kingdom."

Habitat Needed

Strong lion is looking for a roomy home on grassy plains. A large supply of deer, antelope, or zebra is needed, and a refreshing water supply is a must. If available, please call King Leo at 555-0198.

Go Home!

This variation on the game Go Fish! will have students thinking about animal habitats. Organize students into groups of four and assign each member a habitat. Then give each student ten index cards. He writes and draws five different animals found in that habitat on two cards each. He puts the completed cards in a group stack.

To play, a dealer shuffles the cards and gives each group member five of them. Each student locates and removes any matching animal cards from his set. Then Player 1 asks another player for a card, stating the habitat and animal name (pond fish). If the player has the card, she gives it to Player 1, and Player 1 takes another turn. If she does not have the card, she tells Player 1 "Go home!" and Player 1 draws a card from the deck. Then Player 2 takes a turn. Play continues in this manner until all cards are matched or time is up. The player with the most matching pairs wins.

Do you have a desert camel?

polar bear

shark

camel

Name

Research Safari

Please remember to spell correctly!

Fish

_____
_____
_____
_____
_____
_____

Birds

_____
_____
_____
_____
_____
_____

Amphibians

_____
_____
_____
_____
_____
_____

Reptiles

_____
_____
_____
_____
_____
_____

Mammals

_____
_____
_____
_____
_____
_____

Insects

_____
_____
_____
_____
_____
_____

©The Mailbox® • *Superbook*® • TEC61050

Note to the teacher: Use with "Research Safari" on page 159.

Animal Organizer

Use with "From *A* to *Z*" on page 159.

Animal:			
A	B	C	D
E	F	G	H
I	J	K	L
M	N	O	P
Q	R	S	T
U	V	W	XYZ

©The Mailbox® • *Superbook*® • TEC61050

Animal Adaptations

hibernation

groundhog

Survival Sort

Students identify adaptations with this simple partner activity. To prepare, label each of four paper plates with one of the following terms: *camouflage, mimicry, migration,* or *hibernation.* Also obtain a variety of animal pictures from magazines or the Internet, and glue each to a piece of construction paper. Then have each student choose an animal photo and write the animal's adaptation(s) on the back. Stack the completed cards picture-side up and place them with the paper plates at a center. To complete the activity, student partners take turns reviewing each picture. They determine an adaptation appropriate for the animal and place the card on the matching plate. When all of the cards have been placed, the partners flip them over to check their work.

Handy Review

To prepare these student-made reference guides, organize students into groups of four and provide each group with reference materials. Give each student a piece of rectangular cardstock and assign him a vocabulary word. The child writes the word and its definition across the top of the cardstock. Next, he adds a description of an animal that matches his word and definition. Then he passes his paper to another group member, who adds another animal that matches the word and definition. Papers are passed among group members until each group member adds an animal to each adaptation list. Then one group member stacks the papers together and punches a hole in the top left corner. She inserts a metal ring before placing the reference guide at a science center or the class library.

Camouflage

- Colors and patterns on animals that help them blend into their surroundings.

- A zebra uses its stripes to help it hide from lions.

- A tiger uses its stripes to hide in tall grass.

- A walking stick is colored and shaped like a twig.

- A polar bear is white like the snow around it.

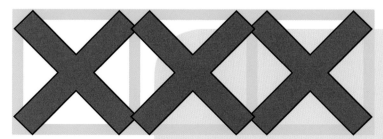

Three in a Row

This variation of tic-tac-toe reinforces vocabulary about animals. Provide students with access to a variety of reference materials as well as discarded magazines and newspapers. Have each student review the activities listed on page 164. He chooses one to complete on a separate piece of paper and uses the reference materials to help him. Then he crosses out the square and continues working on the activities until he has three in a row horizontally, vertically, or diagonally. For an added challenge, have students complete the entire grid.

Tic-Tac-Terms

List two synonyms for *environment.*	Write a question and its answer using the word *prey.*	Find a picture of an animal that is a *predator.* Cut it out and glue it to a piece of paper.
Choose an animal. Write a paragraph describing its *adaptations.*	Draw a picture of an animal that *migrates.*	Write a definition for *instinct.*
Write a riddle, giving clues about an animal that *hibernates.* Include the answer.	Name two animals that use *mimicry.* Also name the animals they mimic.	Choose an animal. Draw and label a picture of the animal in its *habitat.*

OBJECTS IN THE SKY

Planet Particulars

To prepare, gather nonfiction books about the planets. Then give each child a copy of the chart on page 167. The child chooses one planet to focus on as he completes the first two columns on the chart. Next, he reads about his planet in his textbook and the nonfiction books before he completes the third column of the chart. Once he has gathered facts about his planet, the child publishes his facts in a step booklet. To make his booklet, the child stacks two light-colored sheets of construction paper. He slides the top sheet upward an inch and then folds the booklet and staples it in the center along the top fold. He trims the booklet into a circle. Then he uses a black crayon to write one fact about his planet on each layer as shown. To complete the project, he lifts each booklet page and draws an illustration that goes with the fact on that page. Display the completed booklets on a bulletin board titled "Packed With Planet Information."

A day on Jupiter lasts ten Earth hours.

Jupiter has 16 moons.

It takes about 12 Earth years for Jupiter to orbit around the sun.

Jupiter is the largest planet.

Is It Day or Night?

For this demonstration, display a globe in front of the classroom. Dim the classroom lights and have a student volunteer hold a flashlight so the beam is directed toward the globe. Explain to the class that the student represents the sun. Then explain that it is daytime in the part of the earth that is being lit by the sun. Next, direct the child to shine the light on specific locations, such as North America, Europe, or Australia. As the child shines his light on each place, invite other students to point out specific places on the globe. As the second child points to a place, have him look at the area that is lit by the flashlight and then tell whether it is day or night in the place to which he is pointing. Continue the demonstration as time allows.

Waxing and Waning

Demonstrate the different phases of the moon with a Styrofoam ball, a flashlight, and a pencil. Use a black marker or tempera paint to color one-half of the ball. Poke the sharpened end of the pencil into the ball. Darken the room, and then have a student volunteer shine the flashlight on you. Sit about four feet away from the flashlight. Invite the students to sit behind you to observe the phases.

Hold the pencil in front of you, just above your head, with the white side of the ball facing you. Point out that the side of the moon facing you is receiving no light. This represents a new moon.

Slowly turn in a counterclockwise circle, always keeping the white side of the ball facing you. As you turn, direct students' attention to the increasing amount of light shining on the ball, representing the waxing phase. Pause briefly at the full moon stage before showing the moon beginning to wane.

Conclude the activity by asking students to observe the moon during the next few nights. Then discuss the different phases your students observe.

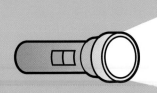

Order Up!

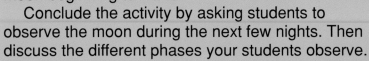

Key

For an individual assessment of students' understanding of the phases of the moon, make a class supply of the reproducible on page 168 and place it at a center along with a basket of moon pies. In addition, complete one copy of the reproducible and place in a manila envelope labeled "key." Have each child follow the directions to complete her copy of the reproducible before checking her work against the key. When she is finished, invite her to enjoy a moon pie before she returns to her desk.

Twinkle, Twinkle in the Sky

This simple demonstration will shed some light on the question of where stars go during the day! Make the classroom as dark as possible and then turn on a flashlight. Have students observe the beam of light made by the flashlight. Next, turn the classroom lights on and shine the flashlight directly underneath an overhead light. Ask, "Can you see the light from the flashlight?" (No.) Then explain that the flashlight is like a star. At night, when there is no light from the sun, we can see the stars shining brightly. During the day, the sun's light is so bright that we cannot see the stars, even though they are still there.

KWL chart

Getting to know _____ planet

What I know	What I want to know	What I learned

Note to the teacher: Use with "Planet Particulars" on page 165.

Name _____

The Moon on the Move

Cut apart the cards below.
Glue the cards in order to show the phases of the moon.
Start with the new moon card.

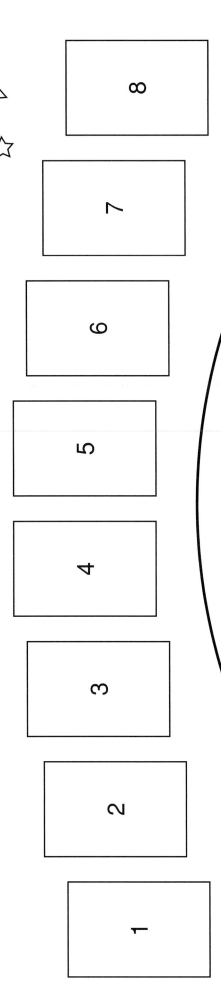

| 1 |
| 2 |
| 3 |
| 4 |
| 5 |
| 6 |
| 7 |
| 8 |

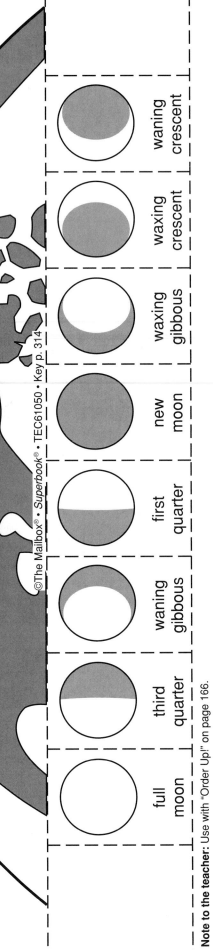

full moon · third quarter · waning gibbous · first quarter · new moon · waxing gibbous · waxing crescent · waning crescent

©The Mailbox® · Superbook® · TEC61050 · Key p. 314

Note to the teacher: Use with "Order Up!" on page 166.

Soil & Rocks

Dig In!

Show your students that dirt is much more than dirt by giving each pair a resealable plastic bag and a spoon. Lead the students onto the playground and direct each pair to scoop several spoonfuls of soil into its bag. As students return to the classroom, give each duo a sheet of waxed paper and four craft sticks. Direct the pair to empty its bag onto the waxed paper, and then have the partners use their craft sticks to investigate their sample. Have them set aside anything they find that's unusual, such as leaves, broken pieces of wood, or insects. To wrap up, guide the class in a discussion of the colors and textures of the soil samples. Then invite each pair to share some of the unusual items it discovered in its sample.

Three Types

Your students may already know that there are different types of soil, but do they know which type of soil holds the most water? To help them find out, give students access to a supply of three soil samples: one that is mostly topsoil, one that is mostly clay, and one that is mostly sand. In addition, make available hand lenses, water, fabric squares, and plastic spoons and tubs. Divide the class into groups and direct each group to make a prediction about which type of soil holds the most water. Next, have each group examine the available materials and develop an experiment to test its hypothesis. Guide the group to work together to perform its experiment. Finally, instruct the group to write a paragraph describing its hypothesis, experiment, and results. Provide time for groups to share and discuss their findings with the class.

Sedimentary Storytellers

Have your students create "fossils" from plaster of paris. Instruct each student to find a small object such as a shell or a leaf. Have the student lightly coat the outside of the object with petroleum jelly. Mix the plaster of paris according to package directions. Pour a small amount into a plastic cup for each student. Tell the student to gently place his object on top of the plaster mixture and then allow the plaster to dry. Help the student carefully remove the object from the dry plaster to reveal a "fossil" of the object.

Name Sarah   Recording Sheet

rock or soil	What is it being used for?
soil	The plants are growing in soil.
gravel	There is gravel in the fish tank.
soil	Soil was used when the bricks were made.
rocks	Rocks were used to make the road.

Note to the teacher: Use with "They're All Around" on page 170.

They're All Around!

To prepare students for this activity, share several photos of uses of rocks and soil. For example, show photos of jewelry made from precious stones, buildings made from granite, and vegetables growing in soil. Next, give each student a copy of the recording sheet on page 171. To get them started, have students look for rocks or soil being used in the classroom. Have volunteers point out the examples they find as each student records the information on his sheet. Then lead students on a walk through the school and playground, encouraging them to list other examples of uses of rocks and soil that they see. When students return to the classroom, invite them to share their findings with their classmates.

The Same, but Different

For this activity, ask each student to bring three to four small rocks to school. Place all of the rocks in a large container and allow each child to choose two different rocks to take back to his desk. As students study their rocks, ask questions such as the following: What color are your rocks? How do your rocks feel, smooth or rough? Are your rocks heavy or light? Next, give each child a copy of the Venn diagram on page 172 and direct him to study his rocks as he completes the page. Allow time for each child to share his work with the class before posting the finished pages on a bulletin board titled "Rocky Comparisons."

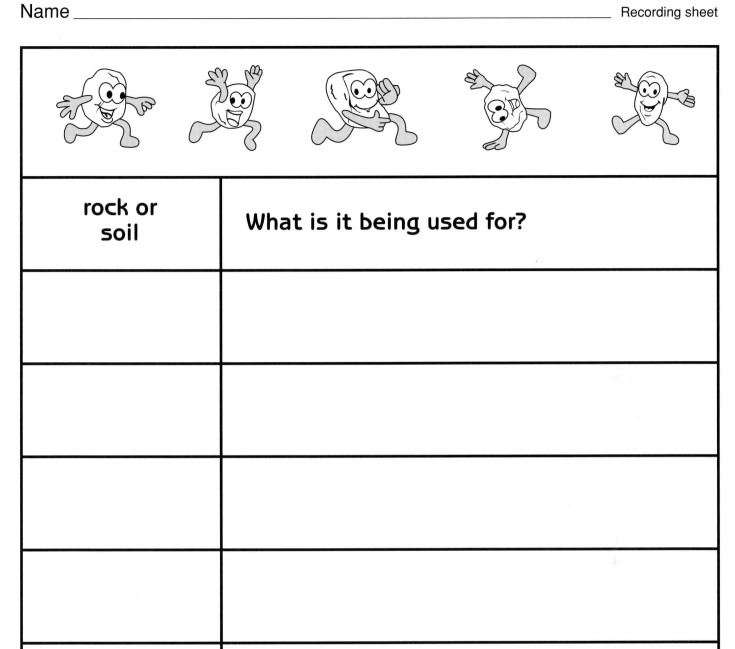

rock or soil	What is it being used for?

A Closer Look

Rock 2

Both

Rock 1

Note to the teacher: Use with "The Same, but Different" on page 170.

Let's Do Lunch!

Invite students to use their lunch period as a learning experience. Have students bring their lunchboxes and trays to the classroom for a conservation discussion over lunch. As students begin to eat, write the words *reusable*, *recyclable*, and *trash* on the board. Ask the students to consider how the items in their lunches fit into the categories. After everyone has finished eating, ask students to study the items remaining from their lunches. Have each student list his remaining items and tell which categories they belong in. Record the responses on the board. After all items have been recorded, have the students discuss the results. Have them offer suggestions for minimizing the *trash* category.

Renoirs of Recycling

Now that your students are aware of the three Rs of conservation, have them use their knowledge to create artistic displays. Ask each student to bring in a collection of clean, unwanted items (such as empty cereal boxes, cardboard tubes, egg cartons, and catalogs) from home. Provide each student with a sheet of 12" x 18" tagboard. Instruct each student to use items from the collection to create a conservation collage. Each collage can contain a message about taking care of the earth, show different items to recycle, or simply display an abstract design. Post the completed projects on a bulletin board with the title "The Renoirs of Recycling."

Get into recycling, or you'll be into garbage right up to your neck.

The Three Rs

Inform students that when it comes to conservation, the three Rs are *reduce*, *reuse*, and *recycle*. Each term describes a very important concept in taking care of the earth.

Reduce the amount of nonbiodegradable products, such as foam and aerosol cans, you and your family use. Also purchase products that use little or no packaging.

Reuse items. Do not discard after only one use. Reuse the product for the same or another function. Grocery sacks are often reused. After unloading your groceries, you can use the sacks as wastebasket liners or overnight bags, or you can take them with you on your next trip to the grocery store and use them again.

Recycle items instead of throwing them away. Aluminum cans, glass jars and bottles, plastic, newspapers and magazines, as well as other items can be recycled into the same product or made into a new product.

To demonstrate each of these concepts, set up three boxes in your classroom. Label each box "Reduce," "Reuse," or "Recycle." Encourage students to bring in examples of items to put in each box. Invite students to take objects from the Reuse box if they can put them to good use. Arrange for the items in the Recycle box to be taken to a recycling center. Then have your students find the best way to discard of the items in the Reduce box, and remind them to be careful of purchasing those items again in the future.

Check out the skill-building reproducible on page 174.

Mother Earth

Use a word from the word bank to complete each sentence.

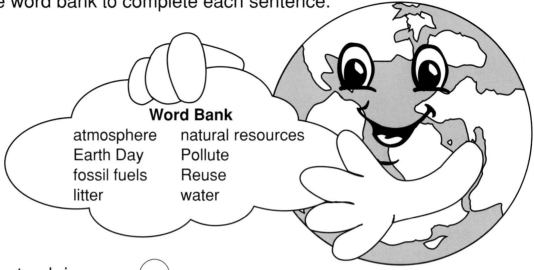

Word Bank

atmosphere	natural resources
Earth Day	Pollute
fossil fuels	Reuse
litter	water

1. Another word for trash is __ __ ◯ __ __ __.

2. ◯ __ __ __ __ __ __ means "to make unclean."

3. The layer of air around the earth is the __ __ __ ◯ __ __ __ __ __ __ __.

4. Fuels formed from dead plants and animals are __ __ __ __ __ ◯

   __ __ __ __ __.

5. ◯ __ __ __ __ means "to use again."

6. __ __ __ __ __ __ __ ◯ __ is celebrated on April 22.

7. Things from nature that people want or need are __ __ __ __ __ __ __

   __ ◯ __ __ __ __ __ __ __.

8. Three-fourths of Earth is covered by ◯ __ __ __ __.

Why did the gardener plant a lightbulb?
To solve the riddle, match the circled letters above to the numbered lines below.

He wanted to grow a __ __ __ __ __   __ __ __ **N** __ !
                      2 3 8 7 5   2 4 6   1

Sensible Snacking

This activity helps students understand the variety of healthful snacks that are available to them. Divide the students into a desired number of groups. Challenge each group to create a list of as many snacks as possible and have each group share its list as you record it on the board. Discuss the results with your students; then have them help you arrange the list into two columns. If desired, make copies of the list for students to take home and share with their parents. Reward students' hard work with a healthful snack of raisins, carrot sticks, or apple slices.

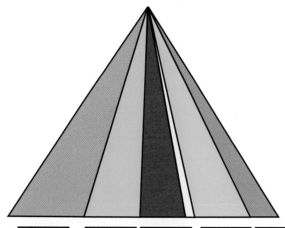

Pyramid Power

What is shaped like a triangle and packed with fabulous food facts? My Pyramid, the food guidance system, of course! Explain to students that the U.S. Department of Agriculture (USDA) and the Department of Health and Human Services (DHHS) have developed a set of guidelines for good eating habits. These guidelines are arranged in a pyramid to show the proportions of a healthful diet. Familiarize students with My Pyramid by having them create a model to display in the classroom. Draw a large triangle on a piece of bulletin board paper and use markers to visually divide it into sections as shown above. Label each section with its name and recommended servings. Divide the class into six groups and assign each group a section of the pyramid. Instruct each group to find or draw pictures of food that belong in its section. Have students glue their pictures on a sheet of construction paper. Then post the pyramid and sheets in a prominent place for students to refer to during their study of nutrition.

Fat is not where it is at!

Explain that besides being high in calories, foods that are high in fat can cause health problems such as heart disease, obesity, and cancer. Make an overhead transparency of a nutrition label and show students where to look for information regarding fat content. Then have students compare labels from candy, chips, cookies, and crackers to see which are highest in fat. (Students may notice that some candies are actually low in fat. That's because sugar, although high in calories, contains no fat.) Then have students use their findings to write a paragraph comparing a lowfat snack to one with a higher fat content. Ask student volunteers to share their paragraphs with the class.

Raiding the Refrigerator

Help your students practice creating well-balanced meals. Draw pictures of cupboard shelves and the inside of a refrigerator on a length of bulletin board paper. Supply students with magazines and instruct them to cut out pictures of healthful foods to glue to the cupboard shelves and the refrigerator. Display the well-stocked shelves in a corner of the classroom. Have student pairs visit the center to write a meal menu using the items displayed on the shelves. If desired, have resources available so that students can determine the fat grams or calories in their meals.

Let's Get Cookin'!

Enlist the help of parents and students in compiling a cookbook that's full of healthful recipes. In advance send a note home to parents asking them to assist their child in locating a healthful recipe to bring to school. Have each student copy his recipe onto a sheet of paper. Afterward, have students help you arrange the recipes into categories such as snacks, main dishes, salads, and desserts. Then, as a class, compose a list that details the dietary guidelines as suggested by the USDA and the DHHS. Bind the dietary guidelines, the completed recipes, and a few blank pages between construction paper covers. If desired, have student volunteers color a picture of the food pyramid to place on the cover. Then let a different student take the resulting cookbook home each night. Encourage each family to try one of the recipes from the cookbook, and invite them to write a comment about the recipe on the blank pages. This book will win rave reviews from students and parents alike!

Sugar, Sugar Everywhere

Surprise students with a sugar-filled fact: Each year the average American eats 125 pounds of sugar! Show students a five-pound bag of sugar and explain that it would take 25 bags of that size to equal 125 pounds. Students may also be surprised to learn that sugar is added to many common foods and labeled as glucose, fructose, maltose, lactose, or corn syrup. Supply students with copies of food labels you have duplicated from cereal, bread, cracker, and chip packages. Have students look at the ingredients list of each label to see if the product contains sugar. Inform students that the ingredients are listed in order from the greatest amount to the least amount. Ask, "Where does sugar appear on each list?" Then encourage students to look for labels at home that show low sugar contents. Have them bring the labels in to share with the class. Post the labels on a bulletin board titled "Here's to Healthy Eating!"

Heritage Banners

Focus on the many different heritages within your community by having students create family banners. Fold a 12" x 18" sheet of construction paper diagonally; then cut along the fold to create two banners. Make a banner for each student in the class. Have each student decorate her banner with a large initial of her family's last name, drawings of flags from her family's country of origin, symbols of favorite family activities, and other important information. Attach the completed banners to a string and display the colorful creations on a classroom wall. If desired, have the class locate each of the countries represented on the banners on a world map.

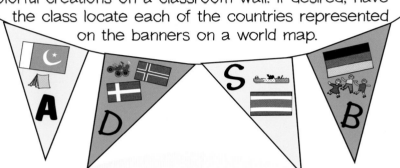

Community Quilts

Share a time-honored tradition with your students by exploring the historical significance of the patchwork quilt. Read either *The Keeping Quilt* by Patricia Polacco or *The Patchwork Quilt* by Valerie Flournoy to your class. Discuss with your students how each piece of the quilt tells about the family's history. Then challenge your students to make a quilt showing your community's history. Help your students research to find important historical events that have taken place in the community. Give each student a square of white construction paper to design a quilt square depicting one of the significant events. When all the individual squares are complete, attach them to a bulletin board paper backing. If desired, have each student use a black marker to add a row of stitch marks around his square. Display the finished quilt in a community center, public library, or courthouse for community members to enjoy.

Cultural Cookbook

Involve your students in a project that will encourage family sharing and yield some tasty results! Have each student interview family members to find out which foods are important to the family's heritage or are considered traditional family favorites. Ask each student to use the form on page 179 to write a copy of the recipe and find out why the food is important to the family, where the recipe originated, and when it is traditionally served. Invite parents to send in samples of some of the foods or assist in preparing one of the recipes with your class. Then help students compile the information they collected into a class cookbook by having each student type or copy the recipe in his best handwriting and compose a sentence or two about its significance to his family. Make a copy of each recipe for every student. Have each student staple the recipes between construction paper covers. The recipe booklet will be a special and useful keepsake for students and their families.

Caption Match

Keep your students aware of community happenings and reinforce reading skills at the same time. Collect several newspaper photos with captions that show events happening in your community. Glue the photos to a sheet of tagboard for durability; then cut the captions away from the photos. Code the backs of the matching pictures and captions for self-checking. Place the pieces in a learning center and challenge students to match each caption with the correct photograph. Students can help update the center by bringing current newspaper photographs from home.

The new post office will open next week.

Rainy skies continue throughout the area.

Current Community Events

Encourage students to keep up with current community happenings. Obtain a class supply of highlighters, or ask each student to bring one from home. Then find a current newspaper article about the community. Copy a class supply of the article and distribute one to each student. Read the article together; then have students locate the sentences that answer the five Ws (who, what, where, when, and why). Ask each student to highlight the key information. Their efforts will make the news article more understandable to them and will provide practice in locating important details.

Spotlighting Local Heroes

Recognize characteristics of good citizenship with this integrated activity. Periodically choose a peer or adult who has made a difference in the lives of your students. Together create a list of ten interview questions to ask the chosen citizen and post them on a sheet of chart paper. Have each child choose three of the questions that are of particular interest to her and record them on her own paper. Next, mail the honored citizen a copy of the note on page 180 along with a copy of the ten interview questions.

When you get a response, share it with the class and have students write the answers that match their chosen questions. Then have students use the information to write a paragraph about the honored citizen. If desired, bind the completed paragraphs into a book, using a copy of the bottom of page 180 as the cover. Present the book to the honored citizen.

Interview Questions

1. Do you volunteer in our community? How?

2. How do you practice good citizenship at home?

3.

Our
Local Hero
Principal Lee

Check out the skill-building reproducible on page 181.

What's Cooking?

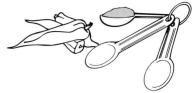

Recipe for _____

Submitted by _____

Ingredients:

Directions:

1. Why is this food special to your family?

2. Does this recipe originate from a special country?

3. Who first prepared this recipe for your family?

4. Is there a special time or occasion when your family uses this recipe?

Hero Note and Book Cover
Use with "Spotlighting Local Heroes" on page 178.

CONGRATULATIONS! • • • • • • • • • • • • • • •

Our class has chosen you as a local hero. We think you are a good citizen, and we want to recognize your efforts through a class project. Please read and answer the questions on the attached page. Then return the form to

_____

_____

_____

_____

We look forward to hearing from you and can't wait to learn more about you!

Sincerely,

_____

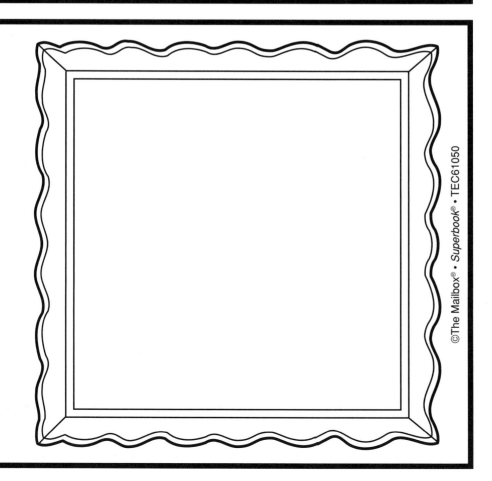

Our Local Hero

Name ______________________________

A Fine Time

Choose four events from your community's history.
Illustrate and describe each event.

_______________ _______________
date
____
____

_______________ _______________
date
____
____

_______________ _______________
date
____
____

_______________ _______________
date
____
____

Constitution Day
September 17

It Takes Time

Students use this center activity to sequence the important dates surrounding the U.S. Constitution. Label the fronts of ten index cards with the different dates and descriptors shown and number the backs to show the order in which the events occurred. Place the cards at a center. To use the center, a student orders the cards by date and turns them over to check. Then he writes a paragraph either telling what he thinks might have happened to the United States if the Constitution had not been written or how he feels about taking so much time to write a plan for something.

May 14, 1787
The Constitutional Convention is to begin. It is postponed when too few men arrive.

May 25, 1787
The Constitutional Convention opens. George Washington serves as the convention's president.

July 16, 1787
The Great Compromise is proposed. It offers a plan for setting up how states will be represented in Congress.

August 6, 1787
The first draft of the Constitution is accepted.

September 17, 1787
The Constitution is signed by 39 delegates.

December 7, 1787
Delaware is the first state to approve the Constitution.

June 21, 1788
The Constitution becomes law when New Hampshire becomes the ninth state to accept it.

February 4, 1789
The first presidential election is held.

March 4, 1789
The first Congress meets in New York City.

December 15, 1791
The Bill of Rights becomes part of the Constitution.

The Constitution is important for our country. It gives us our laws and government. If the Constitution had not been written, we might not be the United States anymore.

Each person should get an equal amount of food and soda.

Students who bring a snack from home should not get any soda or crackers. Kids with no snack will get one cracker and a small cup of punch.

We the students of Ms. Davis' third-grade class

We the Students

Set up a classroom convention to model the challenges of merging delegates who have varying opinions into a decision-making group that creates documents like the U.S. Constitution. Display a jug of punch or a bottle of soda and a box of crackers. Ask student pairs to write a plan to divide the items among class members. Each proposal is written on a sheet of paper, briefly shared with the class, and displayed. As a class, discuss the pros and cons of the various plans. Then write a final "constitution" for distributing the food, and have the class vote. When a decision has been reached, relate the experience to the Constitutional Convention and its purpose.

Check out the skill-building reproducible on page 183.

Constitutional Numbers

Solve.

A. 6 + 7 = _____ the number of original states

B. 10 – 8 = _____ the number of states that had men at the Constitutional Convention on May 14, 1787; the meeting was postponed. Not enough men had arrived.

C. 25 – 13 = _____ the number of states with men at the Constitutional Convention by May 25, 1787, when the work began

D. 42 + 13 = _____ the total number of men at the meeting

E. 40 + 41 = _____ the age of the oldest person present; it was Ben Franklin.

F. 5 + 2 = _____ the number of articles in the Constitution; an article is a numbered section.

G. 22 + 20 = _____ the number of men at the convention on September 17, 1787; this was the day when the Constitution was signed.

H. 27 + 12 = _____ the number of men who signed the Constitution

I. 7 – 4 = _____ the number of men who did not like the Constitution and did not sign it

J. 50 – 41 = _____ the number of states that needed to accept the Constitution for it to become the law of the land

Why do you think the number of men present in May 1787 was different from the number present in September 1787? Explain.

_____

_____

Map Skills

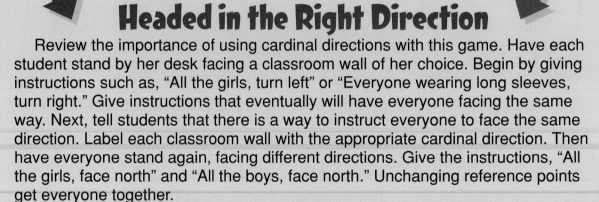

Headed in the Right Direction

Review the importance of using cardinal directions with this game. Have each student stand by her desk facing a classroom wall of her choice. Begin by giving instructions such as, "All the girls, turn left" or "Everyone wearing long sleeves, turn right." Give instructions that eventually will have everyone facing the same way. Next, tell students that there is a way to instruct everyone to face the same direction. Label each classroom wall with the appropriate cardinal direction. Then have everyone stand again, facing different directions. Give the instructions, "All the girls, face north" and "All the boys, face north." Unchanging reference points get everyone together.

Making a Legend

Use the concept of drawing a bird's-eye view to reinforce map keys. Take your students outdoors and have them draw the school playground as it would look from above. Then have each child create a key for his map showing objects such as trees, benches, and the different types of playground equipment. Then challenge each student to use his imagination to design a map of a new playground. Remind him to include a key that explains the objects shown on his map.

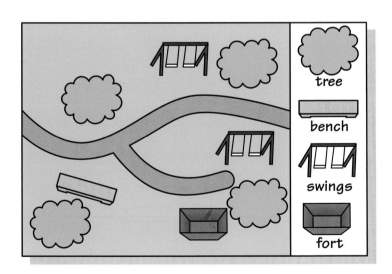

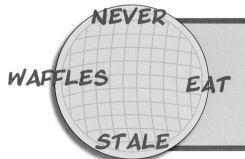

Quick Tip

When teaching cardinal directions, a simple mnemonic device will help each student remember the order. Just remind the class to **N**ever **E**at **S**tale **W**affles!

Shown to Scale

Using a map scale is more meaningful when students are familiar with the location. Obtain a class supply of county or state maps that clearly show points of interest. Give a map and a ruler to each child. After explaining how to use the mileage scale on the map, ask students to determine the number of miles between their city and various locations. Then challenge each child to write a problem relating to distances on the map. Compile the problems into a set of learning-center task cards for students to complete.

Great Grids

Capitalize on students' interests to provide practice with graphing ordered pairs. Create an overhead transparency of the grid on page 186. Use a wipe-off marker to draw a symbol in several of the grid boxes. Then show the transparency to students, demonstrating how to use specific coordinates to identify the location of each symbol. Then make a class supply of the grid pattern and give each child a copy. Call out a series of coordinates and instructions for plotting a point, such as the following:

- (5, C)—Write your first initial.
- (8, F)—Color the square using your favorite color.
- (3, E)—Write the number of people in your family.
- (10, B)—Draw a picture of your favorite fruit.
- (2, G)—Write the day of your birthday.

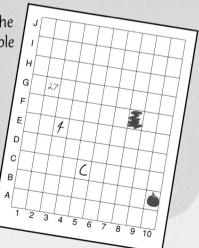

Extend the activity by having students create grids using symbols that relate to their favorite topics. Have each child trade grids with a classmate to determine the coordinates of each symbol. Then have the two students check the answers together.

The Dot Connection

Help your students recognize and locate continents, oceans, major countries, and other places with a package of fluorescent self-sticking dots. When introducing a region on the map, place a colored dot on the area. Also affix a dot of the same color to the corresponding area on the globe. Students will be able to see the same area presented in two different ways, helping to reinforce its location.

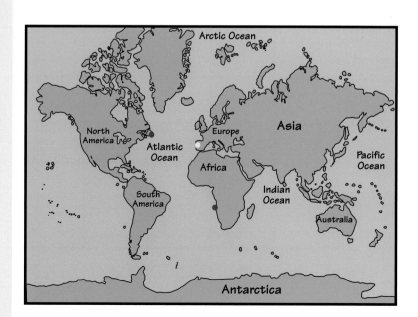

	1	2	3	4	5	6	7	8	9	10
J										
I										
H										
G										
F										
E										
D										
C										
B										
A										

Note to the teacher: Use with "Great Grids" on page 185.

Economic$

Consumer Collages

Reinforce the concept of the three basic consumer needs—food, shelter, and clothing—by having students make a collage of each need. Cut a large shape from bulletin board paper to represent each need. Instruct each child to draw or find an example of a picture that shows each type of need. Have him glue his pictures to the corresponding shapes. Then display the completed collages during your study of economics to help students remember the basic needs.

What About Wants?

Have students look at consumer wants through the eyes of an advertiser. Gather a supply of sale catalogs for students to peruse. Have them circle items that are wants rather than needs. Students may be surprised to find that most items are things a consumer wants but does not necessarily need. Ask students to surmise why advertisers show so many items that people do not have to have in order to survive. Then have each child design an advertisement for a want and a need. Which one is more tempting to the consumer?

Community Goods and Services

Help students recognize the difference between goods and services with this small-group activity. Provide each group with several sheets of construction paper, scissors, glue, and markers. Instruct the group to brainstorm a list of five goods and five services that can be purchased in your community. For each item on the list, the group creates a construction paper symbol and writes a sentence on it telling about the item. The group members label a sheet of chart paper with the categories "Goods" and "Services" and glue each symbol under the correct category.

We bought a dozen doughnuts made fresh by the baker.

Our teacher taught us how to divide.

The landscaper trimmed her trees and bushes.

The butcher had our order ready.

We bought new shoes from the shoe-store clerk.

It's All About Me

To help students distinguish between their own needs and wants, have each child first draw an outline of a person on a sheet of paper. Instruct her to list her needs within the lines on the body. Then direct her to paste or draw pictures of items she wants around the outside of the figure. Completed projects can be displayed on a bulletin board titled "We All Have Wants and Needs."

Red's "Good-ies" and Services

Read or review the tale *Little Red Riding Hood* with the class. Discuss a few goods and services that the grandmother might have needed while sick in bed. Give each small group of two to six students a copy of page 190. Have group members cut out the basket and strips, color the basket, and glue the basket to a sheet of construction paper. Instruct each student to choose several goods and services he would like to send to the grandmother. He writes the gifts on the appropriate strips and glues them to Little Red Riding Hood's basket to provide her grandma with a unique surprise.

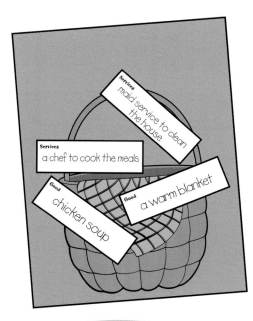

The Planet Glog

Invite your students to close their eyes and join you on an imaginary trip to the Planet Glog. Paint a rich description of a new planet with words to help students visualize a place where basic needs are met but wants are not. After students open their eyes, challenge the class to brainstorm and list a variety of services that would make life on the planet more pleasant. Next, have each child choose a service she would like to see offered on Planet Glog and draw and label a picture of the service being offered there. When complete, pictures can be bound together into an album of the new and improved planet and placed in a center for students to visit again. As a follow up, have each child complete a copy of page 191 as directed.

Basket and Strip Patterns

Use with "Red's 'Good-ies' and Services" on page 189.

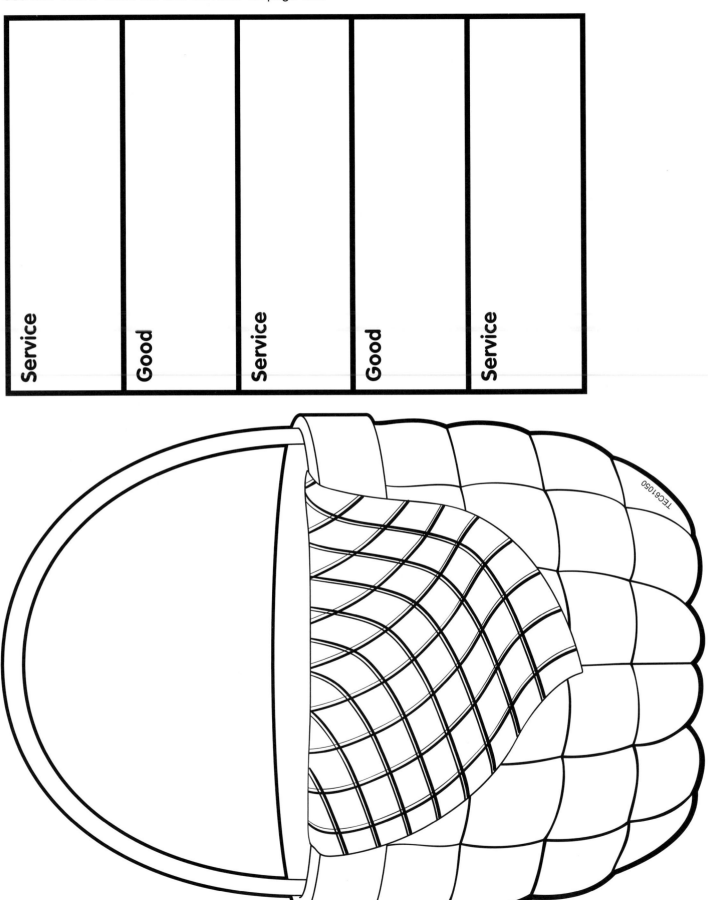

Service

Good

Service

Good

Service

TEC61050

🪐 Planet Glog 🪐

Color the crater red if it describes a good.
Color the crater blue if it describes a service.

1. Ben Glog buys flowers to plant around his space home.

2. Sue Glog pays someone to fix her spaceship's broken window.

3. Will Glog has his glasses repaired.

4. Molly Glog pays for new curtains for her playhouse.

5. Ned Glog has his dog groomed.

6. Holly Glog buys spaceberry pies from her neighbor.

7. Kim Glog buys a dress to wear to the Space Bash.

8. Ed Glog has his computer fixed.

9. Mary Glog pays a boy to sweep space dust from her walkway.

10. Gary Glog gets fresh fruit at the fruit stand.

Graphic Organizers

Storyboard

Use the storyboard on page 194 as a prewriting sheet. When students are planning a how-to paragraph, have each child write her topic on her copy of the page. Next, have her complete the sheet. Then have her refer to it as she writes her paragraph.

Name _____
Under the Stars   Storyboard

Topic:
How to plant a seed.

First:
Get a small shovel, the seed, and some water.

Fourth:
Cover the seed with dirt.

Second:
Dig a small hole

Fifth:
Water the seed carefully.

Third:
Place the seed in the hole.

Sixth:
Wait for the seed to grow.

Beginning, Middle, and End

Give each pair of students a copy of the chart on page 195. Introduce a picture book and direct one partner to write the book's title on the sheet. Read the book aloud. Next, have the partners work together to complete the chart. Provide time for each pair to share its work with the class.

KWL Chart

Before reading a nonfiction passage, give each child a copy of the KWL chart on page 196. Have the child write the topic of the text on the topic line. Next, have him write what he already knows about the topic in the first column. Encourage the child to think about what he would like to know about the topic as he lists his ideas in the second column. After the child has read the text, have him write what he has learned about the topic in the third column.

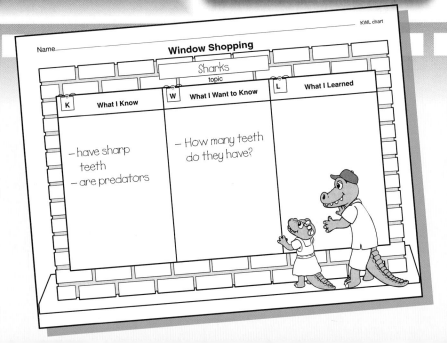

Name _____   KWL chart
Window Shopping

Sharks
topic

K   What I Know   W   What I Want to Know   L   What I Learned

– have sharp teeth
– are predators

– How many teeth do they have?

Idea Web

To increase a child's reading comprehension, have him use the idea web on page 197. When the child is reading a short nonfiction passage, give him a copy of the web. Have him write the main idea of the passage on the cookie jar. Then direct him to write each supporting detail on each of the cookies. Have the child compare his work with a partner who has read the same passage.

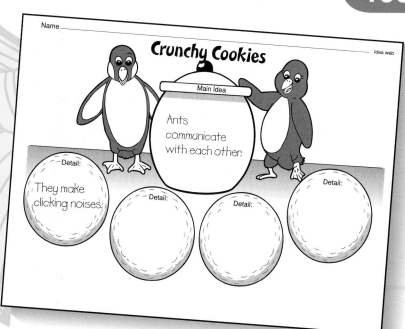

Problem-and-Solution Diagram

Have students use the problem-and-solution diagram on page 198 to predict the outcome of a story. Before reading the end of the book, give each child a copy of the diagram. Have her write the character's name and a description of his problem on the cup. Next, have her write a paragraph describing how she thinks the character will solve the problem. Then read the end of the book and have each child compare her prediction with the actual ending of the book.

Cause-and-Effect Chart

Give each child a copy of the cause-and-effect chart on page 199. As she reads a narrative, have her diagram the cause-and-effect relationships found in the story by completing the page. Invite each child to share her completed work with the class.

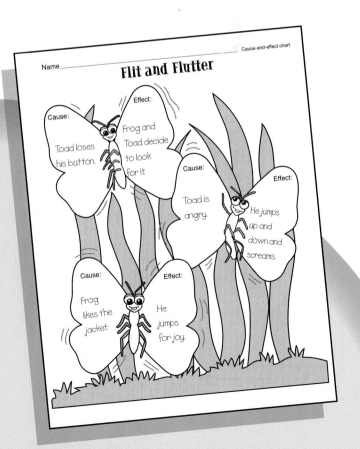

Under the Stars

Topic:

First:

Fourth:

Second:

Fifth:

Third:

Sixth:

©The Mailbox® • Superbook® • TEC61050

Note to the teacher: Use with "Storyboard" on page 192.

Name _____

A TALE TOLD ON TULIPS

Beginning:

Middle:

End:

title _____

©The Mailbox® • Superbook® • TEC61050

Note to the teacher: Use with "Beginning, Middle, and End" on page 192.

195

Name

Window Shopping

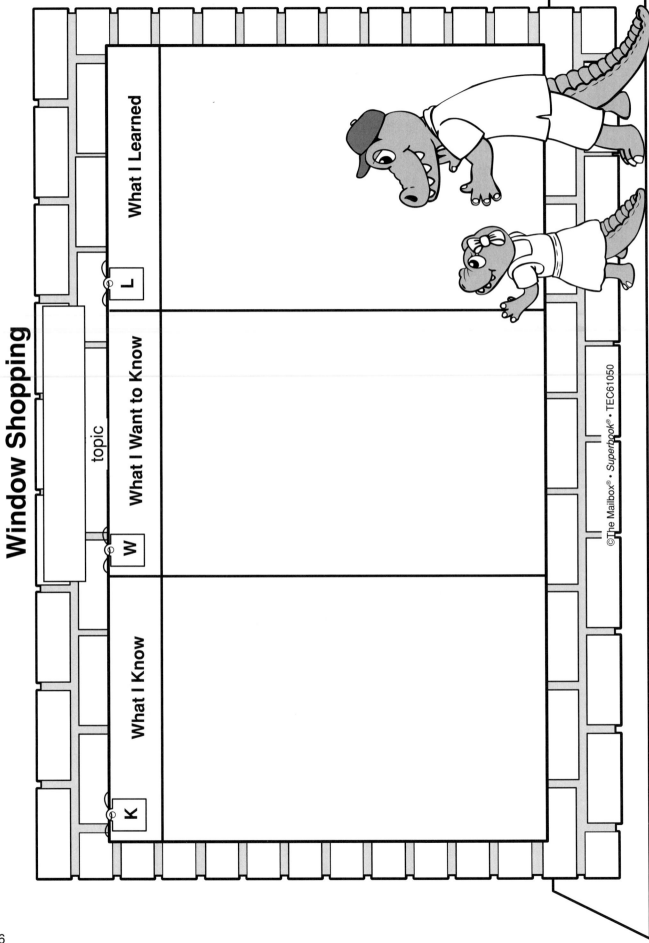

K	W	L
What I Know	**What I Want to Know**	**What I Learned**

topic

©The Mailbox® • Superbook® • TEC61050

Note to the teacher: Use with "KWL Chart" on page 192.

Name _____

Crunchy Cookies

Main Idea

Detail:

Detail:

Detail:

Detail:

Note to the teacher: Use with "Idea Web" on page 193.

Name _____

WHAT'S FOR LUNCH?

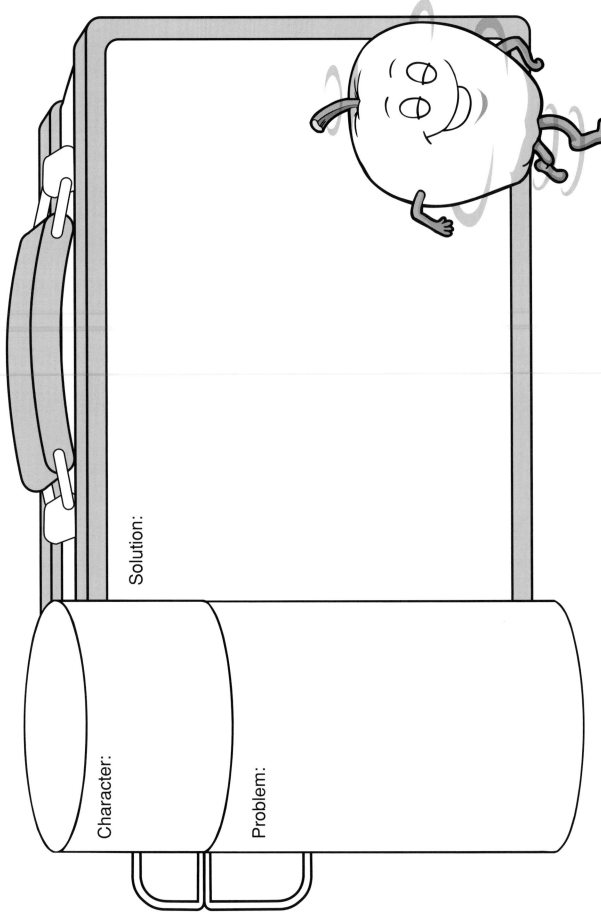

Character:

Problem:

Solution:

Note to the teacher: Use with "Problem-and-Solution Diagram" on page 193.

Flit and Flutter

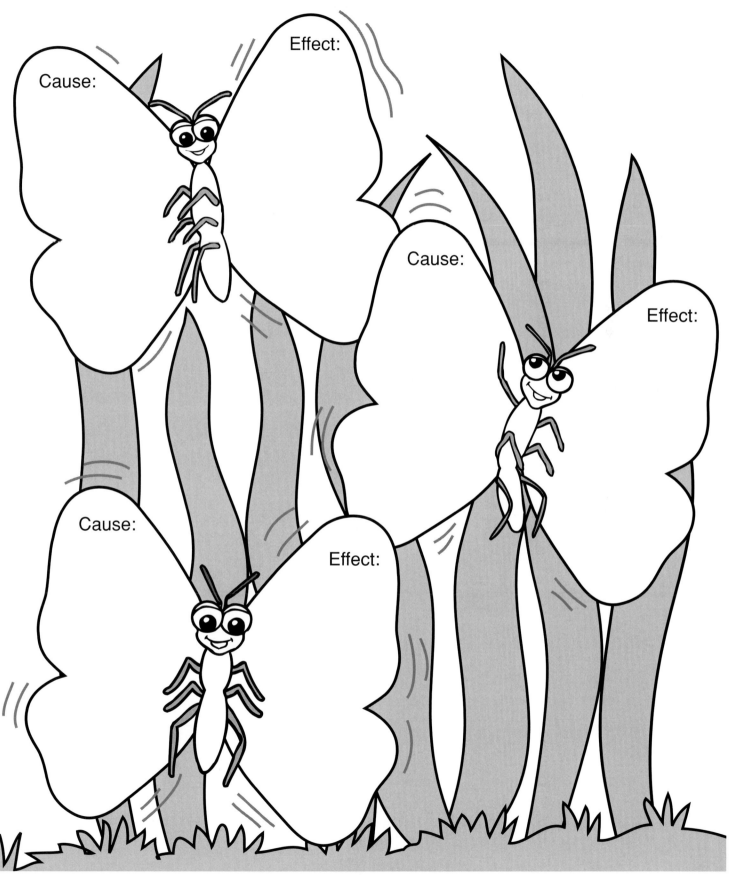

Cause:

Effect:

Cause:

Effect:

Cause:

Effect:

Language Arts Centers

Inviting Writing Centers

Entice students to use writing centers by making them student-friendly. Try the following ideas for setting up writing centers in your classroom:

- Use creative containers—such as sand pails, cookie jars, and jewelry boxes—to hold story starters. Write each story starter on a die-cut shape that matches the theme of the container.

- Cut apart the task cards on page 202 and place them in a decorated box. Challenge students to use the cards as prompts for brainstorming or journal writing.

- Place a class journal in the center. Encourage students to write about a designated weekly topic, such as "Your Favorite Vacation" or "Which animal makes the best pet?" **Writing**

Egg-Carton Parts of Speech

Reinforce the parts of speech with this self-checking center. Program a dozen numbered craft sticks by writing a different word on the middle of each one. Write the word's part of speech on the other end of the stick. (See the example.) Insert the sticks into a clean egg carton, as shown, so that the parts of speech are hidden. Each student numbers his paper from 1 to 12. Then he selects a stick, reads the word, and writes down its part of speech on his paper next to the corresponding number. He removes the stick to reveal the correct response. Provide a new set of words each week, or program sticks with math problems for students to solve. **Parts of speech**

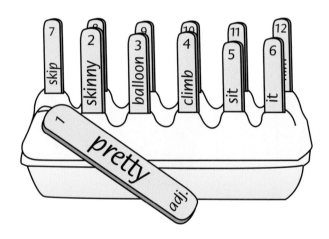

Alphabetical Play-by-Play

Cut apart a copy of the mascot cards on page 203 and tuck them inside a football helmet. Place the helmet, along with a class supply of writing paper, at a center. A student takes the cards out of the helmet, arranges them in ABC order, and then copies the alphabetized words on her paper. Then she returns the cards to the helmet. Provide an answer key for self-checking, if desired. **Alphabetical order**

Scrabble Spelling

Enhance spelling skills by introducing the game Scrabble at your spelling center. Have students follow the rules of the game with these added scoring bonuses: If a student spells a word from a previous spelling list, she doubles her points for that word. If she spells a word from the current list, her points for the word are tripled. Post a list of past and present spelling words at the center for players to refer to during the game. Then ask students to bring Scrabble games from home before each semester review test. Hold a Scrabble Spellathon to help students prepare for the test. Spelling

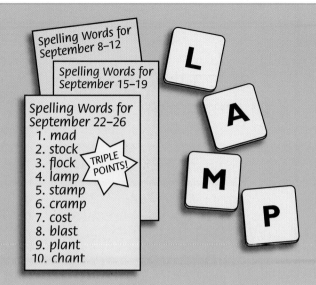

Spelling Words for September 8–12

Spelling Words for September 15–19

Spelling Words for September 22–26
1. mad
2. stock
3. flock
4. lamp
5. stamp
6. cramp
7. cost
8. blast
9. plant
10. chant

TRIPLE POINTS!

Where is m

My favorite color i

Look out for that car

Punctuation in a Cup

Program three plastic cups with ending punctuation marks. Then write different sentences on a supply of craft sticks. If desired, program the sticks for self-checking by writing the punctuation mark on the back of each stick. A student reads the sentence and then places the stick in the cup programmed with the correct ending mark. For additional practice, have students copy five of the sentences on paper, adding the appropriate punctuation. The center can be adapted to practice place value; to identify parts of speech; or to recognize synonyms, antonyms, and homophones. **End marks**

Vocabulary Hangman

To set up this center, gather a list of vocabulary words, a die, a pencil, paper for scorekeeping, a student-size whiteboard, and a dry-erase marker. Invite groups of two to four students to visit the center. One student who acts as the host secretly selects a word from the list and then draws on the board a blank line for each letter of the word. In turn, each remaining student rolls the die to determine the point value of his turn and then guesses a letter in the puzzle. If he correctly guesses a letter, he is awarded the points indicated on the die. If the guess is incorrect, the host draws a section of the hangman on the board and no points are awarded. A student may try to guess the word at the beginning of his turn. If his guess is correct, he can gain ten bonus points by giving the correct definition of the word. When the word has been correctly identified, students add up their points to determine the winner. The person with the highest score acts as host for the next game. **Vocabulary**

Writing Task Cards

Use with "Inviting Writing Centers" on page 200.

List ten flavors of ice cream.

TEC61050

Draw a comic strip to tell what you like to do on a rainy day.

TEC61050

Write a list of things you like to do with your family.

TEC61050

Write directions for making a bed.

TEC61050

Write several ways you can be a good friend.

TEC61050

Write directions for playing your favorite game.

TEC61050

Write a list of things you can do with a cardboard tube.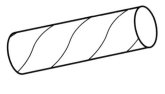

TEC61050

Write a list of animals that live in the ocean.

TEC61050

Make a list of things you can do with a bowl and spoon.

TEC61050

Write directions for making an ice-cream sundae.

TEC61050

Bears

Eagles

Panthers

Cardinals

Giants

Patriots

Colts

Jaguars

Rams

Cowboys

Jets

Ravens

Dolphins

Lions

Vikings

TEC61050

Math Centers

Scrambled Eggs

This center works well as a review of math fact families. Label a supply of plastic eggs, each with a different letter. Fill each egg with three slips of paper that have been programmed with numbers from a fact family. Store the eggs in a basket and place the basket at a center. A student opens an egg, dumps out its contents, and arranges the numbers to create a fact family. She writes the four problems on her paper before replacing the numbers in the egg and returning it to the basket. She repeats the process until she has "cracked" all of the eggs. Provide an answer key for students to check their work. **Fact families**

Special Delivery

Make several colored copies of the mailbox and flag patterns on page 206. Laminate the pieces for durability before cutting them out. Cut a slit in each mailbox as indicated on the dotted line. Then program each mailbox with a math problem and each flag with a corresponding answer. A student matches a flag to the correct mailbox and slides it into the slit. Once all the flags have been placed, check the student's work, or have the student use an answer key for self-checking. If desired, store the pattern pieces in a real mailbox. **Basic facts**

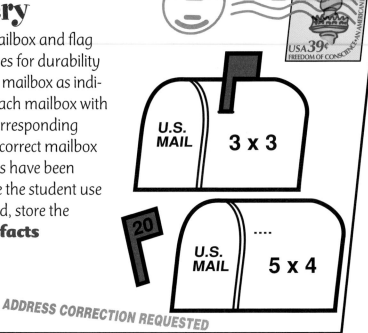

DO NOT BEND

ADDRESS CORRECTION REQUESTED

Punch and Poke

Provide individual skills practice for students with these clever shapes. Select a page-size pattern to color, cut out, and mount on heavy tagboard. Use a hole puncher to make ten to 12 holes around the edge of the shape. If desired, laminate the shape for durability. Program the shape by writing a math fact by each hole. Turn the shape over and write the answer to each problem by the corresponding hole. A student solves each problem; then he checks his work by poking his pencil through a hole, turning the shape over, and checking the answer by the hole. **Skill review**

Connect the Dots

This easy partner game helps students review any math skill. Program each index card in a set with a letter and a fact problem. Create an answer key by writing each letter and the matching answer on a piece of paper. Place the cards, the answer key, colored pencils, and several copies of the grid pattern on page 206 at a learning center.

To play, each student selects a colored pencil to use during the game. Students takes turns drawing one vertical or horizontal line to connect two adjacent dots. If a student draws a line that completes the square, he earns the chance to claim the square by correctly solving a problem from a card. If he answers incorrectly, the square is left blank. The game ends when all the dots have been connected. (Shuffle and reuse game cards if necessary.) The player with more initialed squares is the winner. **Skill review**

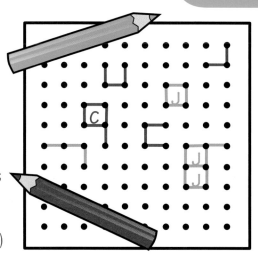

Skill Swatters

Create teams of three students each to practice identifying odd and even numbers. Make two different-colored copies of the flyswatter pattern (page 207) on heavy card stock and cut them out. Attach each cutout to a craft stick to make swatters for the game. Also color and cut out copies of the fly patterns on page 207. Then glue them to the inside of a folder labeled as shown. Make a self-checking list of odd and even numbers. When a team visits the center, one student acts as the caller and reads each number on the list to the other players. As each number is called out, the players swat the fly that represents the correct answer. The player whose swatter is first to hit the correct fly is awarded one point. Play continues until all the numbers on the list have been called out. Players tally their scores to determine the winner of the game. **Odd and even**

Money Bags

Put students' problem-solving skills to work with coin mystery bags. To prepare one bag, label the outside of a paper lunch bag with a money amount and the number of coins used to make that amount. Put the plastic coins needed for that amount inside the bag and fold the bag at the top. Place the bag at a center along with a supply of coin manipulatives. A child uses the clues and coin manipulatives to determine what money is found in the bag. When she thinks she has an answer that matches the clues, she opens the bag to check her work. **Money**

Mailbox and Flag Patterns

Use with "Special Delivery" on page 204.

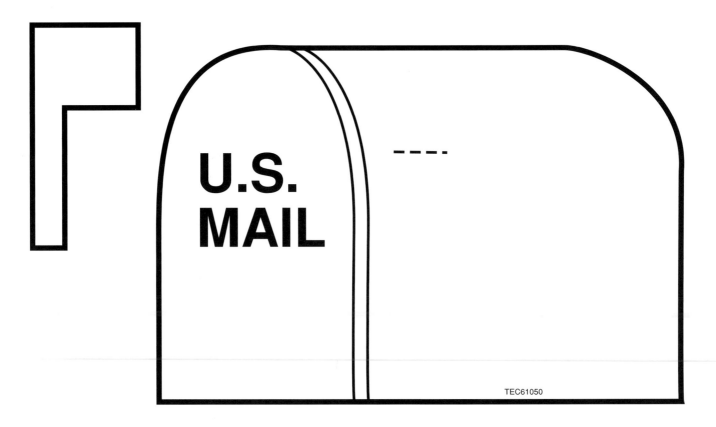

Grid Pattern

Use with "Connect the Dots" on page 205.

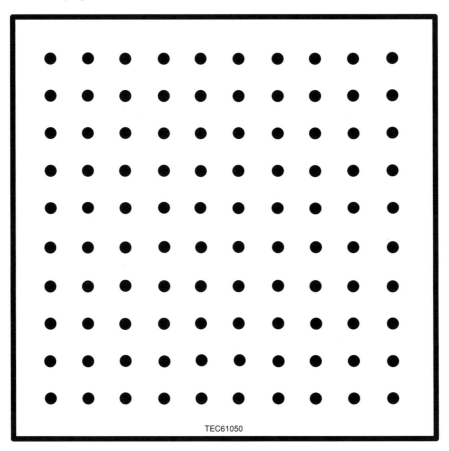

©The Mailbox® • *Superbook*® • TEC61050

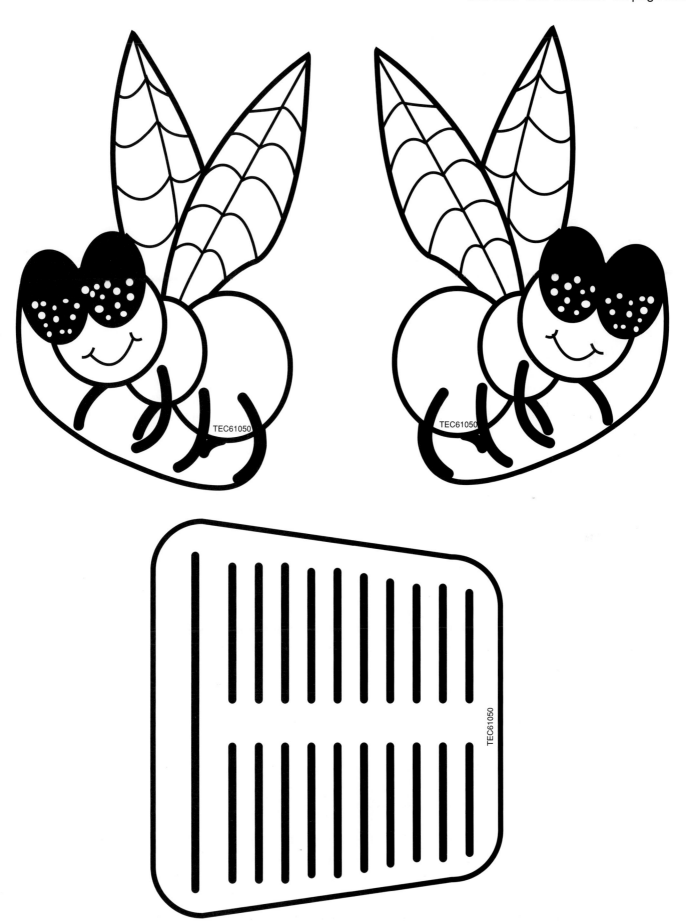

Games

Spin and Say

To prepare this small-group game, program a supply of index cards, each with a different vocabulary or sight word. Then enlarge a copy of the four-section spinner on page 214 and write a number from one to four in each space. Put the spinner, a pencil, and a paper-clip on a playing table. Also stack the cards facedown in the middle of the table. To begin, a player spins the spinner. She draws the corresponding number of cards from the stack. She reads each card aloud and keeps those she read correctly. Cards read incorrectly are placed at the bottom of the stack. Then another player spins. Play continues in this manner until all cards have been read correctly. The player with the most cards wins. **Vocabulary**

Dictionary Decisions

Divide the class into two teams and give a dictionary to each player. Also give each player a small chalkboard or whiteboard and an appropriate writing tool. Assign a letter of the alphabet. Have each child use his dictionary to write on his board a word that begins with the assigned letter. Select a student from each team to come to the front of the room. Have the two students display their chosen words in alphabetical order. Announce that these two words will be the guide words for the round. Each seated child shares the word he wrote. Then he decides whether or not his word would be found on a dictionary page between the chosen guide words. Award a point to each child who makes the correct choice for his word. After each child has shared his word, announce a different letter of the alphabet and repeat the process. Continue as long as desired. The team with more points wins. **Guide words**

Chocolate would be on this page.

synonyms antonyms

Fun in a Flash

In advance, make a list of synonym and antonym pairs. Also, cut out eight circles, four each of two different colors. Label the circles as shown; then glue two like-colored circles to each side of a craft stick to make paddles. Place two desks at the front of the room with a divider, such as a display board or easel, separating them. Then put one paddle of each color on each desk. Divide the class into two teams. A student from each team stands at a desk, facing the class and the teacher. Instruct both children to hold up a paddle as you read a set of words from the list. If a student holds up the correct paddle, she earns a point for her team. Invite two new students to take a turn and continue the game as long as time allows. **Synonyms and antonyms**

Top Secret

Write five unpunctuated sentences inside a supply of file folders and then laminate the folders. Give each small team one folder and an overhead pen. After a starting signal, each student reads a sentence and adds correct punctuation to it. Then he passes the folder to a team member to repeat the steps on the next sentence. If a child sees a sentence that has been incorrectly marked by a teammate, he may change it, but he cannot add punctuation to another sentence. Award a point to the first team to finish. Then review the corrections aloud and give one point to each team for every correct punctuation mark it added. The team with the most points wins.
Punctuation

Roll It!

To prepare this variation of tic-tac-toe, label a copy of the six-section spinner pattern on page 214 with the following sections: noun, verb, adjective, pronoun, adverb, and your choice. Preprogram sticky notes with phrases containing underlined words that match the categories listed on the spinner. Then draw a tic-tac-toe grid on the board and place one of the sticky notes on each section. Divide the class into two teams. One team member spins the spinner and announces a word that matches the category. If correct, she removes the sticky note, places it in a discard pile, and marks an X or O for her team on the space. If she's incorrect, the sticky note stays on the gameboard, and the other team takes a turn. If no match can be made, her team loses a turn. Continue in this manner until a team has three in a row horizontally, vertically, or diagonally or until all spaces have been uncovered. Then replace the sticky notes with new ones and play again. **Parts of speech**

Slowly is an adverb.

Overheard on the Overhead

Encourage good listening while students practice written language skills. Give each small group of students a transparency and an overhead pen. Dictate a short sentence and have a student in each group record it on the transparency. Repeat the process, providing a new sentence for each group member. Allow students a short amount of time to review and confirm their group's work. Then have each group alternate placing their completed transparency on the overhead to check for the desired skill (correct punctuation, capitalization, spelling words). The team with the fewest total errors wins. **Writing sentences**

The Smith family lives in Nashville. −0
They moved there in june. −1

Making Matches

Get students thinking with this game based on an old favorite, Concentration. In advance, use index cards to make a class supply of matching homophone cards. To play, give a card to each student, leaving two students without cards to start the game. Player 1 calls on a classmate to stand, show his card, and read it aloud. Then she calls on another classmate to do the same. If the cards make a homophone pair, those two students give her their cards and team up to help her make another match. If she does not make a match, Player 2 takes a turn in the same manner. Play continues until time is called or until all matches have been made. The team with more cards wins. **Homophones**

Tap on the Top

Use the game of Slapjack to review a variety of classroom skills. Create a deck of cards for the game by programming index cards for the desired skill. Each card should match at least one other card in the deck; for example, program two cards with synonyms so that each card contains one word of the synonym pair. To play, have a group of two to four students divide the deck into equal stacks and keep each stack facedown. Players sit facing each other so that the discard pile will be between them. Each student takes the top card from his stack and turns it over as he places it in the discard pile. If two cards create a match, the first student to tap the cards wins the pile. If they do not make a match, the cards remain in the discard pile. The game ends when one player runs out of cards. The player holding the most cards at that time is declared the winner. Skill review

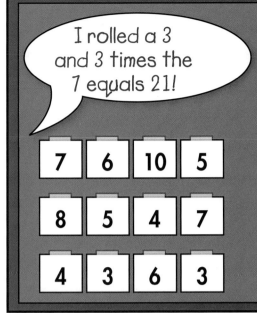

I rolled a 3 and 3 times the 7 equals 21!

7	6	10	5
8	5	4	7
4	3	6	3

On a Roll

Program a class supply of index cards with numbers for the appropriate skill level. Tape the cards to the board. Have each student take a turn selecting a card, rolling a die, and then adding (or multiplying) the numbers together. If the student answers correctly, he removes the card from the board. Play several rounds during the week. Challenge students to earn a specified amount of cards each week, and reward those who meet the challenge with a coupon good for skipping one math homework assignment. **Math facts**

Card Capers

A ♥

Purchase several decks of cards for a variety of skill-review games. Remove the face cards and give a deck of cards to student partners. Call out a task for sorting cards, such as finding all even-numbered red cards, finding all cards with multiples of three on them, or arranging each suit in numerical order. Allow the students a time limit for finding the designated cards; then check each pair's work. Award each pair a point for every task it successfully completes. **Skill review**

NUMBERS

____ , ____ ____ ____

Is the 3 in the hundreds place?

The Spin on Numbers

Paying attention is an important part of this class game. Copy a spinner from page 214. Write a number on a slip of paper and then draw answer blanks on the board to match the number of digits in the number. Next, program the spinner with the same numbers and fill any remaining spaces with digits not found in the number. Then write the word *NUMBERS* on the board. A child uses a pencil and paper clip to spin the spinner. Then he asks to place the number spun in a place-value blank. If correct, write the number on the line and allow another child to spin. If incorrect, cross out a letter in the word *NUMBERS*; then choose another child to spin. Play continues until the number is completed or all of the letters have been crossed out. Place value

71¢

Sarah
2 quarters
1 dime
1 nickel
6 pennies

Weekly Award Winner

Once a week, bring to school an inexpensive item, such as a decorative eraser, silly straw, or puzzle book. Attach a price tag to the item and place the item near a blank sheet of chart paper. Give each child a sticky note. During free time, a child writes a coin combination that equals the price of the item and posts it on the chart paper. At the end of the week, remove all of the correct answers from the chart and place them in a bag. Draw one sticky note and award that child the item as the prize. Reward the other students who had the correct answer. Coin combinations

Watching the Time

To prepare this whole-class game, make a supply of the clock and time cards on page 215. Draw hands on the clockfaces and add lengths of time to the time cards. Next, divide the class into four teams. A player from one team chooses a card from each pile. She names the time on the clockface and then calculates the time elapsed. If needed, she may get help from her teammates. If she names the correct time, her team gets two points. If she incorrectly names the time on the clock, no points are awarded to her team, but another team may try to answer. If she names the correct clock time but wrong elapsed time, another team can solve and get one point. If responses are still incorrect, the card is returned to the pile and the next team chooses two cards. The first team to earn ten points wins.
Telling time

_15_ minutes before

Is it 2:20?

Bird's-Eye View

Materials for each pair of students: copy of the gameboard on page 216, calculator, 2 different-colored crayons

Directions:
1. Player 1 chooses a product and names a matching multiplication fact.
2. Player 2 uses the calculator to check Player 1's answer.
3. If correct, Player 1 writes the problem on the window and lightly colors it. Then his turn is over. If incorrect, Player 1 does not write an answer or color, and his turn is over.
4. Player 2 takes a turn in the same manner.
5. Players continue taking turns until all windows have been colored. The player with more colored windows wins. **Multiplication**

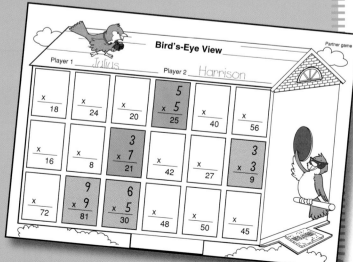

Name That Unit

Revisit previous units of study with this quick categorizing game. Throughout the year, record terms related to units of study on an index card. Store the cards in a resealable plastic bag. Read the words from one of the cards when the class has a few minutes of free time. Students try to name the unit associated with the words. If a student correctly names the unit, award a point to the class and choose a new card to repeat the process. If the unit is not correctly named after three tries, return the card to the bag and choose another card. Encourage students to score as many points as possible in the time available. As an extra review, have students list related terms at the end of a unit of study instead. **Skill review**

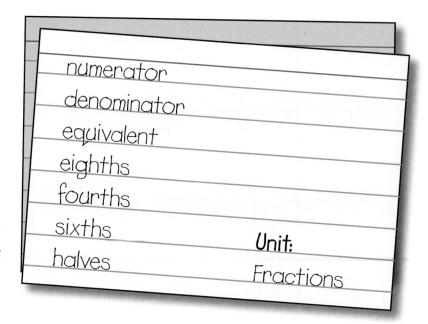

numerator
denominator
equivalent
eighths
fourths
sixths
halves

Unit:
Fractions

Proper Nouns

A | bby
B | en
C | hicago
D | elaware
E | mpire State Building
F |
G | eorgia
H | ilton Head
I |
J | efferson Elementary
K | rispy Kreme doughnuts
L | EGO construction toys
M |
N |
O |
P |
Q |
R |
S |
T |
U |
V |
W |
X |
Y |
Z |

Alphabetical Inventory

Give each small group a sheet of paper and have one member list the alphabet on it. Name a category—such as verbs, landforms, or sky objects—and have a group member write it as the title. Next, have each student list a word that matches the category and then pass the paper to a group member. If a student can't name a word for a given letter, he leaves it blank and passes the paper to another student. After a predetermined length of time, have students orally share the words on their lists one letter at a time. Groups receive a point for each word if no other group has the same word listed. **Skill review**

Spinners

Use with "Spin and Say" on page 208, "Roll It!" on page 209, and "The Spin on Numbers" on page 211.

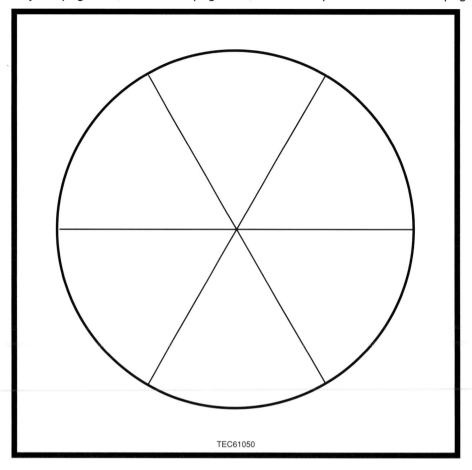

TEC61050

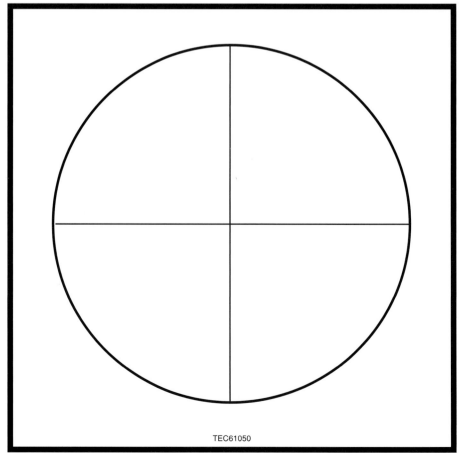

TEC61050

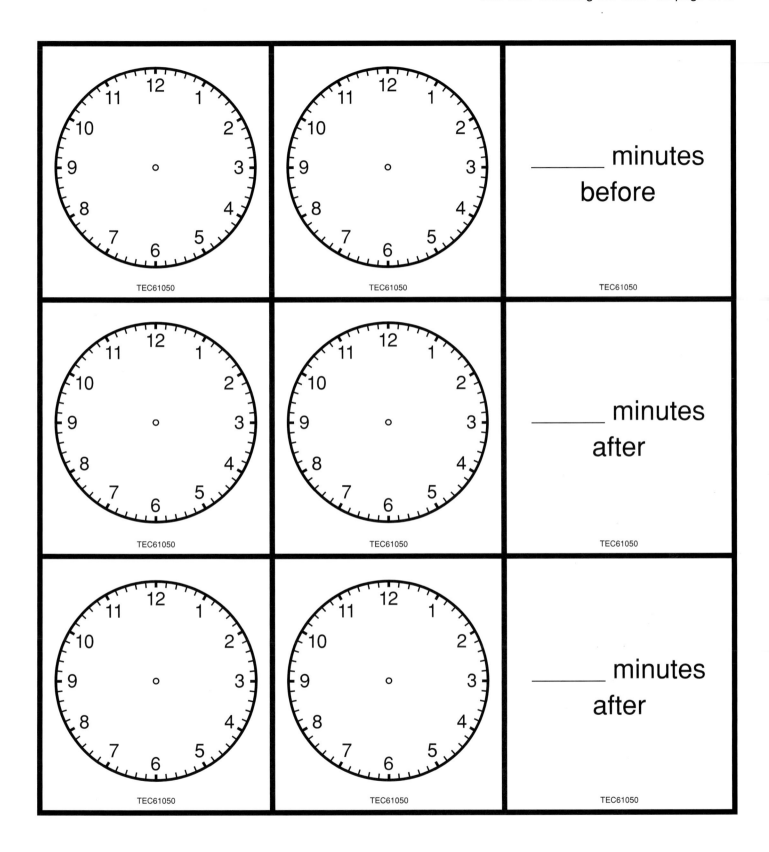

_____ minutes before

_____ minutes after

_____ minutes after

TEC61050

Bird's-Eye View

Player 1 _____

Player 2 _____

x 18	x 24	x 20	x 25	x 40	x 56
x 16	x 8	x 21	x 42	x 27	x 9
x 72	x 81	x 30	x 48	x 50	x 45

Note to the teacher: Use with "Bird's-Eye View" on page 212.

Differentiation Tips

A Tubful of Reinforcement

To help students get the skills practice they need, gather a supply of learning games, file folder centers, and flash cards that reinforce several different skills. Place the activities for each skill in a separate plastic tub. Next, laminate several index cards and attach a different one to each tub. Use a dry-erase marker to program each card with the appropriate skill. When a child needs reinforcement in a specific skill, direct him to the matching tub. Periodically change the contents of the tubs and erase and reprogram the index card labels.

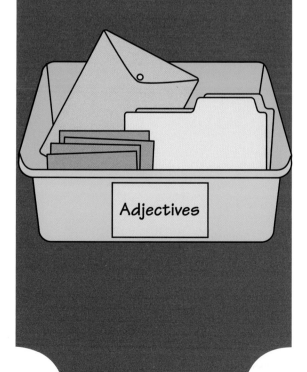

Adjectives

Resourceful With Resources

Be prepared for students' needs by keeping a variety of resource books on hand. Purchase skill books for the grade levels just above and just below the grade level you teach. Or partner with teachers in those grade levels and agree to share materials. When a student needs reinforcement, extra practice, or reteaching, you'll always have a reproducible that is appropriate for his needs!

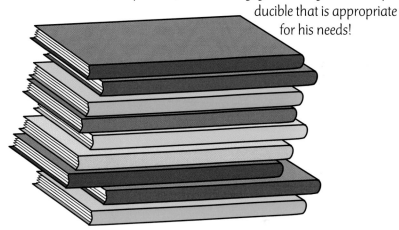

Math Mastery

Keep students' learning progressing at their own rates by giving a short pretest at the beginning of each new math unit. Assign children to groups based on the results of the test. Next, prepare different packets of textbook pages and reproducibles for each group. Each day, distribute the packets and, as children are working, meet with each group for a mini lesson that's tailored to the group's needs. In addition, check students' progress in their packets and answer any questions that students may have. If a child masters or needs more reinforcement on a set of skills, she can be moved to a different group.

A Total of Ten

Give students flexibility by designing tests based on the ten-point system. At the end of a unit, develop a test that has questions with varying difficulty. Then assign a point value of two or four to each question. Distribute the test and tell students they can choose the questions they would like to answer, but the questions they answer must total ten points.

(2 points) 1. What does Toad lose while the friends are walking?

(2 points) 2. Toad is happy when the raccoon brings him a square button. true/false

(2 points) 3. Where does Toad find his button?

(2 points) 4. What does Toad make for Frog?

(4 points) 5. How do you think Toad feels when he finds his button?

(4 points) 6. Why do you think Toad made a gift for Frog?

Spelling Activities

To give students a variety of spelling practice options, make a class supply of the activity sheet on page 220. Give each child a copy of the sheet with her new spelling list. Have her write her words on the sheet, and then meet with the child to determine a number of activities for her to complete. During the week, have the child sign her name on the line in each box as she finishes each assignment and then place the assignment in a folder or a folded 9" x 24" sheet of construction paper. Before she takes her spelling test, have her turn in her sheet and her folder of work.

Indicating Interests

When it's time to begin a new unit of study, gather center materials and reproducibles based on three or four different themes. For example, a subtraction unit could be taught using gardening, video game, and automobile themes. Place each set of materials in a different basket or box. When it's time for students to practice or reinforce skills, they can choose activities from the theme that interests them most.

Ready Record

Keep students' spelling words, vocabulary lists, math facts, and more at your fingertips with these handy recording sheets. Each week, program a copy of page 221 with the date and then make a class supply. (To save time, write spelling words, vocabulary lists, and math facts that students may share before photocopying the sheet.) Fill out the rest of each sheet, hole-punch it, and then store the sheets in a three-ring binder for easy access. If desired, send home a copy of each child's sheet for parents to review.

Making Skill Sheets Work

If students struggle with reproducibles, have them try one of these tips. (Each suggestion is for a fill-in-the-blank reproducible that has a word bank but could be adapted to another format.)

- Use a pencil and a ruler to make a dashed line between the words in the word bank. Next, copy the page. Have the child cut apart the words in the word bank and then glue each one on its matching blank.
- Write a different letter in front of each word in the word bank. Direct the child to write the letter on its matching blank.
- Use crayons to make a different-colored dot in front of each word in the word bank. Have the student use her crayons to make a matching dot on the corresponding blank.

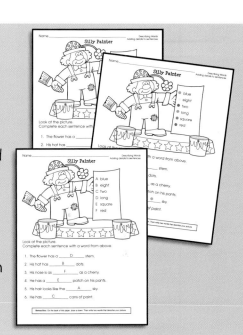

Highlighting Highlights

Use these highlighter tips to improve your students' organizational skills!

- Have students highlight operational signs on computation problems before they begin their work.
- When a student receives a reproducible, have him highlight the key words in the directions.
- Before giving a child a multiple-choice activity, modify the page by highlighting two answer choices (one correct and one incorrect) per question.

Name _____

Word List

_____

_____

_____

_____

_____

_____

_____

_____

_____

Write a silly story using all of your spelling words.	Write each of your spelling words using stairstep spelling: m mo mos most
Make a set of flash cards for your spelling list. Use the cards to study your words.	Write each of your spelling words. Then rearrange some of the letters in each word to make new words.
Write your spelling words in ABC order.	Find each spelling word in a magazine. Cut out the word and glue it on a sheet of paper.

Make a comic strip that uses at least five of your spelling words.

Write a sentence for each of your spelling words. Make at least three of the sentences questions.

If you are right-handed, write your list with your left hand. If you are left-handed, write your list with your right hand.

©The Mailbox® • Superbook® • TEC61050

Note to the teacher: Use with "Spelling Activities" on page 218.

Name ____________________

Week of ____________________

Spelling Words

____________ ____________ ____________
____________ ____________ ____________
____________ ____________ ____________
____________ ____________ ____________
____________ ____________ ____________

Math Facts to Master

____________ ____________
____________ ____________
____________ ____________
____________ ____________
____________ ____________
____________ ____________

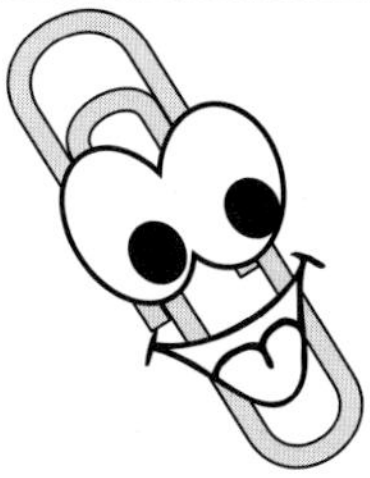

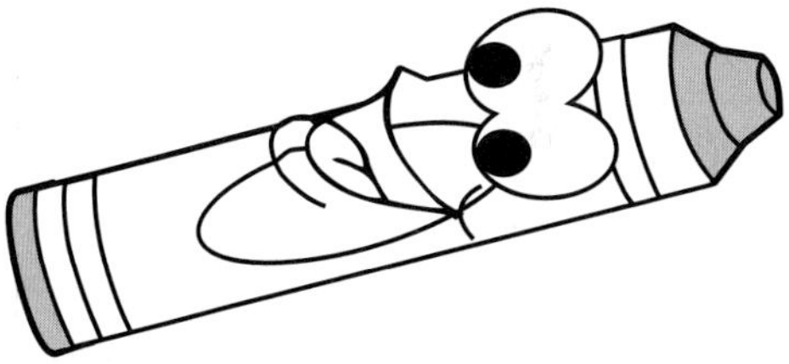

Vocabulary Words

____________ ____________
____________ ____________
____________ ____________
____________ ____________
____________ ____________

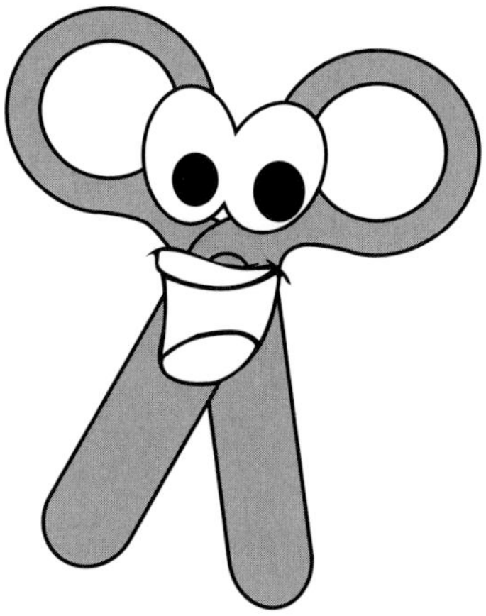

Notes

____
____
____

Note to the teacher: Use with "Ready Record" on page 219.

ASSESSMENT

P.S. See You Soon!

Begin assessing your students before you even meet them! As soon as you receive your class list, write a short letter to each child. Include several questions in your letter, including a simple math question. Encourage the child to respond to your letter. To ensure a response, tuck a self-addressed stamped envelope into each student's envelope. As each letter arrives, you'll be able to assess the student's punctuation, capitalization, and spelling skills. In addition, the child's answers to your questions will provide a peek into her thinking skills.

July 5, 2006

Dear Yolanda,

I am looking forward to having you in my class! Have you had a good summer? What was the most exciting thing you did? Did you read any good books?

I spent a lot of time with my family. I went to the beach and worked in my yard. I also read some books by Kevin Henkes. I want to buy 24 new books for our classroom before school starts! I have already bought 9 books. How many more do I need to buy?

Please write back to me and tell me what you would like to learn in the third grade.

See you soon!

Sincerely,
Ms. Clay

A Rainbow of Reinforcement

Take a colorful approach to assessing your students' journal-writing assignments. Gather highlighters in several colors and develop a positive color code. For example, mark correct capital letters with a pink highlighter or a punctuation mark that is in the correct place with a green highlighter. Use a yellow highlighter to draw a line through a difficult word that is spelled correctly. If a student uses descriptive language or strong details, highlight the phrases with a blue highlighter. Students are sure to appreciate the positive reinforcement and you'll be able to see at a glance the things that they are doing well.

On Friday my brother and I built a fort. My dad helped us too. First, we had to buy some wood. Then my dad helped us make the frame. We used lots of nails and screws! My brother and I nailed all the boards on the frame. Our fort has three windows and a big door. We painted it with brown paint. We had fun making our fort.

HIGHLIGHTER

HIGHLIGHTER

HIGHLIGHTER

HIGHLIGHTER

What We Know

Assess students' progress in a new unit by using a class KWL chart. Create and laminate a large KWL chart as shown. Display the chart in front of the class and use a dry-erase marker to write the topic of the new unit on the topic line. Lead the class in a discussion of what they already know about the topic as you write each idea on a separate sticky note. Place the sticky notes in the first column on the chart. Next, make a pad of sticky notes available to students. Encourage each child to write on a sticky note a question he has about the topic and then have him place the note in the second column. As the class progresses through the unit, have students record the answers to their questions, along with other things that they learn, on new sticky notes. Students then place the last set of notes in the third column.

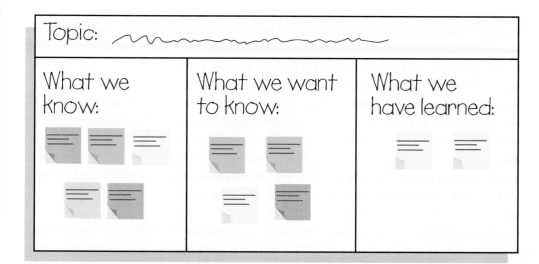

Choosing to Read Aloud

Even shy children have an easier time reading aloud when they have a choice! Before a child begins to read, have him announce whether he will be reading a sentence or a paragraph. You'll have the chance to assess each child's reading, and students' understanding of the meanings of *sentence* and *paragraph* will be reinforced!

This assignment helped me learn my multiplication facts.

Share and Tell

Put a twist on an old favorite by having students replace their show-and-tell time with an assignment-sharing time. Invite each child to select her favorite assignment from those she has finished in a week. Next, have the child share her assignment with the class. As she shows her work, ask the child questions such as the following: "Why did you choose this assignment?" "What did you learn while you were doing this assignment?" "What kind of grade do you think you should receive on this assignment?" The child's answers will give you an assessment of her understanding as well as an insight into her view of her own progress.

Red or Green?

This handy tool gives you a quick assessment of students' understanding of a lesson or concept. For each student, cut out a four-inch diameter red construction paper circle and a four-inch diameter green construction paper circle. Laminate each pair of circles. Then glue the circles back-to-back with a craft stick sandwiched between them to make a paddle as shown. Give one paddle to each child. As you present new information or review information, periodically ask the class, "Red or green?" Students who understand the concept hold up their paddles so that the green side is showing. Students who feel that they may need some more explanation or extra help hold up their paddles so that the red side is showing. Make a note of those students who need more help and meet with them at a later time.

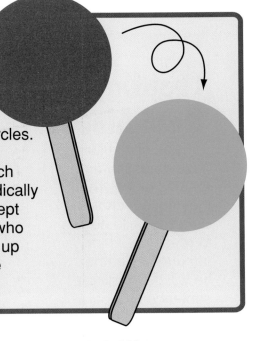

Self-Assessment

Give students the opportunity to add their insight to report card time. Meet with each child to discuss his progress, behavior, and goals for the rest of the year. Next, have the child complete a copy of the self-report card on page 225. Review the report card with the child and then send it home with his regular report card. This form gives you and the child's parents insight into a child's self-esteem and his feelings about school and about his progress.

Self-Report Card

Date January 5, 2007

Name Nikki

Subject	Grade	Subject	Grade
Math	B	Science	A
Reading	A	Music	A
Spelling	A	P.E.	A
English	B	Art	A
Social Studies	B		

My behavior is good. Sometimes I talk with my friends too much. I am a good helper for my teacher.

My goals are I want to do better in math. I need to learn my multiplication facts.

Field Trip Follow-Up

After your students return from a field trip, assess their understanding of the experience with this quick writing activity. Write a writing prompt and a word bank on the board as shown. Direct each student to use the prompt and word bank as she writes a paragraph or story about the field trip. Allow time for each child to share her work with the class.

What happens in a typical day at the Thompson Farm?

milking machine
rooster
pasture
garden
pumpkin patch
chickens

Self-Report Card

Name _____   Date _____

Subject	Grade	Subject	Grade

My behavior is _____

_____

_____

_____

My goals are _____

_____

_____

_____

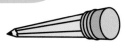
Test-Taking Tips
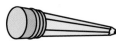

Quick Tips

These quick tips are sure to help students have a more successful testing day!

- Cover an empty aerosol can with construction paper. Use construction paper scraps and craft supplies to decorate the can to look like a can of "brain spray" as shown. Pretend to spray it over your students before they begin testing.

- Reduce trips to the water fountain by asking each child to bring a water bottle to class on the day of the test.

- Begin the day with a cheerleader's chant! Have the class stand and perform this chant with you:

Teacher: Give me a *T!*

Class: *T!*

Teacher: Give me an *E!*

Class: E!

Teacher: Give me an *S!*

Class: S!

Teacher: Give me a *T!*

Class: *T!*

Teacher: What do we want?

Class: To do our best!

Teacher: What will we do?

Class: Do our best!

Together: Go class!

Brain Spray

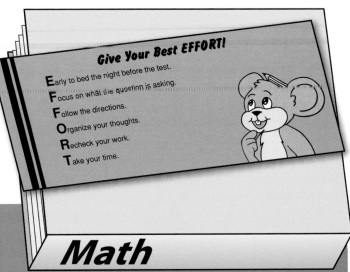

Give Your Best EFFORT!

Early to bed the night before the test.

Focus on what the question is asking.

Follow the directions.

Organize your thoughts.

Recheck your work.

Take your time.

Math

Effort-Filled Bookmarks

Give each child a copy of the bookmarks on page 228. After he colors his bookmarks, have him use them while reading during his free time or to mark his place in his textbooks. If desired, let him keep one on his desk during class to remind him to do his best as he works.

Test-Taking Tools

In advance, make a large toolbox-shaped cutout and post it in the center of a bulletin board that's titled as shown. Next, lead students in a discussion of their favorite test-day tips and list each suggestion on the board. Then give each child a tool-shaped cutout and have the child copy his favorite tip on his cutout. Staple the cutouts on the display for an at-a-glance reminder of the best test-taking tips!

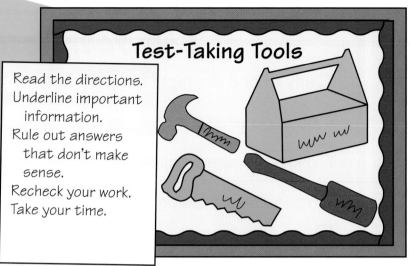

Test-Taking Tools

Read the directions.
Underline important information.
Rule out answers that don't make sense.
Recheck your work.
Take your time.

Shhhh! We're Working!

Help children understand the need for quiet during testing by creating testing folders for each child. Give each child a colorful file folder and have her write on one side, as shown, her name and "Shhhh! I'm working." Collect the folders and then, on testing days, redistribute them. Direct each child to set up her folder on her desk, creating a wall that she can work behind. Explain to students that when the folders are up, no one may talk or get out of his seat. This serves as a great reminder to students that although each child works at his own pace, each student should respect the others' right to work in a quiet, still environment.

Shhhh! I'm working.

Carlie

A Test About Testing

Before the big day, reinforce testing procedures with students by having them complete a copy of the reproducible on page 229. To begin, direct the child to cut the answer strip off of his copy. Next, have him write his name on the test and answer strip, and then remind students how to fill in the bubbles as they answer the test questions. As children are working, act as if they are taking an actual test by having them work quietly and remain in their seats.

Bookmarks

Use with "Effort-Filled Bookmarks" on page 226.

Give Your Best EFFORT!

Early to bed the night before the test.

Focus on what the question is asking.

Follow the directions.

Organize your thoughts.

Recheck your work.

Take your time.

©The Mailbox® • *Superbook*® • TEC61050

Give Your Best EFFORT!

Early to bed the night before the test.

Focus on what the question is asking.

Follow the directions.

Organize your thoughts.

Recheck your work.

Take your time.

©The Mailbox® • *Superbook*® • TEC61050

Give Your Best EFFORT!

Early to bed the night before the test.

Focus on what the question is asking.

Follow the directions.

Organize your thoughts.

Recheck your work.

Take your time.

©The Mailbox® • *Superbook*® • TEC61050

Taking the Test

Follow your teacher's directions.

1. You read the first question on the test, and you know the answer. What do you do next?
   A. Close the test booklet.
   B. Raise your hand.
   C. Mark the answer on your answer sheet.
   D. Circle the answer in your test booklet.

2. You are erasing an answer, and you tear a hole in your answer sheet. What do you do next?
   A. Throw the answer sheet away.
   B. Put tape over the hole.
   C. Throw your pencil away.
   D. Tell your teacher right away.

3. You are working on your test when you realize that time is almost up. What do you do?
   A. Fold up the test and take it home with you.
   B. Keep working at your own pace until your teacher tells you to stop.
   C. Mark C for the rest of the answers.
   D. Start working faster.

4. You finish answering all of the questions on the test. What do you do?
   A. Go get a puzzle and bring it back to your desk.
   B. Check your answers.
   C. Talk with your friend.
   D. Raise your hand.

5. You are having trouble choosing an answer for a question. What should you do?
   A. Mark two answers on the answer sheet.
   B. Don't mark any answers on the answer sheet.
   C. Ask your teacher which answer to mark.
   D. Mark the best answer on the answer sheet.

6. You don't know how to do a math problem on the test. What should you do?
   A. Stop working and put your pencil down.
   B. Mark C on the answer sheet.
   C. Skip the problem and come back to it later.
   D. Cross out the problem on the answer sheet.

Name _____

1 Ⓐ Ⓑ Ⓒ Ⓓ

2 Ⓐ Ⓑ Ⓒ Ⓓ

3 Ⓐ Ⓑ Ⓒ Ⓓ

4 Ⓐ Ⓑ Ⓒ Ⓓ

5 Ⓐ Ⓑ Ⓒ Ⓓ

6 Ⓐ Ⓑ Ⓒ Ⓓ

Note to the teacher: Use with "A Test About Testing" on page 227.

English LANGUAGE Learners

Keeping It Real

To keep English language learners engaged throughout the school day, try incorporating real-life objects into your lessons! For example, before beginning a unit about communities, share familiar items such as a town map, coupons or advertisements from local businesses, or a tourist brochure with pictures from around the town. To introduce a lesson on solid figures, display a real-world example for each shape beside its model. Then, throughout each lesson, use the objects to enhance the child's understanding.

Listen to Me

Boost reading skills and help each English language learner share her school success. After reading a book with a child, guide her to record herself as she reads the book aloud. Then send the tape and the book home in a plastic resealable bag. At home, the student can replay the tape for her family and then read along with it to build her reading skills!

Crafting New Skills

Use simple craft projects, such as the flying bookmark on page 232, to help English language learners with their learning. In advance, assemble the craft and stock the center with the sample, project materials, and a copy of the directions for each student. Then guide the child to follow the steps on the cards to create his own version of the craft. As the child works, encourage him to read the steps and study the sample to clarify any misunderstandings.

Take-Home Kit

To help English language learners participate in at-home reading projects, put together a kit that can be checked out right along with the book. Inside a large resealable plastic bag, place the student's book, simplified project guidelines, and supplies the child will need to complete the project. Then, before sending the kit home, review the instructions with the student, pointing out that the materials are included. Encourage the child to bring in his project a day or two early to check for any missed details or ask any questions.

Spell It Out

Turn your listening center into a spelling review center with a recording of your weekly list. To make the recording, read each word, pausing to allow the child time to write it. Next, repeat the word and spell it, so that the student can check his work. If desired, provide an alphabet strip to remind the child how to form each letter.

In a Snap

When your English language learner is ready to start writing, have her use pictures to get started. Collect several interesting pictures from old magazines and cut several small sticky notes into narrow strips. Next, have the child choose a picture and glue it to a sheet of construction paper. Guide the student to label colors, objects, and actions in the picture using the sticky note strips. Then help the child use the labels to describe the picture or write a story about what is happening in the picture and glue it to the picture's flip side.

Check out the skill-building reproducibles on pages 233–234.

Flying Bookmark and Direction Card Patterns

Use with "Crafting New Skills" on page 230.

direction card

Finished sample

Taking Off!

To make a bookmark, follow the steps.

Steps:
1. Color the bird and its beak.
2. Cut out the bird's beak.
3. Glue the beak to the bird.
4. Cut out the bird.
5. Color the bookmark.
6. Cut out the bookmark.
7. Glue the bird to the bookmark.

TEC61050

bird

bird's beak

TEC61050

bookmark

Glue here.

How Do You Feel?

Draw a picture for each sentence.

This is a time
when I felt **happy.**

This is a time
when I felt **sad.**

This is a time
when I got **mad.**

This is a time
when I was **confused.**

Words to Know

Write a word from the word box to finish each sentence.

1. We read a ☐☐☐☐ about horses.

2. I ☐☐☐☐☐ a letter to my grandmother.

3. I like to ☐☐☐☐ pictures of dogs.

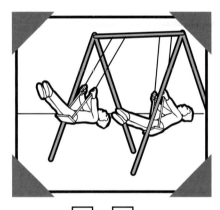
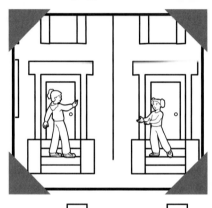

4. We ☐☐☐☐ to swing during recess.

5. My ☐☐☐☐☐☐ lives next door.

6. This glass of ☐☐☐☐☐ is cold.

7. His ☐☐☐☐☐☐☐ came to school to see the show.

8. Use the crayons to ☐☐☐☐☐ the picture.

Word Box

parents   book
friend   like
write   draw
color   water

Bulletin Boards

Welcome

This display offers a special welcome to parents at open house. Prior to the event, take a picture of each student. Have the student cut around her likeness in the photo and glue it to a schoolhouse cutout. The student also writes a sentence stating one of her strengths at school. Post the completed projects on a board. As families arrive for open house, each student removes her schoolhouse from the display and gives it and a pin to a parent to wear as a nametag. This will help you associate each parent with the right student, and parents have a special keepsake of the event.

We All Fit Together!

This first-day activity will have students working together to put the pieces in place for a great year. Supply each student with a marker and a square of white paper for each letter in her first name. Instruct the student to print one letter of her name on each square. Then have students work together to arrange their names in a crossword puzzle format. Help them staple the arrangement to a bulletin board. Add the title, and the display is complete!

Enlarge the Columbus pattern on page 247. Color the pattern and attach it to a bulletin board covered in blue background paper. Have each student add to the display by completing a copy of the ship pattern on page 247 with information about a book. Have students color the ships; then staple them to the board. Invite students to discover new books by reading their classmates' reports.

Dress up your board for Halloween with descriptions that are good enough to eat. Provide each student with a candy pattern from page 248. Instruct him to describe his favorite candy using his senses and then color and cut out the shape. Attach the finished patterns and a colorful trick-or-treat sack to a bulletin board as shown.

Your class can show gratitude with a bounty of letters. Have each student write a note expressing appreciation to a special friend or family member. Mount the writing on a student-made woven mat for display. Before Thanksgiving, each student removes his project from the board and delivers it for a fulfilling Thanksgiving surprise.

Cover your board with red background paper. Use a black marker to draw a brick design on the paper so that it resembles a fireplace mantel. Have each student create a stocking and personalize it. Then ask her to write a holiday wish on the foot portion of the stocking and add decorative designs. Hang the completed stockings on the mantel with a string of garland.

Each student draws or brings in a picture of himself with family or friends. He mounts the picture on a package cutout. Next, he writes a caption for the picture on a gift tag made from an index card and uses a length of ribbon to attach it to the package. Staple the packages to a gift-wrap covered board.

Celebrate Hanukkah with an interactive math display. To make a star, each student cuts two aluminum foil triangles and positions them as shown. Then she lays the star on the sticky side of clear adhesive paper and sprinkles a layer of glitter around the outside edge of the star. She lays a second adhesive paper on top of the star (sticky side down) and trims around the star shape, leaving a one-inch glitter border. Collect the stars and program them with math problems for students to complete during free time.

Create a winter display that reinforces that differences are special. Have each child fold and cut a sheet of white paper to create a snowflake shape. Spread a thin coat of glue on the snowflake and sprinkle with iridescent glitter. Glue each student's photo in the center of her shape. Then on an index card have each student write why she is unique and special. Add the cards to the display.

Instruct each child to trace a copy of the pattern on page 249 on a sheet of accordion-folded construction paper. Then have him cut along the pattern and unfold the resulting paper-doll chain. Have each student decorate his chain of dolls to resemble members in the community. Staple the completed projects to a bulletin board to create a border. Next post each student's New Year's resolution that tells how he will participate in the community.

Provide each student with a copy of one pattern from page 249 and the form at the top of page 250. Instruct the student to decorate the pattern in her own likeness and then complete the form with her thoughts on creating a peaceful world. Display the completed projects on a bulletin board in honor of Martin Luther King Jr.

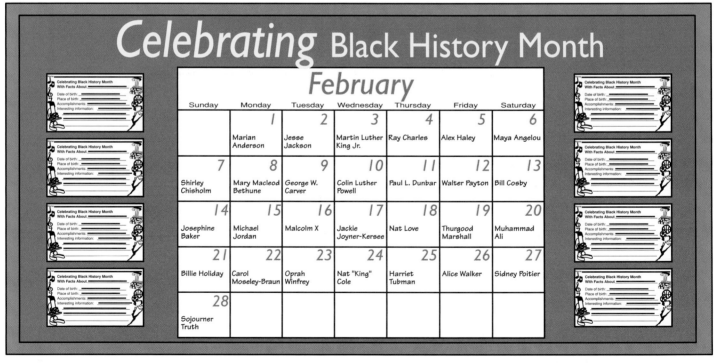

This bulletin board will do double duty as a Black History Month calendar. Cover the board with background paper, and illustrate it with a calendar grid and the title. Program each square of the grid with the appropriate date and the name of a famous Black American. Assign each student a name on the calendar to research. Have him record information about the assigned person on a copy of the form at the bottom of page 250. Provide time for each student to present the information to the class on the day designated on the calendar. After each presentation, staple the form to the calendar display.

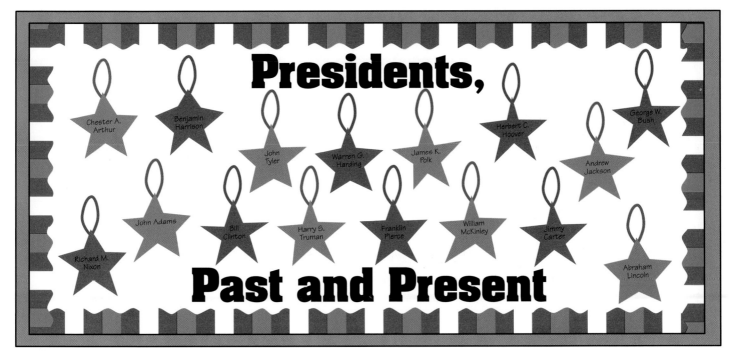

Assign a different U.S. president to each student to research. Make a supply of red and blue stars, and give a star to each student. Instruct each student to write his assigned president's name on the front of the star and a fact about him on the back. Attach a loop of yarn to each star and attach the stars to a bulletin board covered in white background paper. Encourage students to visit the display to learn more about presidents, past and present.

Instruct each student to fold a sheet of construction paper in half and trim it to form a heart shape. Have her unfold the shape and add a red sponge-painted border. After the paint has dried, have each student compose a valentine couplet and write it in the center of the heart. Mount the completed projects on a board covered in pink background paper. Add the title and a border made from valentine cards.

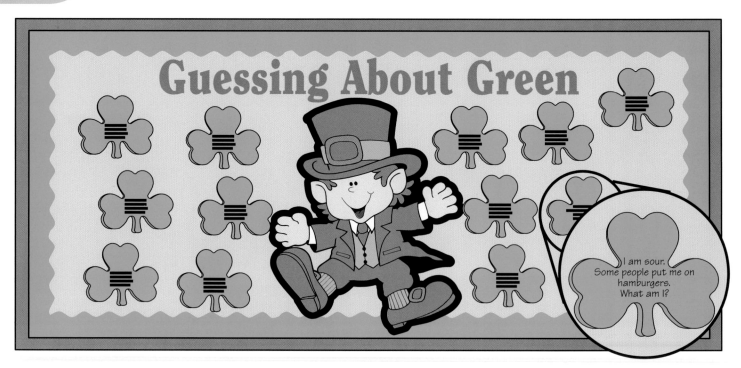

Present a puzzling project for St. Patrick's Day with a focus on green. Each student cuts two identical shamrock shapes from a folded sheet of green construction paper and staples them together at the top. Then he writes a riddle about something green on the front of the shape and writes the riddle's answer on the inside. Mount the riddles on a bulletin board as shown.

Each student lightly sketches a butterfly on a sheet of black construction paper. Then she squeezes liquid glue onto the lines. After the glue dries, she cuts out the butterfly and colors in each section with brightly colored chalk. Spray the butterfly with a fixative before mounting it on a bulletin board. If desired, add student-written paragraphs about a favorite spring occurrence.

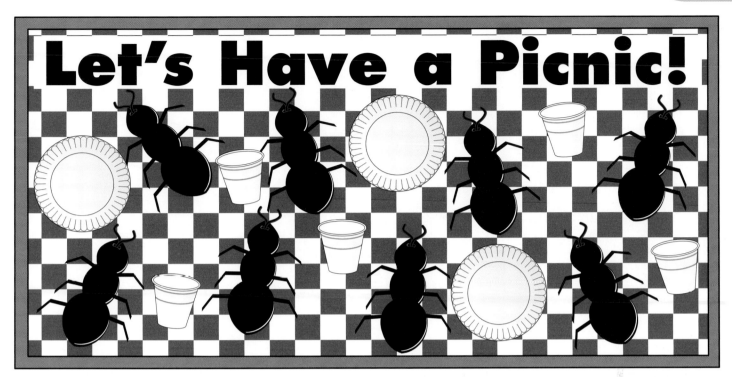

Each student cuts out a large ant body from black construction paper. He uses the ant as a template to make three ants from white paper and another from black paper. Then he staples the white pages between the black cutouts, punches two holes in the head, and threads a black pipe cleaner through as antennae. To complete the project, he adds six black legs to the back cover and then writes a summertime story on the white pages. Mount the ants on a display as shown.

End the year with a cool collection of third-grade memories. Provide each student with a copy of the pattern on page 251. Have each student write her favorite memory of the third-grade year on the pattern before coloring it and cutting it out. Decorate a bulletin board with the completed patterns, and have a cool summer!

Enlarge the airplane pattern on page 248. Color, cut out, and laminate the pattern before mounting it on a bulletin board. To display students' papers, have each student cut out and personalize a white construction paper cloud. Staple the clouds to the bulletin board, and then attach samples of the students' work.

Post a clown character on a board titled as shown. Attach a sample of each student's best work to the board. Have each student create an ice-cream cone out of colored construction paper. Program a student's name on each cone; then write a comment praising the student's handwriting, quality of work, or area of improvement. Staple the cone beside the student's paper. When it's time to replace the work on the board, attach the cone to the paper for the student to take home.

Post the title on a bulletin board covered with yellow paper. Staple an example of each student's best work on the board. Then have each student make a paper topper by placing her hand, palm down, in poster paint and pressing it on a sheet of white construction paper. When the prints are dry, trim around the hand-print. Attach the print to the top of the student's paper.

Cut a supply of three-inch circles from purple construction paper and store them in a resealable bag pinned to the board. Attach a stem programmed with the date of the weekly spelling test to the board. When a student scores above a predetermined grade on his weekly test, he writes his name on a circle and staples it to the board as shown. When the board is full, have each student collect all the circles with his name on them to redeem for minutes of free time.

Our Work Is on Target!

Create a target design in the center of a bulletin board. Post examples of each student's best work around the target. Then cut out an arrow shape for each paper on display. Cut the arrow in half and attach it to the paper as shown. Students will be proud to make their mark with good work!

Step up to good habits with this record of class progress. Create a ladder from brown construction paper and attach it to a bulletin board. Label the top of the ladder with a classroom goal, such as turning in homework on time. For each day the class achieves the goal, move a paper cutout of the school mascot up one rung of the ladder. When the mascot reaches the top, celebrate your class's success with a special reward.

Everyone Turning in Homework

Steps to Success

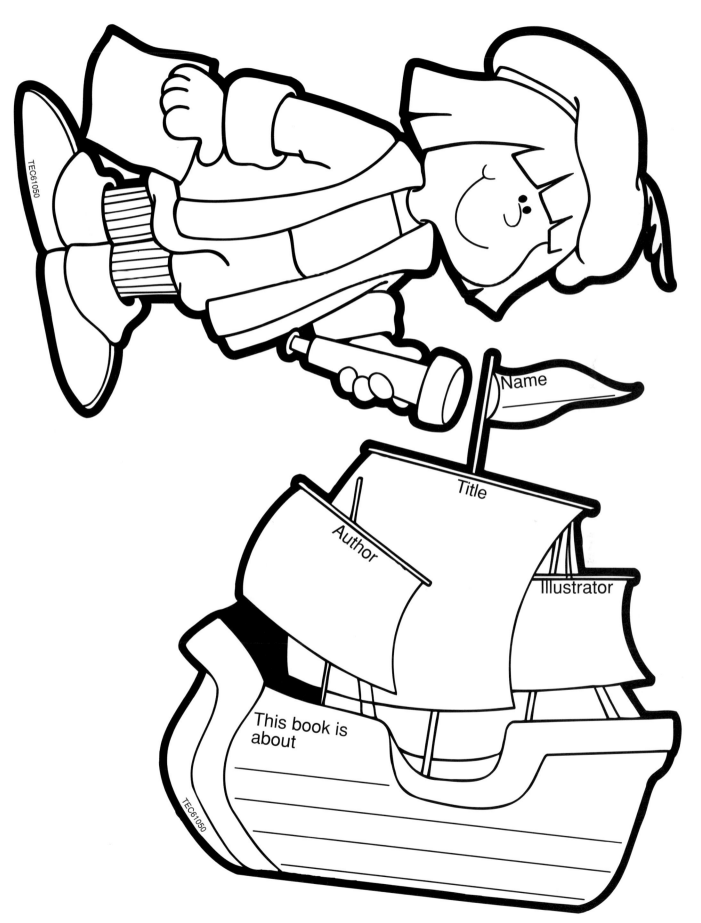

Name

Title

Author

Illustrator

This book is about

Candy Patterns

Use with "Have a Tasty Halloween!" on page 236.

Airplane Pattern

Use with "High-Flying Work" on page 244.

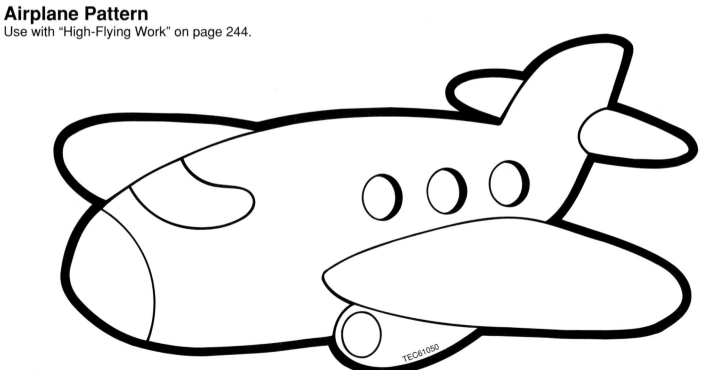

People Patterns
Use with "The New Year Will Be Great If We All
Participate" on page 239 and "Working Toward
a Peaceful World" on page 240.

Place on fold.

Place on fold.

Place on fold.

Place on fold.

TEC61050

TEC61050

Form

Use with "Working Toward a Peaceful World" on page 240.

Martin Luther King Jr. wanted people to live peaceably. I can help make a peaceful world by

_____

_____

_____

_____

_____

_____

Name _____

TEC61050

Form

Use with "Celebrating Black History Month" on page 240.

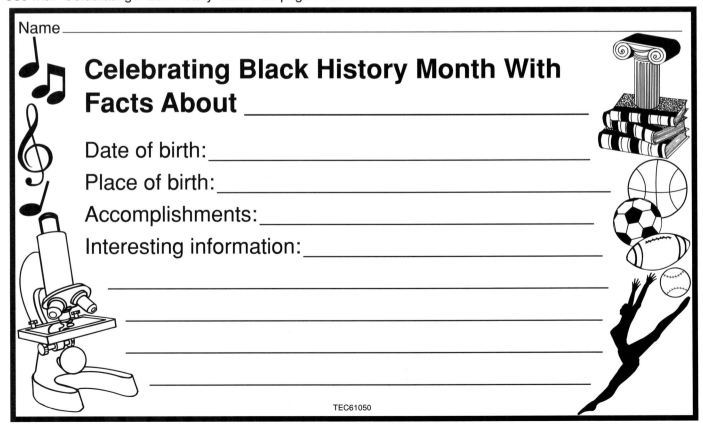

Name _____

Celebrating Black History Month With Facts About _____

Date of birth: _____

Place of birth: _____

Accomplishments: _____

Interesting information: _____

_____

_____

_____

_____

TEC61050

CLASSROOM MANAGEMENT

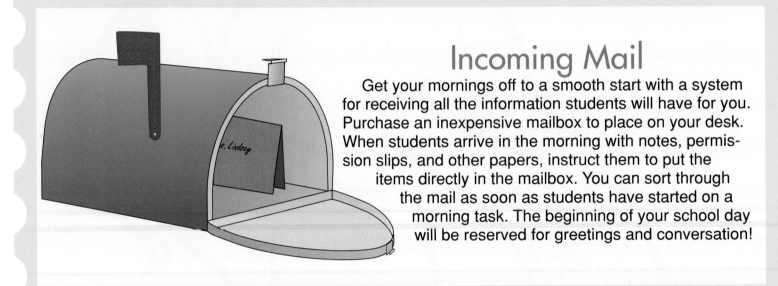

Incoming Mail

Get your mornings off to a smooth start with a system for receiving all the information students will have for you. Purchase an inexpensive mailbox to place on your desk. When students arrive in the morning with notes, permission slips, and other papers, instruct them to put the items directly in the mailbox. You can sort through the mail as soon as students have started on a morning task. The beginning of your school day will be reserved for greetings and conversation!

Exit Board

Stay on top of the comings and goings in your classroom with a nametag charting system. Attach self-adhesive hooks to a bulletin board, and label each hook with a title such as restroom, speech class, library, or office. Distribute to each student a cardboard tag with a metal ring attached. Have him personalize the tag and keep it at his desk until he needs to leave the classroom. Before leaving the room, the student places his tag on the appropriate hook. When he returns, he removes the tag and stores it at his desk.

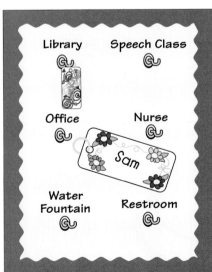

The Name Cup

For a great timesaver, program a class set of wooden tongue depressors or craft sticks each with different student's name. Store the sticks in a decorated cup or tin. When it is time to randomly choose a student's name, place students in small groups, choose partners or teams, or select a student to go first in an activity, simply pull a stick from the cup. Students will know that the selection was done fairly, and you won't have to make the decision!

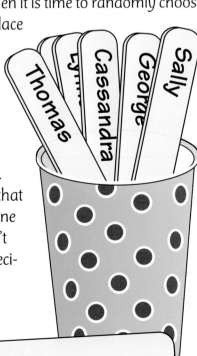

Absences/Tardies

Pam	9/6	(9/7)						
Greg	9/2							
Katie								
Tim								
Ashton								
Paul								
Carly								

Attendance Made Easy

Make attendance-taking an easy task with this quick tip. Instead of marking each student present in your grade book each day, write down only the dates each student is absent. Place the date in a blank square by the name of the absent student. If the student comes in late, draw a circle around the date to indicate a tardy. Absences and tardy marks will be easier to count, and your daily record keeping will be much simpler.

Lesson-Plan Checklist

A checklist is the perfect way to keep your daily plans within reach. Use the form on page 259 to make a generic schedule of your daily routines and then make several copies. Cross off items as they are completed. Make notes next to activities that went well or concepts that need to be reviewed. At the end of each day, look over the checklist. Any unfinished items can simply be clipped to the next day's planning sheet.

Class Information

Have a list of important details ready when you need it by creating a class information list. Make one copy of the form on page 258. Program it with the desired information, such as students' birth dates, parents' names, and phone numbers where parents can be reached. Attach the completed list to your attendance or lesson plan book for easy access after making a copy of the list to take home with you.

Color-Coded Grade Book

This system for color-coding your grade book will allow you to see at a glance which scores are daily grades, homework assignments, or test scores. Select a different-colored highlighter for each type of grade to be recorded. Before recording a set of grades, use the appropriate highlighter to color in the column in your grade book. The color-coded page will help you evaluate students' progress and simplify grade averaging.

MATH	p. 13	p. 14	p. 15	quiz	p. 16	test 1	project				
Mary	✓+	95	95	91	✓+	93	A+				
Tina	✓	90	90	94	✓+	94	A				
Miguel	✓	90	90	86	✓	90	A-				
Eric	✓+	85	85	91	✓+	89	B+				
Tanya	✓	88	88	89	✓+	86	B				
Andrew	✓+	93	93	94	✓	95	A				

▢ = daily homework grade   ▢ = quiz grade   ▢ = test grade   ▢ = project grade

Anecdotal Notecards

Keep anecdotal records right at your fingertips with this easy idea. Begin by labeling a class supply of large index cards each with the name of a student as shown. Next, tape the top of the cards to a clipboard, as shown, overlapping the cards until each student's card is attached. Tape a blank card at the top to keep your notes private. When you need to assess a skill or make note of a behavior, flip your records open to the appropriate student card. The cards will quickly fill up with comments to share on report cards, at parent conferences, and with students.

Caitlyn
Doug
Elizabeth
Clevell
Susan
Jennifer
Rob
Amy
Scott
Alex
Tia

Absentee Assignments

When a student is absent, use this simple system for collecting class work that he has missed. Program a folder with the absent student's name and place it on his desk. As papers are passed out during the day, have a designated classmate place a copy of each assignment in the student's folder. At the end of the day, the folder will contain all the day's work and be ready to send home to the student. If desired, have classmates sign the folder and add get-well wishes.

If you are going to introduce a new concept, begin a new unit, or give an oral test when a student is absent, you may want to tape-record the lesson. The tape can be sent home with the student so he can be kept up-to-date on the information discussed in the lesson. When he returns to school, the student can make up any oral testing by listening to that portion of the tape.

Traveling Nametags

If your grade level is departmentalized, use traveling nametags to help identify students during the first few weeks of school. To make a nametag, fold a large index card in half to create a tent shape. Write a student's name on both sides of the nametag and then place it atop the student's desk. Invite the student to decorate her tag as desired. When it's time to change classes, the student carries the nametag with her and places it on her desk in the next classroom. Have students carry their nametags to music class and the cafeteria as well, so that everyone on staff can become familiar with students' names.

Shared Responsibility

Help students keep up with homework assignments with "Buddy Books"—small spiral notepads for keeping track of homework information. Provide time at the end of the day for each student to copy the necessary homework information in her Buddy Book. The book is then read by a classmate buddy who checks the information for accuracy. After any corrections have been made, the buddy initials the notepad and passes it back to its owner. Students have the information they need to complete their assignments, and they develop a feeling of teamwork as well.

File-Folder Storage

For a simple way to keep track of file-folder games or centers, store the contents of each activity in a manila envelope. Label the envelope to identify the contents; then file it with the appropriate month or unit it is used with. This serves as excellent storage when the activity contains separate pieces or cards, and it will be easy to locate the materials when you are ready to set up the center.

Handy Reminders

Students will have a reminder of the classroom rules when they complete this activity. Distribute a piece of colored construction paper to each student. Instruct her to trace her hand on the paper and then cut out the shape. On each of the fingers, have her copy a classroom rule, such as the ones shown. Have her write the title "Handy Rules" in the center of the palm. Tape the completed projects to each desk for a visual reminder of behavioral expectations.

Handy Rules

Respect others.
Keep my hands and feet to myself.
Raise my hand to speak.
Be responsible for my belongings.
Use self-control.

"Carroty" Conduct

Teach classroom expectations with the help of Captain Carrot, a cute character that promotes positive classroom conduct. Create a display, as shown, using an enlarged copy of the pattern on page 260. Discuss the expectations with your students. When you are ready to take down the display, keep Captain Carrot close at hand. Have him pay an occasional visit to reinforce positive classroom behavior.

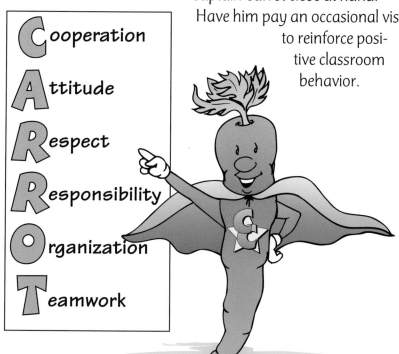

Cooperation
Attitude
Respect
Responsibility
Organization
Teamwork

Pocket Organization

A pocket folder is the perfect tool for helping you keep track of which activities and reproducibles you have used. Purchase a two-pocket folder for each of your thematic files. Label one pocket of each folder "Activities to Use" and the other pocket "Completed

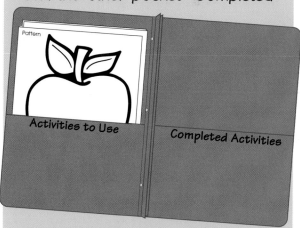

Activities." Store your ideas, activities, and worksheets in the first pocket. When an activity has been used, transfer it to the other side of the folder. At the end of each unit, transfer all pages back to the first pocket, and you'll be ready to go for the next year.

Extra Storage Space

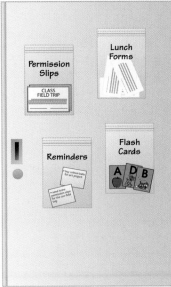

Create additional storage space in closets and cabinets by attaching stick-on pockets to the insides of the doors. Label the see-through pockets according to contents and use them for storing flash cards, lunch forms, tardy slips, and daily reminders. You'll have access to the items you use most in a space-saving place!

Be Prepared!

Be prepared for unexpected situations by keeping an emergency kit on hand. In addition to a basic first-aid kit, stock a lockable drawer or box with the following items:

- a sewing kit
- a screwdriver
- a hammer
- a package of assorted nails
- resealable plastic bags
- a flashlight
- nail scissors and clippers
- tweezers
- a smock or old shirt
- safety pins
- a nail file
- matches or a lighter
- a ball of string
- packing tape

Additional Storage Ideas

Keep your classroom clutter-free by utilizing some of the following storage ideas:

Use a silverware tray to hold paintbrushes, colored pencils, and markers in your art center.

Ice-cube trays and egg cartons make handy organizers for storing tiny craft items or game pieces. They also work well for holding small amounts of tempera paints.

Cardboard tubes from wrapping paper or paper towels are perfect for storing charts, maps, and posters. Roll up each poster and place it inside a tube. If desired, label the tube's contents before putting it away.

Use margarine tubs and whipped-topping tubs to hold paints, clay, or small manipulatives.

Cardboard shoe organizers are just the thing for holding sets of papers or serving as cubbyholes.

Check craft stores for plastic, multidrawer containers. Use the drawers for holding sequins, buttons, pom-poms, beads, and other small craft items.

Clever Clothespins

Keep a supply of spring-type clothespins handy. They can be used in a variety of ways!

- Use a clothespin when a paper clip is too small for the job.

- Display a chart or poster by clipping the poster to a clothes hanger.

- Program clothespins with students' names. Use the clips as nametags and manipulatives.

- Glue magnets on the back of several clothespins. Then use the clothespins as message holders or to hold posters, charts, and displays.

- Use the clothespins to hold art projects that need to dry.

- Program a set of clips to be used as passes to the office, library, and restroom. When a student needs to leave the room, he clips the appropriate clothespin to his shirt.

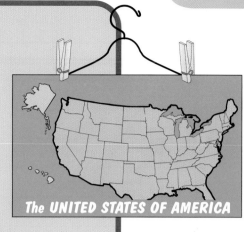

The UNITED STATES OF AMERICA

Who has a ...
cat
dog
both

Jason leaves today at 2:00.

Library

Super Shoe Organizers

A clear multipocket shoe organizer can serve a variety of purposes in your classroom! For an at-a-glance classroom job chart, use a permanent marker to label each pocket of the organizer with a different job. Next, program a class set of index cards each with a different student's name. To assign jobs, place a name card in a pocket. Jobs can easily be reassigned by rearranging the cards!

Hang a shoe organizer at your art center and stock it with supplies needed for the current project. It will be easy for students to find each item, and cleanup will be a simple task!

Keep a shoe organizer hanging near your desk. It can be used to hold

- lunch tickets
- medical forms
- office passes
- markers
- chalk
- reward stickers

- scissors
- rubber bands
- index cards
- calculators
- glue bottles
- die-cut letters for bulletin boards

Class Information

	Name				

Note to the teacher: Use with "Class Information" on page 253.

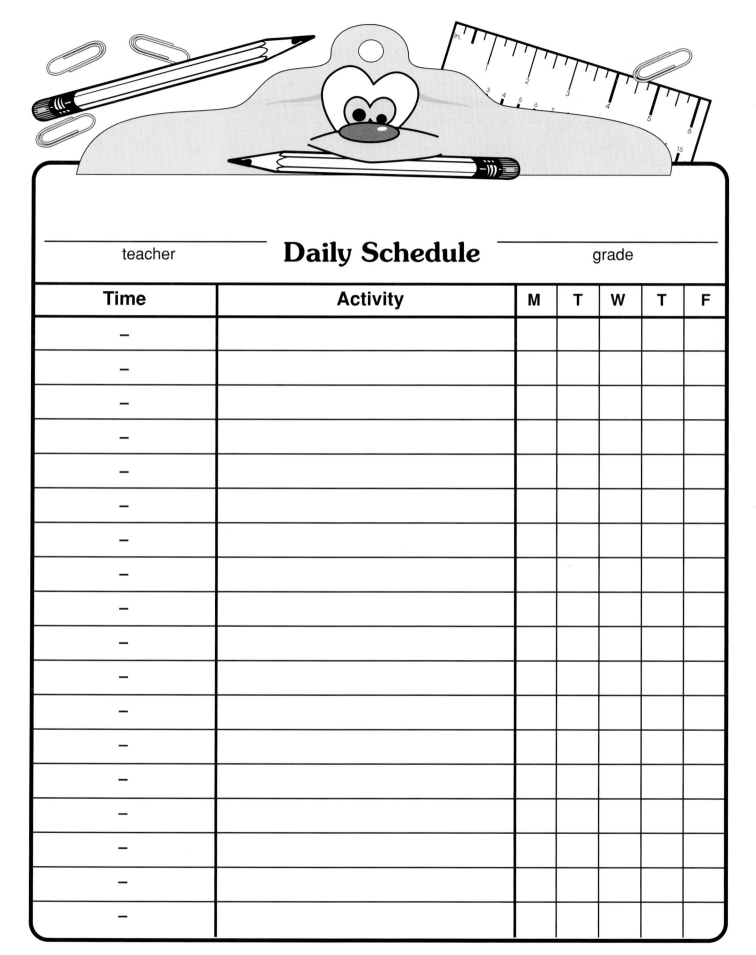

Daily Schedule

teacher _____   grade _____

Time	Activity	M	T	W	T	F
–						
–						
–						
–						
–						
–						
–						
–						
–						
–						
–						
–						
–						
–						
–						
–						
–						
–						

Note to the teacher: Use with "Lesson-Plan Checklist" on page 253.

Carrot Pattern

Use with "'Carroty' Conduct" on page 255.

Our Classroom Rules

We have discussed the rules we need in order to have a positive learning environment. We agree to

_____

_____

_____

_____

_____

_____

Note to the teacher: Duplicate this page; then program it with the necessary information. If desired, enlarge and color the page before displaying it.

261

Homework Policy

_____

_____

_____

_____

_____

_____

_____

Rewards

_____

_____

_____

_____

_____

Note to the teacher: Duplicate this page; then program it with the necessary information. If desired, enlarge and color the page before displaying it.

Discipline Policy

Severe situations will be handled by

Note to the teacher: Duplicate this page; then program it with the necessary information. If desired, enlarge and color the page before displaying it.

Motivation & Positive Discipline

Marvelous Motivation

Set the stage for learning by creating a positive environment for your students. See the lists below for ideas about letting each student know how special she is. Use copies of the rewards and coupons on page 268 to recognize positive student behavior and encourage each student to do her best.

Recognize students for:

- helping a classmate
- making a new student feel welcome
- acting cooperatively
- using nice handwriting
- learning math facts
- consistently turning in homework assignments
- keeping an orderly workspace
- perseverance with a difficult assignment
- consistently following classroom rules
- a good attendance record

Ways to Reinforce Positive Behavior

Program copies of the coupons to be redeemed for
- the opportunity to sit by a friend during a lesson
- choosing a classroom job for the week
- being first in line for a day
- choosing a game for the class to play
- selecting bonus words for the spelling list
- skipping a homework assignment
- selecting music to be played during art time
- eating lunch with the principal or another member of the faculty

For Good "Bee-havior"

Cover a bulletin board with blue paper and mount a construction paper flower programmed as shown. Make a class supply of copies of the bee pattern on page 269 and store them near the bulletin board. When a student notices a classmate displaying one of the behaviors shown, she writes on one of the bees a sentence describing the situation, colors and cuts out the bee, and then staples it on the display.

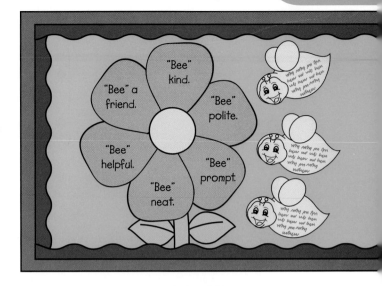

Stamps of Approval

Use an individualized progress card to motivate each student to work on a specific area of improvement while reinforcing her strengths. Meet with each student to discuss both strong points and areas that need to be improved. Personalize an index card for each student and write a goal for the student. At the end of each day, stamp the card with a motivational rubber stamp if progress has been made toward the goal. After a predetermined number of stamps have been earned, reward the student with a special treat or privilege.

Ann
Use your best
handwriting all week.

WOW!   #1

Self-Esteem Supply

Give a copy of page 270 to each student. Instruct the student to cut out the shape and write her name on the label. Collect the patterns and redistribute them in random order. The student reads the name on the jar she receives and then writes on the pattern a positive comment, as shown, about that student. Continue collecting and redistributing the jars until each jar is full of favorable comments. Provide time for each student to read the statements written about her; then display the jars on a bulletin board decorated with a construction paper shelf.

Chris is a good sport.
Chris is good at math.
Chris has cool shoes.

Chris

Chris uses his manners.
Chris knows a lot about snakes.

It's in the Cards

Add a spark of excitement to positive reinforcement. Purchase a deck of playing cards and divide it into the four suits. Place two of the suits in a container. When you notice a student displaying positive behavior, allow the student to reach into the container and draw out two cards. If the cards are a matching pair, the student may take a prize from the prize box. If the cards do not match, offer a smaller prize such as a sticker or bookmark. Aside from the treat, the element of chance will make reaching into the jar a special reward of its own.

Sticking With Good Behavior

Provide a place for each student to display the incentive stickers she receives by covering a small area of her desk with a square of Con-Tact covering. This allows the students to affix the stickers to her desk without placing them directly on the furniture. The stickers will easily peel away from the Con-Tact covering, enabling students to remove them and take them home.

Choose a sticker from your teacher.

Be the leader in line.

Encouraging Organization

For an easy and effective way to encourage students to keep their desks in tip-top order, cut out a supply of seasonal shapes. On each shape, write a reward such as being first in line, using a colored pen on an assignment, or spending extra time at a learning center. Choose a time when the students are out of the room to inspect each desk for being neat and orderly. If a student has a well-organized desk, leave a reward shape on his desk. When students return to the room, they will be surprised to find rewards on some of the desks. Continue to make random inspections to encourage students to keep their desks orderly at all times.

Spend ten extra minutes at any learning center.

Dressed for Success

Recognize your students' outstanding behavior and work habits with a special privilege. Invite students who have exhibited desired behaviors to participate in a special dress-up event such as hat day, sunglasses day, or pajama day. Provide a special table in the cafeteria for these well-attired students to eat their lunches. Then take pictures of the students in their special garb. Display the photographs as a reminder of what fun good behavior can be!

Book Order Incentives

Student book order forms can be an incentive to encourage proper classroom behavior. Post a list of books from the current order that could be purchased with bonus points for the classroom library. When you *see* a student modeling good conduct, allow her to cast a vote for one of the books on the list by making a tally mark beside it. As an extra bonus, reward students who have earned the most tally marks by giving them first opportunities to read the new books when they arrive.

Reward Raffle

Encourage students to maintain good conduct with a classroom raffle. At the beginning of each week, enlist students' help to create five certificates for classroom privileges. Have students suggest the types of rewards, such as a homework pass, the chance to eat lunch in the classroom, or the chance to choose a free-time activity. Program each certificate with one reward. Then, each time a student displays outstanding behavior during the week, write his name on a slip of paper and place it in a raffle jar. At the end of the week, draw five names from the jar. Present each winner with a certificate, redeemable anytime the following week.

Conduct Celebration

Motivate the class to work together to earn a special reward. Plan an event, such as a popcorn party, a video showing, or an extra recess to celebrate classwide behavior. On the board, write a blank for each letter in the name of the reward. For each day the class works together to maintain good conduct, fill in a blank with a letter of the reward. When all the blanks have been filled, it's time to celebrate!

You did a bang-up job and I'm proud of you!

To: _____ From: _____

TEC61050

#1

Award-Winning Efforts

Presented to:

_____

Keep up the good work!

TEC61050

Three cheers for _____!

Hip Hip Hooray!

TEC61050

You're on a Roll!

To: _____

From: _____

TEC61050

This coupon is good for

_____

_____

_____

TEC61050

This coupon is good for

_____

_____

_____

_____

TEC61050

THIS COUPON IS GOOD FOR

_____

_____

_____

TEC61050

THIS COUPON IS GOOD FOR

_____

_____

_____

TEC61050

knows how to "bee"

TEC61050

Jar Pattern
Use with "Self-Esteem Supply" on page 265.

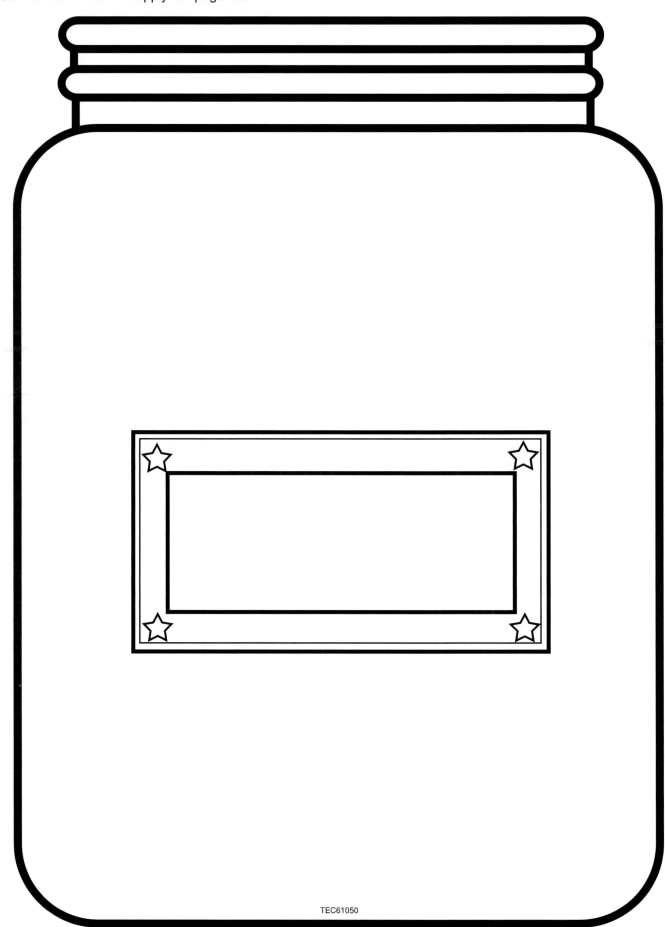

TEC61050

Five-Minute Fillers

Line-Up Lesson

Students are lined up at the door, but there are still a few minutes before it's time to leave. Why not initiate a brainstorming session? Name a category that students are familiar with. Have students name an item in the category for each letter of the alphabet. By the time everyone has volunteered an answer, it will be time to go!

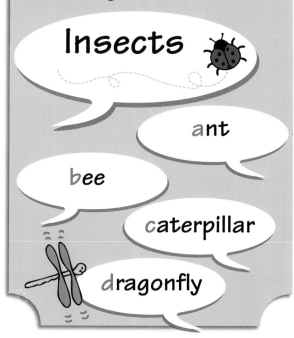

Operation, Please!

Use spare moments to reinforce problem-solving strategies. Give each student two index cards. Instruct the student to write one of the four basic operation signs (addition, subtraction, multiplication, or division) on each side of the index cards. When a few extra minutes arise, read a story problem to the class. Each student holds up the sign for the correct operation needed to solve the problem. Not only will this provide extra practice, but you can also see at a glance who is having trouble with the concept.

Instant Graphing

Fill spare minutes with a graphing activity. Prepare for the activity by drawing a bar graph on poster board and then laminating it for durability. To use the graph, write the topic and categories of the graph on the poster board with a wipe-off marker. Then give a self-stick note to each student. The student writes his name or response on the note and then posts it in the correct column on the graph. If time allows, have students discuss the results, making comparative or observational statements about the findings.

FAVORITE COLORS

blue	red	green	yellow	purple	orange
Tim				Clevell	
Carly		Brian		Angie	
Sue	Scott	Leann	Adam	Rob	
Joey	Kendall	Jessie	Becky	Kim	Tanya
				Mandy	

Number-Concept Practice

Students can practice number concepts in the extra minutes between classes. Write four numerals on the board. Call on volunteers to come to the board and write numbers that can be made using the four numerals. After several numbers have been made, ask students to identify the greatest number written, the smallest number written, or the number that has a certain numeral in a designated place-value position.

8	4	9	2
9,842	4,298		2,984
2,489	9,248		4,829
8,429	2,894		8,942

Making Words

Engage students in a word-building challenge during the transitional time between classes. Choose a vocabulary word from a current unit of study. Write the word on the board. Challenge students to use the letters in the word to create other words. As a student discovers a word, have him write it on the board. As students' skills improve, reverse the activity by providing a list of words and challenging the class to discover the longer mystery word.

kitchen

kit	nice	hen
chin	kite	tick
think	ten	ice

Review With Riddles

Create a supply of riddles that reinforces a variety of skills. Compose riddles relating to the curriculum. (See the examples below.) Write each riddle on an index card. Store the cards in a file box or on a metal ring, and keep them in a handy location. When you need a time filler, the riddles will be ready to go!

- Can you name the root in the word *unchecked*?
- Can you name an animal that hibernates?
- Can you name one part of a plant?
- Can you name a synonym for the word *said*?
- Can you think of two kinds of maps?
- Can you explain the difference between a good and a service?
- Can you name the value of three quarters, one dime, and four pennies?

Can you name the shape with eight sides?

Can you think of a mammal with three syllables in its name?

Can you name a difference between Jupiter and Mercury?

Word-Skills Search

Review basic word skills with this easy activity. Announce a specific type of word, such as compounds, contractions, or four-syllable words. Have students look through their library books for examples of that type of word. When a student locates a word, ask her to write it on the board. Leave the list on the board for students to copy for handwriting practice.

Four-Syllable Words

elevator
interesting
situation
January
alligator
information

Twenty Questions

When it comes to polishing thinking skills, keep the game of Twenty Questions in mind. To guess the object you are thinking of, have students formulate questions that can be answered with *yes* or *no.* Keep track of the number of questions asked by having a student write tally marks on the board. If students identify the object before 20 questions have been asked, challenge them to supply five facts about the object. If the students are not able to identify the object after 20 questions, provide facts about the object until students are able to guess what it is.

Is it alive?

Is it smaller than a bread box?

SCHOOL MENU

sloppy joes
french fries
green beans
applesauce
milk

Menu Activities

Use the school lunch menu for a variety of fast filler activities. Write the daily menu on the board and challenge students to

✔ name an item from each food group

✔ alphabetize the items

✔ predict which item is the class favorite and then vote to determine the answer

✔ count the number of syllables in each item

✔ categorize the menu into solids and liquids

✔ name the ingredients in an item

✔ think of ways to categorize the items

VITAMIN D MILK VITAMIN D MILK

Student Similarities

Generate positive bonds between your students with an activity that focuses on similarities. Select a student to come to the front of the room. Have each classmate identify one thing that he has in common with the student. If desired, have the student record the responses on the board. The students may be surprised at how much they have in common with their fellow classmates!

Mystery Student

Have each student write her name on a slip of paper. Collect the papers and place them in a container. Choose a student to draw a name from the container. Without revealing the person's name, the student makes three statements about the mystery student. His classmates have three chances to identify the mystery student. If the name is identified, the person who guessed correctly will draw the next name from the container. If no one guesses the name, the mystery student becomes the next player.

The mystery student has a brother.

He likes ketchup on his pizza.

He also plays the piano.

Vocabulary Booster

As new vocabulary is introduced throughout the year, copy each vocabulary word and its definition on an index card. Store the cards in a file box; then fill spare minutes with a vocabulary review. Randomly pull a card from the box and read aloud the vocabulary word. Award the student who can define the word with a sticker or a point toward a larger prize.

Memory Test

This activity will enhance students' observational skills. Write ten vocabulary words on the board in a random arrangement. Have students study the words for one minute. Then ask students to put their heads down while you erase two of the words. Have students study the remaining words and try to identify which two have been erased.

And the Answer Is...

Challenge students to practice math by having them create a list of problems. Designate a numeral that will be the answer to the problems and write it on the board. Then have students come up with as many problems as they can think of that yield that answer. If desired, specify an operation for students to use in creating the problems.

21

$10 + 11 =$ $42 - 21 =$

$7 \times 3 =$ $15 + 6 =$

$29 - 8 =$ $21 \times 1 =$

Arts & Crafts

Tricks & Tips

Many art projects involve a variety of materials, and organizing the supplies can be a challenge. Arrange your materials in easy-to-use ways to help make art time more enjoyable for you and your students.

Keep balls of yarn and string tangle-free with a plastic funnel. Place the ball inside the funnel and pull the string out through the spout.

Use baby-wipe containers to hold cotton balls, sponge shapes, paint-brushes, and craft sticks. The containers will stack neatly in your closet or cupboard.

Make individual sets of paint by pouring leftover tempera paint into the sections of an ice cube tray. Allow the paint to dry. Reuse the paint by moistening a paintbrush with water and running it over the desired color.

Store seasonal craft supplies in see-through plastic shoeboxes. Felt, pipe cleaners, and glitter in seasonal colors will be easier to locate when grouped together.

Stock Up

Stock up on project materials when you find them on sale. Some items to keep on hand are:

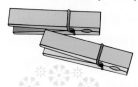

clothespins   coffee filters   cotton balls

doilies   paper cups   paper lunch sacks

paper plates   pipe cleaners   wiggle eyes

Other materials can be obtained by asking parents to send specific items to school. Use a copy of the form on page 282 to request donations for special projects.

Personalized Posters

Student individuality will shine with this colorful poster project. Give each student a sheet of art paper. Instruct him to wet the paper using a sponge. While the paper is still wet, have him paint designs on the paper with water-colors, allowing the colors to bleed and run. After the paper is dry, have each child trace the letters of his name with stencils. Then have him cut out the letters and glue them to a sheet of colored construction paper. Have students cut additional shapes from any leftover painted paper and add them to the poster. Hang the posters in your room for a colorful display.

Glowing Ghosts

Set up a "spook-tacular" display with these glowing ghosts! Give each student a sheet of black construction paper. Instruct her to lightly sketch a ghost shape onto the paper. Tape the paper to a piece of cardboard; then have each student use a thumbtack to punch holes on the pencil outline. When the entire shape has been punched, remove the cardboard and tape the paper to a window. As the light shines through the tiny holes, the ghosts will appear to glow!

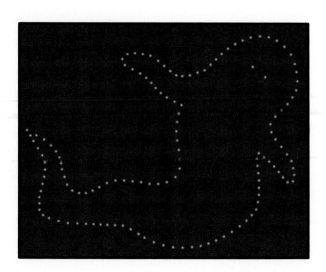

Colorful Corn

These Indian corn projects will fill your room with a harvest of fall colors. Have each student trace a copy of the corn pattern on page 283 onto a piece of tagboard and then cut it out. Then have each student trace the husk patterns on page 283 onto a brown paper grocery sack. Have her cut out the husk shapes and set them aside.

Place several shallow dishes of tempera paint on a table. Have students take turns dipping their pinkies into a color and pressing it onto their tagboard ears of corn. Have your students repeat this step using different colors until the ears of corn are covered. While the paint is drying, have each child crumple her husks into a ball and then unfold them. To complete the project, have each child attach her husks to the bottom of the corn using a brad.

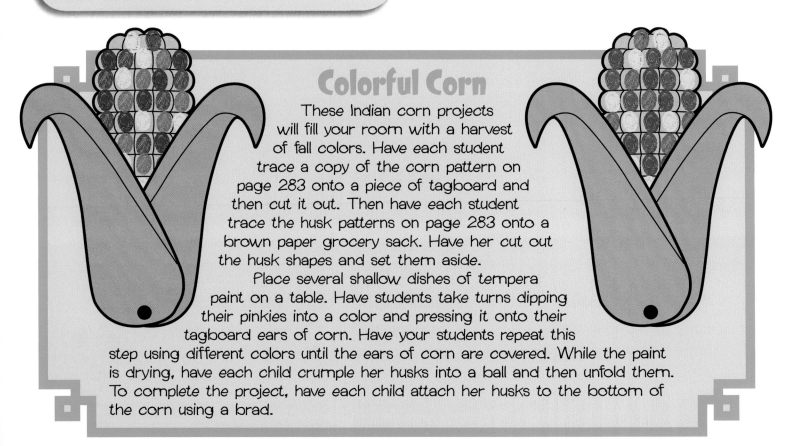

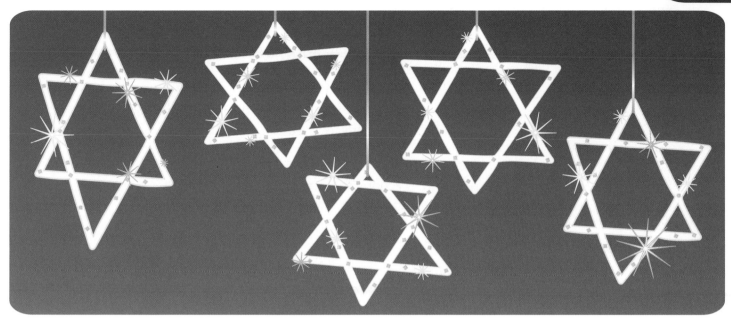

Shining Stars

Celebrate Hanukkah with a display of sparkling stars. Show your students how to make a star by drawing two overlapping large triangles. Give each student a piece of waxed paper, and have him draw the star shape on the paper with liquid glue. After each student sprinkles his design with glitter, let it dry for an hour. Have each student add another line of glue to the project to thicken the outline, and sprinkle again with glitter. Allow the designs to dry overnight; then gently peel the waxed paper away from the shapes. Create a hanging loop for each star using metallic thread. Suspend the stars from the ceiling for a shimmering display.

Framed Photographs

Class photographs will become treasured keepsakes when presented as holiday gifts. Take a picture of your class and have a copy made for each student. Help each student glue her photo in the center of a piece of construction paper. (Allow at least a ½-inch border to show around the picture.) Have each student sign and date the back of her project. Then have each child decorate the border by gluing on holiday-shaped confetti or sequins. If desired, have each student pass her picture around and have her fellow classmates sign their names in the border. Laminate the pictures for durability and attach a piece of magnetic tape to the back of each project.

Trim a Tree

Spruce up the classroom with trees that are measured to perfection. Prepare a supply of one-inch-wide green paper strips, and give each student eight strips. To make a tree, each child measures and cuts one strip to eight-inches long and glues it to the bottom of a sheet of construction paper. Next, he measures and cuts the second strip to seven inches long and glues it above the first strip. He continues cutting each strip an inch shorter until the last piece is one inch long. Decorate with various shapes of ornaments and packages.

Pretty Page Holders

Have each of your students create this simple Valentine's Day project to give to family members, friends, or someone else special. Provide each student with a white business-size envelope, and have him sketch heart shapes at the bottom corners of the envelope. Have each child decorate the heart shapes with colored markers. Then have him cut the heart shapes from the corners so that the tips of the hearts are still joined together. Each heart shape can slip over a page corner to mark a valentine's place in a book!

Lucky Leprechauns

Combine an art project with a writing assignment to create some very lucky leprechauns. Have each child write a paragraph telling about his luckiest day on a copy of the form on page 282. Then give each student a nine-inch paper plate, a sheet of green construction paper, construction paper scraps, and a supply of orange yarn. Students will also need access to glue, scissors, a hole puncher, and a black marker.

To assemble the leprechaun:
1. Punch 20 holes along the bottom edge of the plate.
2. Cut the yarn into eight-inch pieces. Tie a piece through each hole to form a beard.
3. Cut the eyes, nose, and ears from colored construction paper and glue to the plate as shown. Use a marker to draw a mouth.
4. Cut a hat from the green construction paper. Glue the paragraph to the top of the hat. If desired, create a band and buckle for the hat with colored construction paper.
5. Glue several strands of yarn to the back side of the hat brim. Then glue the hat to the paper plate.

March Weather Windsocks

Show students that March comes in like a lion and goes out like a lamb with this wild and woolly windsock project. Each student will need scissors, glue, paper plates, a 12" x 18" sheet of yellow construction paper, a length of yarn, and assorted colors of crepe-paper streamers. To decorate the windsock, supply each child with 9" x 12" sheets of light brown, dark brown, white, and black construction paper. Provide copies of the pattern pieces on page 284 for students to trace.

To make a lion, have each student trace and cut the face and lion ear patterns from light brown construction paper. Have her glue strips of dark brown paper behind the face to create a mane. Attach the face and ears to a paper plate.

To complete the windsock, have each student roll the yellow sheet of construction paper into a cylinder and staple it together. Have each child glue the faces on opposite sides of her cylinder. Create a handle by having each child staple a length of string to the top as shown. Provide crepe paper for students to add streamers to the bottoms of their windsocks, and they're ready to sail in the March breeze.

To make the lamb, have each child trace the face and lamb ear patterns on black paper. Have the student glue behind the face strips of white paper that have been curled around a pencil. Attach the face and ears to a paper plate.

Using scraps of paper, have each student add eyes, a nose, and a mouth to each face.

Mother's Day Magnets

This scented kitchen magnet will make a sweet Mother's Day surprise. Mix dough from 2 cups of applesauce and 12 ounces of cinnamon. Roll out the dough on a sheet of waxed paper. Have each student cut out a shape by tracing around a butterfly pattern with a plastic knife. Place the cutouts on a wire rack. When dry, have each child decorate his butterfly with touches of paint (do not varnish them). Attach a magnet to the back of each shape. Have each student present the magnet to his mother, explaining that it should be attached to the metal hood over the stove. While dinner is cooking, the heat from the stove will release the cutout's spicy scent.

RECIPES

Create a variety of art materials for your classroom with the following collection of recipes for glue, dye, paints, dough, and papier-mâché.

SPARKLE PAINT

light corn syrup
food coloring
glitter

In each of several small containers, mix corn syrup, a few drops of food coloring, and glitter. Have students use the mixture to paint on construction paper, paper plates, tagboard, or other heavy paper. Allow several days drying time.

EASY DYE

rubbing alcohol
food coloring

Use this simple method to color pasta, rice, seeds, or dried flowers. Put a small amount of rubbing alcohol into a container with a tight-fitting lid. Add the desired amount of food coloring. Place the objects to be dyed inside the container and secure the lid. Gently shake the container for one minute. Spread the objects on paper towels to dry.

PASTEL PAINT

evaporated milk
food coloring

Pour evaporated milk into several small containers. Add a few drops of food coloring to each container and mix. When painted on construction paper, the paint has a creamy, pastel appearance.

WET-LOOK PAINT

1 part white liquid glue
1 part tempera paint

Mix the paint and glue together, and apply to paper with a paintbrush. This paint retains a shiny, wet appearance when dry.

SIMPLE PAPIER-MÂCHÉ

1 part liquid starch
1 part cold water
newspaper torn into strips

Mix together the starch and water. Have students dip strips of newspaper into the mixture before applying to a balloon, chicken wire, or other form.

COLORED GLUE

white glue
food coloring

Pour glue into a small container and add the desired amount of food coloring. Stir until the glue is blended. Have students apply the colored glue with a paintbrush to a variety of materials.

COOKED PLAY DOUGH

1 cup flour
1/2 cup salt
2 teaspoons cream of tartar
1 cup water
1 teaspoon vegetable oil
food coloring

Mix the dry ingredients. Stir in the water, oil, and food coloring. Place the mixture in a heavy skillet and cook over medium heat for two or three minutes, stirring frequently. Knead the dough until it is soft and smooth. Store in an airtight container.

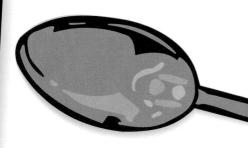

NO-COOK MODELING DOUGH

2 cups flour
1 cup salt
water
tempera paint powder

Mix the ingredients, adding enough water to make the dough pliable. This dough will air-dry to harden or can be baked at 300°F for an hour, depending on the thickness of the object.

My luckiest day was when...

_____

_____

_____

_____

_____

_____

DEAR PARENT,

For our upcoming art projects, we will need the supplies indicated below. If you are able to donate any of these items, please send the materials to school with your child. We appreciate your help!

____ aluminum foil
____ plastic baby-food tubs
____ buttons
____ cardboard tubes
____ coat hangers (metal)
____ craft sticks
____ cotton balls
____ empty plastic milk jugs
____ fabric scraps
____ glitter
____ magazines or catalogs
____ newspapers
____ paper plates
____ paper sacks

____ pipe cleaners
____ empty plastic margarine containers
____ plastic six-pack rings
____ plastic soft-drink bottles
____ ribbon
____ sandpaper
____ plastic drinking straws
____ foam packing pieces
____ foam plates
____ sponges
____ wallpaper samples
____ wrapping paper
____ yarn

Other:

____ _____

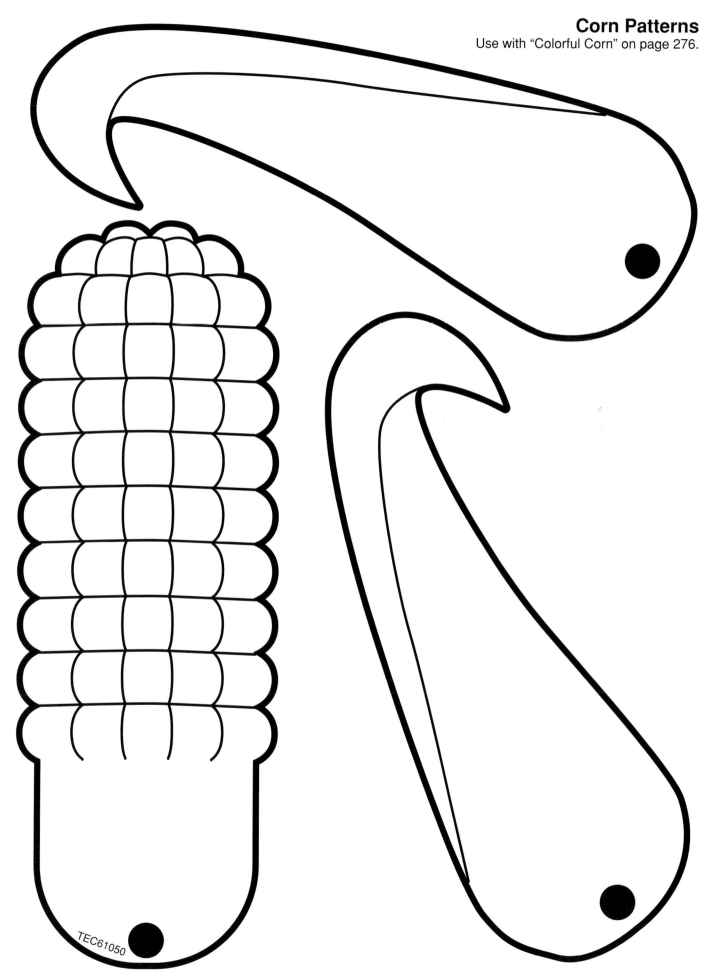

TEC61050

Lion and Lamb Patterns

Use with "March Weather Windsocks" on page 279.

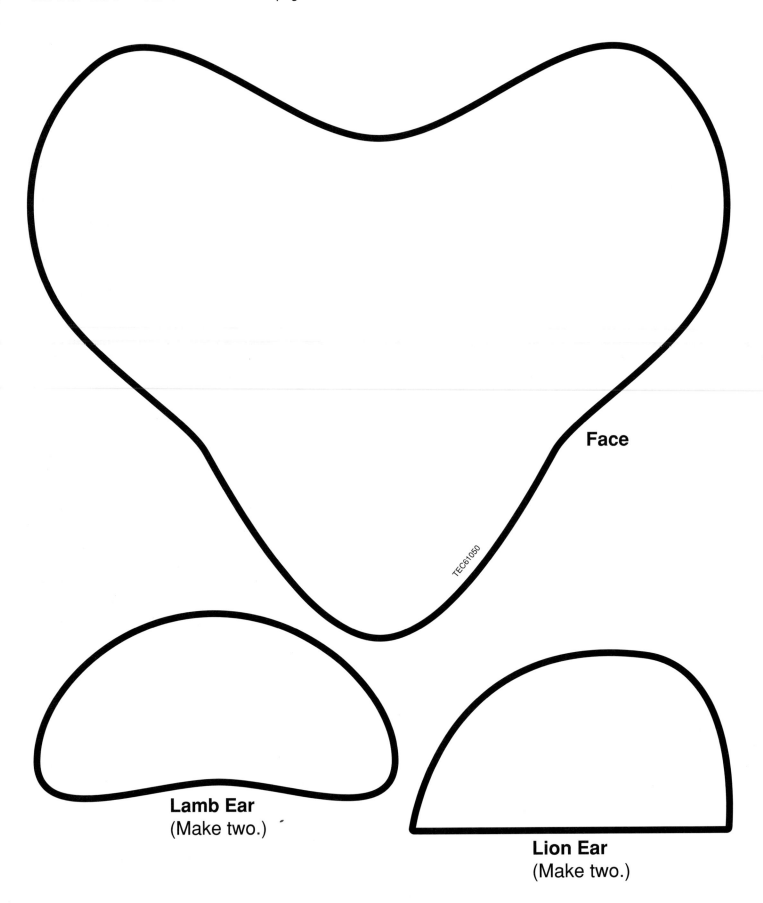

Face

TEC61050

Lamb Ear
(Make two.)

Lion Ear
(Make two.)

FALL

Traveling With Johnny

Introduce your students to a character known for his love of apples—Johnny Appleseed. Share the adventurous tall tale *Johnny Appleseed* by Steven Kellogg with your students. Then challenge your class to travel along Johnny's route by recording his journey on a map of the United States. Provide each student with a map and a red crayon. Read the story a second time, having students draw an apple on a state each time it is mentioned. After reading the story, have the students draw lines to connect the apples. Extend the activity by having students research to find which states are currently major apple producers. Instruct them to color those states on their maps with a green crayon.

Name _____					Weather
Fall Weather					
City	Monday	Tuesday	Wednesday	Thursday	Friday
Boston, Massachusetts	☀ 55°F				
Atlanta, Georgia	☁ 73°F				
Boise, Idaho	☀ 60°F				
Los Angeles, California	☁ 82°F				
Honolulu, Hawaii	☂ 81°F				

Autumn All Around

Help students picture fall weather in communities all over the United States with this graphing activity. Make a copy of page 287 and cut out the weather cards. Duplicate more weather pieces as needed. Use a map of the United States to help your students choose five cities from various parts of the country to "visit" over the next week. Each day, share with students a national weather map (found in most newspapers) and discuss the weather observed in each of the five cities. Record the high temperature on the corresponding weather card and glue it to the graph. At the end of the week, discuss the results and have students share which city they'd most like to visit in autumn.

He's wearing a rainbow-colored wig and large green shoes. He has on a polka-dotted suit, and he is carrying a balloon.

A clown!

Costume Clues

Reinforce descriptive language with this whole-class activity. To prepare, cut out a class supply of costume pictures (found in store circulars and online) and place them in a stack. A child pulls a picture from the stack and describes it for the class. Students try to identify the costume based on the description. If it is not correctly identified after three guesses, the picture is returned to the stack and another child chooses a picture to describe. Play continues in this manner until all pictures are identified, until each child has a chance to describe a picture, or until time is up.

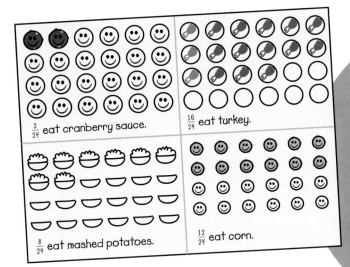

$\frac{2}{24}$ eat cranberry sauce.

$\frac{16}{24}$ eat turkey.

$\frac{8}{24}$ eat mashed potatoes.

$\frac{12}{24}$ eat corn.

Fraction Feast

To start this holiday activity, ask each student to share three foods he eats each Thanksgiving. Record the results in a tally chart on the board. Then have each student fold a sheet of construction paper into fourths. He chooses four of the foods from the chart and uses the data to create a fraction showing the students who celebrate Thanksgiving with that food. After each fraction is written and the food labeled, he draws a picture to represent the fraction. When completed, post the projects on a board titled "Feasting on Fractions."

World Hello Day

Encourage students to help spread cheerful greetings on World Hello Day (November 21). Explain to students that the purpose of this day is to promote peace through communication. To participate, each student should extend a greeting to ten or more people during the day. Add a decorative touch to the affair by having students create posters featuring salutations from around the world. Provide your class with poster boards, markers, and this list of world-class greetings:

Buenos dias Spanish

Guten tag German

Morn Norwegian

Hallo Dutch

Ciao Italian

Bonjour French

National Author's Day

Who are the most popular authors among third-grade readers? Find out by having students create a display of their favorite authors' works for National Author's Day (November 1). Ask each student to look in the library for books written by a favorite author. Have her select several books and create a poster showing the covers and characters from the stories. Display the posters in the hallway, cafeteria, or library. For added fun encourage each student to dress as a character from one of the stories featured on her poster. Have her tell about the story from the character's point of view.

Check out the skill-building reproducibles on pages 288–292.

Name _____

Fall Weather

Weather _____

City	Monday	Tuesday	Wednesday	Thursday	Friday

_____ °F TEC61050

_____ °F TEC61050

_____ °F TEC61050

_____ °F TEC61050

_____ °F TEC61050

_____ °F TEC61050

_____ °F TEC61050

_____ °F TEC61050

_____ °F TEC61050

_____ °F TEC61050

_____ °F TEC61050

_____ °F TEC61050

Note to the teacher: Use with "Autumn All Around" on page 286.

Capitalize on Johnny Appleseed!

Read each sentence.
Circle the letters that need to be capitalized.
The number of capitals needed is written in
   the apple by each sentence.

 1. johnny appleseed was born on september 26, 1774.

 2. his real name was john chapman.

 3. he traveled through ohio and indiana planting apple orchards.

 4. there are many stories about johnny's adventures.

 5. some people claim he was a medicine man to the native americans.

 6. others say he wore a pot on his head instead of a hat.

 7. still others claim johnny never wore shoes, summer or winter.

 8. none of these stories about johnny have been proven true.

 9. we do know that he owned about 1,200 acres of orchards.

 10. until his death in 1845, he kept traveling and planting apple trees.

Name_____

Autumn Addition

Add.
Color by the code.

1. 125
+ 237

2. 358
+ 112

3. 156
+ 129

4. 160
+ 279

5. 154
+ 29

6. 214
+ 159

7. 136
+ 127

8. 109
+ 27

9. 265
+ 225

10. 237
+ 115

11. 127
+ 36

12. 253
+ 186

13. 197
+ 53

14. 169
+ 193

15. 138
+ 126

16. 371
+ 99

Sum Color Code	
yellow = 100–200	red = 201–300
brown = 301–400	orange = 401–500

Name _____

Pumpkins in Print

Use the table of contents to answer the questions.

1. Which chapter tells where pumpkins grow? _____

2. Which chapter tells how pumpkins grow? _____

3. How many pages are in Chapter 1? _____

4. How many pages are in Chapter 2? _____

5. How much longer is Chapter 4 than Chapter 3? _____

6. Which chapter would tell the size of a pumpkin? _____

7. Which chapter would tell about jack-o-lanterns? _____

8. Where would you look for the meaning of *pulp?* _____

Name_____

Tasty Treats

Color the larger number.

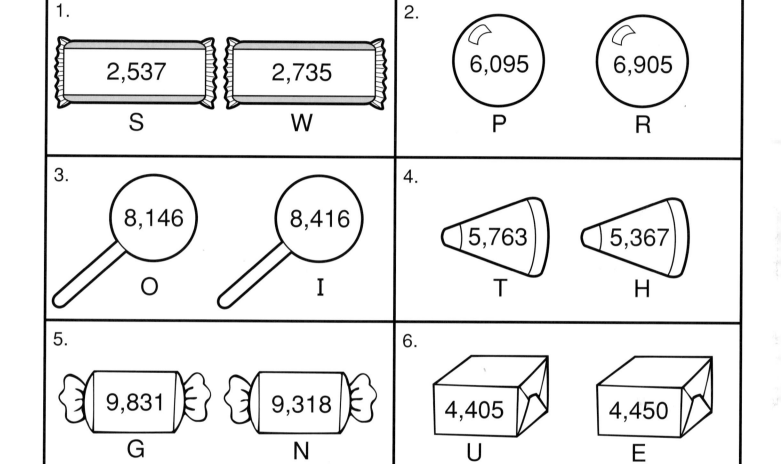

1.

2,537
S

2,735
W

2.

6,095
P

6,905
R

3.

8,146
O

8,416
I

4.

5,763
T

5,367
H

5.

9,831
G

9,318
N

6.

4,405
U

4,450
E

7.

3,947
B

3,974
A

8.

7,626
O

7,266
C

What do little trees say on Halloween?

To solve the riddle, match the letters under the colored candies to the numbered lines below.

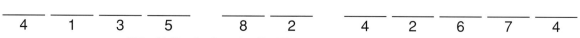

__ __ __ __ __ __ __ __ __ __ __!
4 1 3 5   8 2   4 2 6 7 4

A Friendly Letter

Use editing marks to correct each capitalization and
punctuation mistake.

Dear Elizabeth

   I hope this letter finds you well in england. I wanted to tell you
about the celebration we had this fall We had a three-day feast
to give thanks for our healthy corn crop. we ate wonderful foods
such as Fish geese and corn bread. Our feast was held outdoors
because we had so many guests Along with the Pilgrims, 90 native
people joined in the celebration. They brought deer I wish you
could have been here to enjoy the good food and good company.
please keep in touch!

                                                    Your friend

                                                    mary

Editing Marks

≡ **make uppercase**
   N
   november
   ≡

/ **make lowercase**
       d
   the Ḋog

⊙ **add a period**

   I like corn⊙

˄ **add a comma**

   Plymouth˄Massachusetts

What part of the letter is missing?

_____

Add it to the letter.

Winter

Seasonal Stories

Students will warm up to writing with this simple story-starter idea. To begin, write on the board six to eight seasonal nouns. Explain that each student must choose one of the words to serve as a main character in a story. Then challenge students to write a story that contains all of the words listed. If desired, model a short story on the board before having each student write her own. Instruct her to underline each seasonal noun in her story. After sharing the completed stories, bind them in a book and place it at your reading center.

Holiday ABCs

This holiday-inspired book makes a great gift for loved ones. To prepare one book, fold a sheet of construction paper in half. Then fold seven pieces of white paper in half. Place the white papers inside the folded construction paper and staple them to make a book. Next, list on a sheet of chart paper each letter of the alphabet. Brainstorm with the class things that bring joy, and write them by the appropriate letter on the chart paper. To complete the book, each student chooses a favorite word for each letter and writes it on a page. He illustrates the pages and writes the title "The ABCs of Joy." His holiday gift is complete!

Fred the Snowman
by Olivia
My neighbor is a snowman! His name is Fred, and he lives in the yard next door. I have a lot of fun playing with Fred! Yesterday, he found a sled and took me for a ride in my backyard. I lost my left mitten, but I still had a good time. We're going to get Fred a new hat and maybe go skating on the pond. Fred loves to wear ice skates! He says they're more fun than boots.

Holiday Wreath

Decorate your classroom for the upcoming season with a student-made wreath. To make one wreath, cut an 18-inch circle from a piece of tagboard. Gently fold the circle and cut out the center section to form a wreath shape. Provide a supply of three-inch squares of construction paper in seasonal colors. Have each student cut three or four holiday shapes—such as ornaments, stockings, or hearts—from the squares. Attach the shapes to the tagboard circle for a colorful, class-made door decoration.

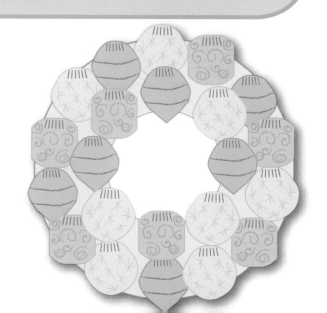

Gift of Knowledge

Students share the symbols of Kwanzaa in this easy-to-make book. Prior to the activity, post on the board the names of the seven symbols of Kwanzaa and their meanings. Discuss them with the class. Then have each student stack eight pieces of 4" x 6" construction paper. Keeping the pages together, have her cut off two corners to make the rectangles resemble gift tags. Help her hole-punch two holes through the short side of the paper. Then she feeds a length of yarn through the holes to bind the pages together. She labels the cover with a title and then writes the name of each symbol on the remaining pages. She includes each symbol's meaning and, if desired, adds an illustration. Finally, she uses red, black, and green crayons to decorate the borders of each page.

Seven Symbols of Kwanzaa

Mazao: harvest fruits

Mkeka: a special mat on which to place the fruits

Kinara: a candleholder

Mishumaa saba: candles

Muhindi: ears of corn, one per child in the family

Kikombe cha umoja: a unity cup

Zawadi: gifts

1929 Dr. King was born in Atlanta, Georgia.

1944 He started college at age 15.

1953 He married Coretta Scott.

1963 Dr. King gave his "I Have a Dream" speech.

1968 Dr. King died.

Happy Birthday, Dr. King!

In advance, cut for each child five 4" x 1" paper rectangles to resemble candles. After sharing a story such as *A Picture Book of Martin Luther King, Jr.* by David A. Adler, review important events from Dr. King's life. List the events and their dates on the board. To complete the timeline, give each student five paper rectangles and a sheet of construction paper. He chooses five events from Dr. King's life and writes one across each paper rectangle, leaving a small margin at the left. Then he adds decorative touches to the sheet of paper to resemble a birthday cake. Next, he glues the rectangle candles in chronological order to the back of the cake. If desired, he glues a tissue paper oval to the top of each candle. Have students share the timelines aloud in small groups, and wrap up the activity with a round of "Happy Birthday."

Presidents and Their Pets

Build an appreciation for presidential trivia with this interactive display. To begin, post on a display the names of several presidents who had pets. Assign each child a presidential pet and provide him with research materials. Then give each student an index card and have him fold it in half as shown. He writes a clue about the animal on the outside of the card and writes the type of pet on the inside. Post the cards below the corresponding president's name, and provide time for students to visit the display.

President Abraham Lincoln

This animal likes to cool itself in the mud. It is a smart animal.

a pet pig.

I hope you will "bee" mine! Happy Valentine's Day! Love, Kendra

"Bee" Mine

Create a buzz for Valentine's Day with these easy-to-make cards! To make a card, fold a piece of yellow construction paper in half and then trim it to an oval shape. Cut strips of black paper and glue them to the front of the oval as shown. Cut two more strips of black paper and curl each around a pencil. Glue these strips to the back of the folded yellow paper (card) to resemble antennae. Next, cut two hearts from white tissue paper and fold each one in half. Glue each folded heart to the back of the card as shown. Glue wiggle eyes to the front of the card and add facial features as desired. Finally, write a Valentine's Day message on the inside of the card and deliver it to that special someone.

Brushing Up

Challenge your students to show off their dental health knowledge with this fun project. Brainstorm dental health–related words for each letter of the alphabet, and list students' responses on the board. Each student selects a word and writes it across a sheet of folded construction paper, leaving space between each letter. Then he creates flaps by cutting between each letter, stopping at the fold. Next, he writes under each flap a dental health statement that corresponds to each letter of his word, using the student-generated list if necessary. He illustrates each statement and glues the paper to a long strip of colored construction paper to make a toothbrush. Post the completed projects on a display titled "Brushing Up on Dental Health."

E is for enamel. Enamel makes up the outside of each tooth. It is very hard.

S m i l

Check out the skill-building reproducibles on pages 296–301.

Count on Winter!

Complete each sentence with information about winter.

One winter sport is _____ .

Two winter holidays are _____ .

Three winter months are _____ .

Four types of winter clothing are _____

_____ .

Five kinds of winter weather are _____

_____ .

Six things to do in the winter are _____

_____ .

Seven things you see in winter are _____

_____ .

Eight words to describe winter are _____

_____ .

Nine things that keep you warm are _____

_____

_____ .

Ten things that are as cold as winter are _____

_____ .

Snow Day!

Color the mitten that completes the sentence.

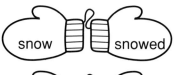 snow | snowed

1. It _____ yesterday!

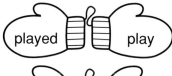 played | play

2. School was called off, so Barry _____ outside.

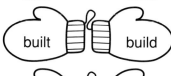 built | build

3. First, he _____ a snowpal.

 make | made

4. Then he _____ a snow fort.

 try | tried

5. Barry _____ to go sledding, but the hill was crowded.

 go | went

6. So he _____ ice fishing instead.

 caught | catch

7. Barry _____ two fish.

 join | joined

8. Then he _____ a game of ice hockey.

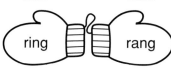 ring | rang

9. Finally, Barry's mom _____ the dinner bell.

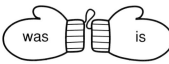 was | is

10. He _____ "bear-y" hungry after his busy day!

Scrambled Sleighs

Read the words on each sleigh.
Write the words in ABC order on the lines.

1.
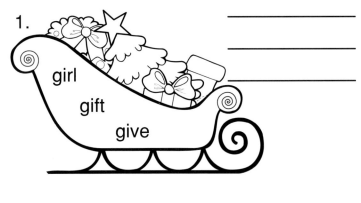
girl
gift
give
_____
_____
_____

2.

sneak
snow
sniffle
_____
_____
_____

3.

rip
ring
ribbon
_____
_____
_____

4.

wrap
write
wreath
_____
_____
_____

5.
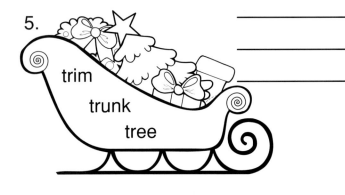
trim
trunk
tree
_____
_____
_____

6.

sled
slush
slippery
_____
_____
_____

7.
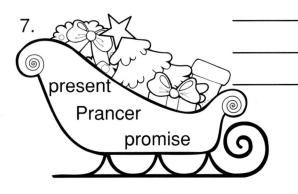
present
Prancer
promise
_____
_____
_____

8.
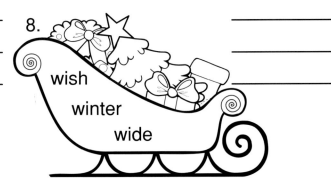
wish
winter
wide
_____
_____
_____

Count Down the New Year!

Look at each clock.
Write the time for each event on the line.

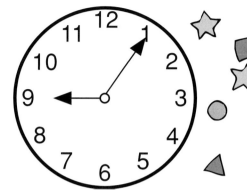
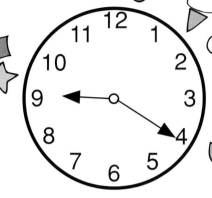

1. _____
The last guest arrives.

2. _____
Everyone puts on a funny hat.

3. _____
We sit down to a late supper.

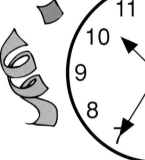

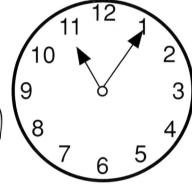

4. _____
We recall happy times of the year.

5. _____
Is anyone getting sleepy yet?

6. _____
There's less than an hour to go!

7. _____
Make your New Year's resolution.

8. _____
Pass out the noisemakers!

9. _____
Happy New Year!

Night Job

Multiply.

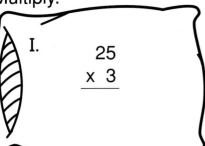
I.
25
x 3

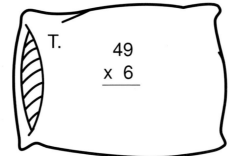
T.
49
x 6

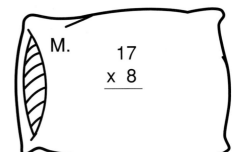
M.
17
x 8

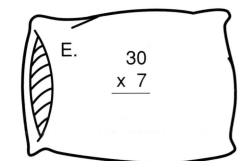
E.
30
x 7

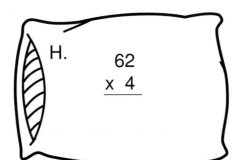
H.
62
x 4

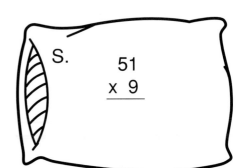
S.
51
x 9

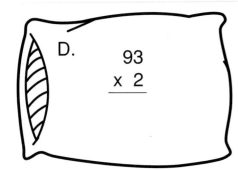
D.
93
x 2

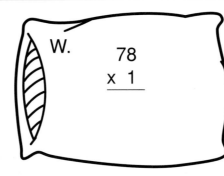
W.
78
x 1

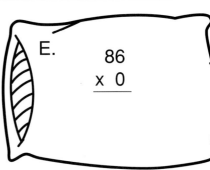
E.
86
x 0

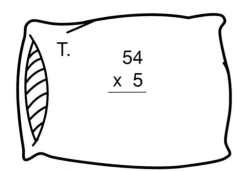
T.
54
x 5

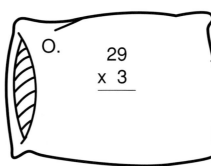
O.
29
x 3

Why is the tooth fairy so smart?
To solve the riddle, match the letters above to the numbered lines below.

She has a lot of

___ ___ ___ ___ ___ ___   ___ ___ ___ ___ ___ .
78 75 459 186 87 136   270 0   210 294 248

©The Mailbox® • Superbook® • TEC61050 • Key p. 316

Valentine Values

Find the prices of the items on the chart.
Add the prices together.
Then tell if $5.00 is enough money to
  buy the items.

$4.25 $2.65 $ .50

$1.85 CANDY HEARTS $ .75 $ .95

1.

Total cost _____

Could you buy it? _____

2.

Total cost _____

Could you buy it? _____

3.

Total cost _____

Could you buy it? _____

4.

Total cost _____

Could you buy it? _____

5.

Total cost _____

Could you buy it? _____

6.

Total cost _____

Could you buy it? _____

7.

Total cost _____

Could you buy it? _____

8.

Total cost _____

Could you buy it? _____

SPRING

Stamp of Approval

Honor women during Women's History Month with this notable March display. Have each child choose one woman who has made a difference to honor on a stamp. Give him an eight-inch construction paper square and provide references to help him illustrate his chosen honoree. Then have him write a short description explaining why she is being honored. Post the completed stamps and descriptions on a board titled "Women Who Left Their Stamps on History."

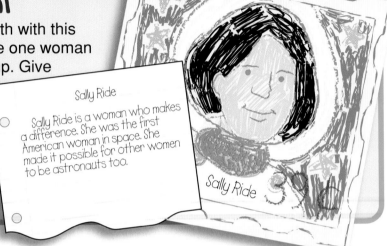

Sally Ride

Sally Ride is a woman who makes a difference. She was the first American woman in space. She made it possible for other women to be astronauts too.

Picnic Paragraph

A Picnic to Remember
by Kelsey
One day last year, I went on a wonderful picnic with my grandparents. We went to Leesville Lake and rented a boat. After we sailed out to the middle of the lake and back, we ate a delicious lunch of fried chicken, fruit salad, and brownies. My grandparents and I rested in the warm sun before heading home. That picnic day was fun and relaxing.

This writing project serves up a great springtime display. In advance, cut a six-inch circle from lined paper for each student. Then have students brainstorm a list of words related to picnics, and write the words on the board. Students use the words to write a paragraph titled "A Picnic to Remember." After drafts are edited, each student writes her paragraph on a precut circle. Then she glues the paragraph to a nine-inch paper plate and glues the plate to construction paper. If desired, also glue or draw other picnic items, such as a napkin or a plastic fork. After the paragraphs have been shared, post them on a display titled "A Picnic to Remember."

Kite Caboodle

Bring outdoor fun inside with this prefix review activity. To prepare, cut two 12-inch construction paper squares. Turn them to resemble kites and write a prefix on each. Tape a length of yarn to the back of each, and post the kites on a low wall. Also copy to make a supply of the kite bow patterns on page 304 and store them near the display. Ask students to be on the lookout for words that use each prefix. When a word is found, have each student write the word on a bow and outline the cutout with a crayon. Then he cuts out the bow and tapes it to the matching kite string. Periodically review the completed kites, making note of any newly added words.

mis-

misjudge

misplace

Treasure Chest

These precious booklets will make moms feel as good as gold on Mother's Day. Explain to students that to treasure someone means to value or appreciate that person. Brainstorm with students activities or gestures their moms do that they appreciate, and write the ideas on the board. Then give each student a construction paper copy of page 305 and four index cards. Have her complete the cover patterns and cut them out. Next, she completes the sentence "I treasure my mom's __ because __." on each card. When finished, she sandwiches the cards between the covers and staples them together to complete her booklet. If desired, have her glue plastic gems to the bottom of the booklet.

You're treasured!
Love, Melissa

You're treasured!
Love, Melissa

I treasure my mom's hugs because they make me feel safe.

Surfing Through Good Books

Create a wave of reading interest with this incentive. To begin, cut a class supply of long ovals from 3" x 9" construction paper and laminate them. Each student uses an oval as a surfboard bookmark while reading a book. For each book he finishes, he adds a small sticker to the surfboard. Once he has collected a predetermined number of stickers, post his surfboard on a display titled "Surfing Through Good Books." Then give him a new surfboard to start again. If desired, fill a plastic fish tank with treasures and place it under the display. Allow students to select a reward each time they post a surfboard.

Just Ducky

Post students' summer plans on this fine-feathered display. Give each student a copy of the duck pattern on page 304 to color and cut out. Then have each child write a paragraph or more describing her plans for the summer. Staple the duck and paragraph to blue paper and title the display "Waddle We Do This Summer?"

I can't wait to start my exciting summer! First, I am going to visit my cousin, Lara, in Colorado. I get to fly on a plane, and I've never done that before. I can't wait! When I get back from Colorado, I will head off to camp in New York. My little sister is going too, so I don't think I will get homesick. Finally, after camp is over, my family and I will spend a week at Myrtle Beach. I think this will be my best summer yet!

Check out the skill-building reproducibles on pages 306–308.

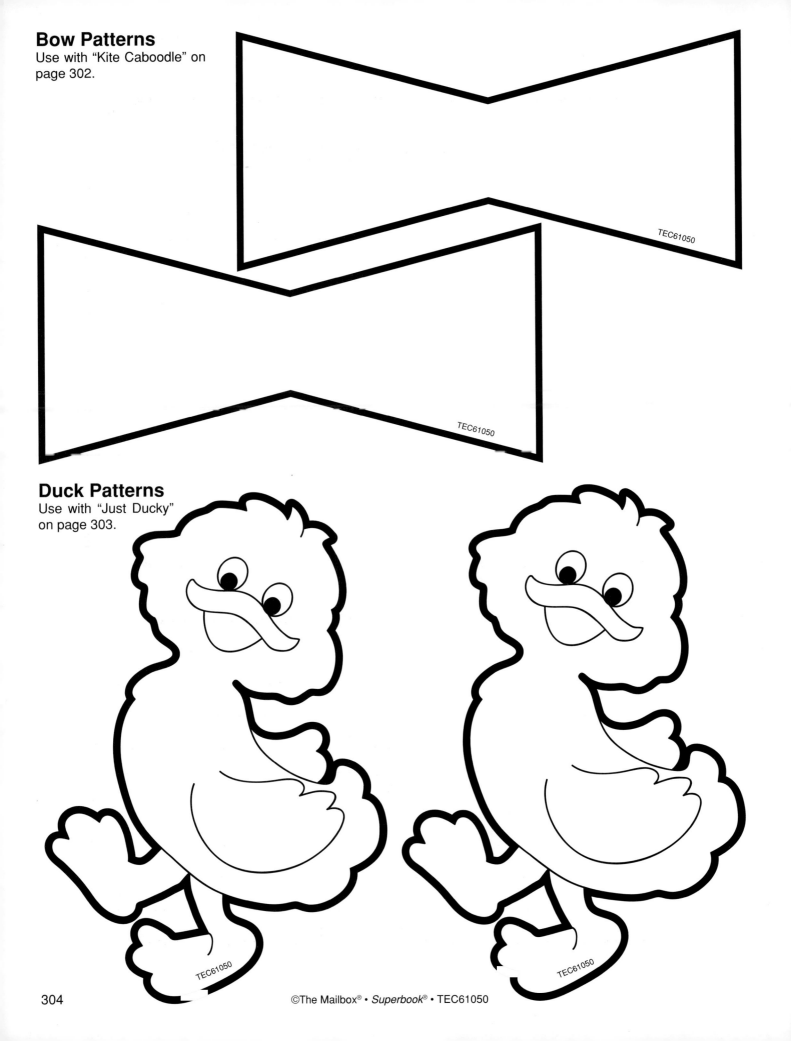

Bow Patterns
Use with "Kite Caboodle" on page 302.

TEC61050

TEC61050

Duck Patterns
Use with "Just Ducky" on page 303.

TEC61050

TEC61050

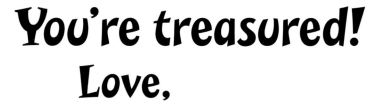

You're treasured!
Love,

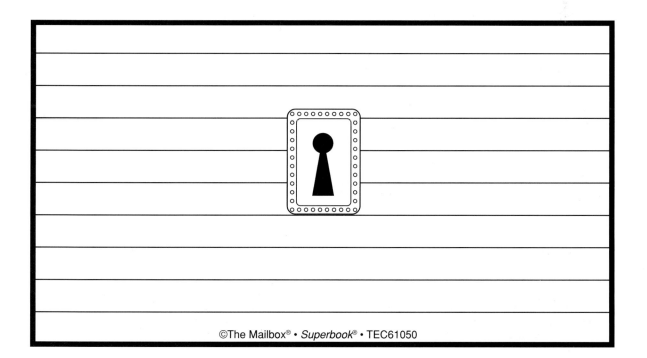

"Eggs-tra" Special Fractions

Follow the directions for coloring the eggs.
Then write a fraction to answer each question.

---

1. Color two eggs pink and three eggs green.

What fraction of the eggs are pink? _____

2. Color four eggs yellow and one egg red.

What fraction of the eggs are yellow?_____

---

3. Color two eggs blue and four eggs purple.

What fraction of the eggs are blue? _____

4. Color three eggs yellow and five eggs red.

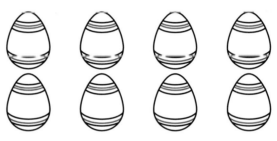

What fraction of the eggs are red? _____

---

5. Color six eggs orange and one egg pink.

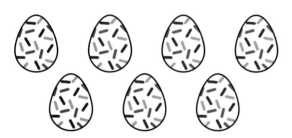

What fraction of the eggs are pink? _____

6. Color three eggs pink and two eggs yellow.

What fraction of the eggs are pink? _____

---

7. Color one egg blue and three eggs green.

What fraction of the eggs are blue? _____

8. Color four eggs purple and four eggs green.

What fraction of the eggs are purple?_____

Celebrate Cinco de Mayo!

Color the piñata.
Use the word box for help.

azul

rojo   morado   rojo

verde

azul   azul

morado   verde   anaranjado   verde   morado

azul   azul

azul   azul

amarillo

verde

morado

rojo   rojo

azul

Synonyms for Super Dads

Read each sentence.
Use the word box to find a synonym for each word in bold.
Write the synonyms on the lines following each sentence.

Word Box				
intelligent	construct	stream	great	correct
repair	forest	glad	chef	grin

1. My dad is a **wonderful** guy! _____

2. Just thinking of him makes me **smile**. _____

3. He is always **happy** to spend time with me. _____

4. Sometimes we go fishing at the **creek**. _____

5. Other times we camp out in the **woods**. _____

6. My dad showed me how to **build** a birdhouse. _____

7. He also taught me how to **fix** a flat tire on my bike. _____

8. Dad is also a very good **cook**. _____

9. I think my dad is very **smart**. _____

10. When I ask him a question, he always knows the **right** answer. _____

©The Mailbox® • Superbook® • TEC61050 • Key p. 316

Answer Keys

Page 35

Page 36

1. ◐ Settlers came to America to find gold and silver.
   ○ Settlers learned to raise hogs and grow corn.
2. ○ The settlers chose swampy land.
   ◐ The settlers did not plan to farm corn.
3. ○ The settlers tried to grow grapes.
   ◐ Many settlers got sick.
4. ◐ Captain John Smith took charge.
   ○ John Smith helped the settlers survive their first winter.
5. ○ The settlers began to learn how to survive in the New World.
   ◐ The settlers came to find gold and silver.

Page 37

Black bears are the smallest bears in North America.

They are smaller than grizzly bears and polar bears.

Grizzly bears are the scariest bears.

Black bears are the best bears.

Most black bears live in forests.

Black bears use their sharp claws to climb trees.

Climbing trees is hard work.

All bears should eat honey.

Black bears look for insects under rocks.

Page 38

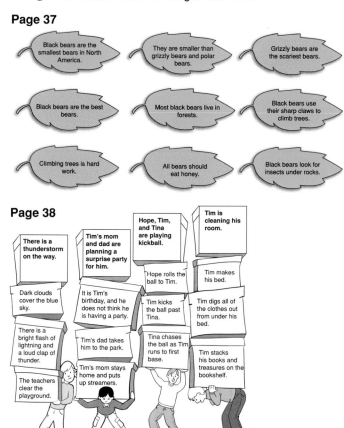

Page 61

1. Ⓘly and Ⓛester will drive in a race on Ⓢaturday.
2. The last time they raced was in Ⓜarch.
3. This is the biggest race in Ⓜay.
4. The race is the day before Ⓜother's Ⓓay.
5. Ⓘly trained for the race on Ⓜondays and Ⓦednesdays.
6. Ⓛester liked to train on Ⓣuesdays and Ⓣhursdays.
7. Many people will drive to Ⓢpeedy Ⓒity to see the race.
8. They may come from as far away as Ⓢouth Ⓣown.
9. If Ⓘly wins, the two cats will race again in Ⓙune.
10. If Ⓛester wins, the next race will be on the Ⓕourth of Ⓙuly.

M	F	S	C	L	E	M
L	S	T	E	J	L	S
S	M	L	W	L	T	L
T	L	M	J	D	R	T

The winner is <u>Lester</u>.

Page 62

1. .	6. .	11. !	
2. ?	7. ?	12. .	
3. !	8. .	13. .	
4. .	9. .	14. ?	
5. !	10. ?	15. !	

Page 63

		yes	no
1. Have you ever been to a rodeo here?		Ⓝ	**Ⓚ**
2. No, but I have always wanted to go to a rodeo.		**Ⓓ**	Ⓝ
3. I went to a rodeo with my mom, my dad, and my sister.		**Ⓣ**	Ⓢ
4. Rodeo cowboys use rope to lasso cattle.		**Ⓜ**	Ⓐ
5. They can lasso cattle very quickly?		Ⓞ	**Ⓖ**
6. Wow, it would be really fun to see that?!		Ⓘ	**Ⓙ**
7. It must be hard to lasso the biggest cattle.		**Ⓣ**	Ⓞ
8. Do rodeo clowns lasso cattle too?		Ⓨ	**Ⓝ**
9. A clown will lasso a cow if a cowboy falls from it.		**Ⓕ**	Ⓚ
10. Boy, the clowns must be very brave!		**Ⓐ**	Ⓗ
11. The rodeo clowns are brave, funny, and quick.		**Ⓦ**	Ⓗ
12. Can we get some tickets to the next rodeo?		**Ⓖ**	Ⓒ

<u>OH NO, "KNOT" AGAIN</u>!

Page 64

1. My favorite colors are <u>red</u>, yellow, and <u>blue</u>.
2. I love to wear <u>shirts</u>, pants, and <u>shoes</u> that are these colors.
3. I wear these colors when I <u>play</u>, go to school, or <u>stay home</u>.
4. <u>My bike</u>, coat, and <u>bedroom</u> are yellow.
5. My hobby is <u>making</u>, painting, and <u>fixing</u> model cars.
6. I put my cars <u>on shelves</u>, in cases, and <u>on my desk</u>.
7. I win <u>prizes</u>, ribbons, and <u>trophies</u> at model-car shows.
8. My best cars are gifts from <u>my dad</u>, mom, and <u>best friend</u>.
9. My favorite subjects at school are <u>math</u>, spelling, and <u>art</u>.
10. I like to <u>add</u>, subtract, and <u>spell</u> at school.
11. I like books that are about <u>dogs</u>, space, and <u>sports</u>.
12. I am happy when I <u>paint pictures</u>, draw posters, or <u>make things with clay</u>.

309

Page 77

Answers may vary. Possible answers include the following:

1. friend, pal, companion
2. drink, swallow
3. shoes, boots
4. trails, lanes
5. beware of, guard against; creatures, critters
6. toss, pitch; garbage, litter
7. near, within a short distance
8. morning, sunrise; evening, sunset

Page 78

1. Do
2. for
3. plain
4. choose
5. Some
6. blue
7. son
8. wait

Page 79

1. unlock
2. unsure
3. misuse
4. mismatch
5. unsafe
6. miscount
7. misplace
8. unknown
9. unlucky
10. unscented
11. unusual
12. misbehave

Page 80

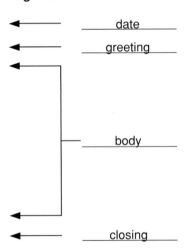

	er	est
1. biggest		est
2. kindest		est
3. taller	er	
4. softer	er	
5. fastest		est
6. cleaner	er	
7. stronger	er	
8. smartest		est
9. brightest		est
10. cooler	er	

Rabbit City, SD — Albunny, NY

Page 81

1. asteroid
2. eclipse
3. launch
4. Mercury
5. planet
6. rocket
7. shuttle
8. star map
9. Venus

Page 96

Today <u>i</u> woke up early. My mom ~~M~~ade pancakes

for me_⊙ *Pancakes* 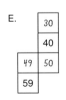 are my favorite breakfast food! I

put on my coat and went outside. My friends and I

played
~~playeed~~ at the park all day. We jumped‸skipped, and

ran. We threw a foot~~B~~all to each other.

Later, it was time to go home_⊙My favorite show

was on television. <u>on</u> the show, they tell ~~say~~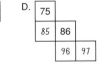

funny stories, do magic tricks‸and sing songs.

great
It was a ~~grate~~ day!

Page 102

date
greeting

body

closing
signature

1. greeting
2. signature
3. date
4. body
5. closing

Page 105

A.

54		
63	64	65
74		

B.

35	36	37	38
			48

C.

5	6	7
	16	
	26	

D.

75		
85	86	
	96	97

E.

	30
	40
49	50
59	

F.

9	
19	20
29	30

G.

12		14
22	23	24

H.

87	88	89	90
		99	

I.

	73
	83
91	92	93

J.

33				
42	43	44	45	46

K.

58		
67	68	69
	79	

L.

2	3
11	12	13

Page 106

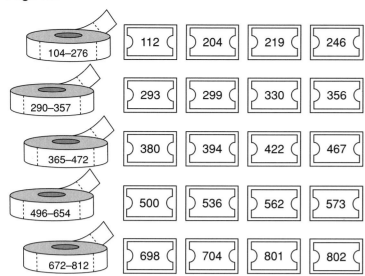

104–276	112 204 219 246
290–357	293 299 330 356
365–472	380 394 422 467
496–654	500 536 562 573
672–812	698 704 801 802

Page 107

A. 730
B. 312
C. 794
D. 128
E. 224
F. 903
G. 356
H. 703

Page 108

A. 300	B. 700	C. 500
D. 100	E. 800	F. 200
G. 500	H. 800	I. 400
J. 100	K. 700	L. 900
M. 400	N. 200	O. 600
P. 600	Q. 900	R. 300

Page 113

D	26	H	11	O	43
	+ 43		+ 17		+ 54
	69		28		97

S	40	S	57	N	61
	+ 39		+ 32		+ 32
	79		89		93

R	44	A	10	W	24
	+ 52		+ 23		+ 21
	96		33		45

F	20	L	16	I	12
	+ 75		+ 30		+ 66
	95		46		78

SWORDFISH AND LIONFISH

Page 114

28	32	46	25
+ 19	+ 18	+ 37	+ 45
47	50	83	70

13	37	56	18
+ 58	+ 14	+ 25	+ 16
71	51	81	34

39	25	37	24
+ 27	+ 28	+ 45	+ 19
66	53	82	43

43	29		
+ 37	+ 36		
80	65		

34	57		
+ 38	+ 37		
72	94		

Page 115

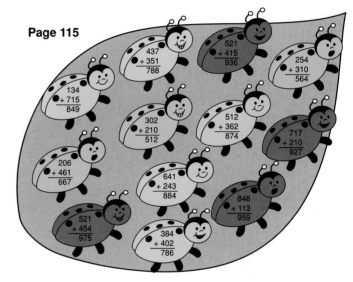

Page 116

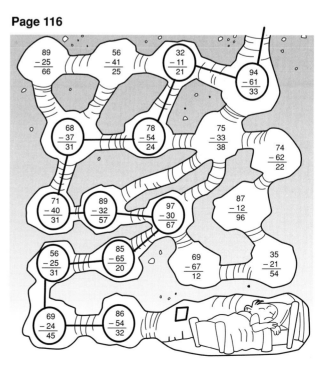

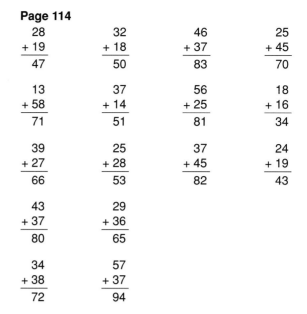

311

Page 117

32 − 19 13 D	64 − 28 36 S	81 − 37 44 R	50 − 32 18 R
74 − 35 39 E	87 − 59 28 E	76 − 18 58 W	93 − 28 65 A
68 − 49 19 R	71 − 68 3 C	83 − 26 57 V	92 − 67 25 I

A SCREWDRIVER!

Page 118

A. 282	B. 619	C. 346	D. 281	E. 561
F. 257	G. 527	H. 94	I. 95	J. 304
K. 87	L. 429	M. 137	N. 819	O. 212

Page 123

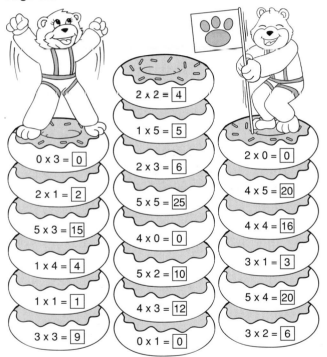

2 x 2 = 4
0 x 3 = 0
2 x 1 = 2
5 x 3 = 15
1 x 4 = 4
1 x 1 = 1
3 x 3 = 9

1 x 5 = 5
2 x 3 = 6
5 x 5 = 25
4 x 0 = 0
5 x 2 = 10
4 x 3 = 12
0 x 1 = 0

2 x 0 = 0
4 x 5 = 20
4 x 4 = 16
3 x 1 = 3
5 x 4 = 20
3 x 2 = 6

Page 124

Ⓘ 7 x 6 = 42   Ⓜ 9 x 3 = 27   Ⓔ 7 x 5 = 35

Ⓨ 8 x 7 = 56   Ⓚ 8 x 9 = 72   Ⓤ 6 x 8 = 48

Ⓓ 6 x 5 = 30   Ⓝ 6 x 4 = 24   Ⓡ 7 x 7 = 49

Ⓗ 8 x 8 = 64   Ⓟ 8 x 0 = 0   Ⓒ 9 x 6 = 54

Ⓣ 7 x 9 = 63   Ⓐ 7 x 3 = 21   Ⓘ 6 x 6 = 36

Ⓑ 8 x 2 = 16   Ⓗ 9 x 9 = 81   Ⓣ 8 x 5 = 40

PUT HIM IN THE BACKYARD!

Page 125

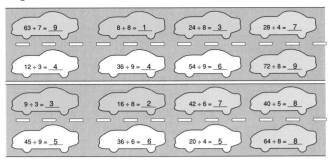

63 ÷ 7 = 9   8 ÷ 8 = 1   24 ÷ 8 = 3   28 ÷ 4 = 7

12 ÷ 3 = 4   36 ÷ 9 = 4   54 ÷ 9 = 6   72 ÷ 8 = 9

9 ÷ 3 = 3   16 ÷ 8 = 2   42 ÷ 6 = 7   40 ÷ 5 = 8

45 ÷ 9 = 5   36 ÷ 6 = 6   20 ÷ 4 = 5   64 ÷ 8 = 8

Page 126

8 x 5 = 40
5 x 8 = 40
40 ÷ 5 = 8
40 ÷ 8 = 5

3 x 6 = 18
6 x 3 = 18
18 ÷ 3 = 6
18 ÷ 6 = 3

6 x 9 = 54
9 x 6 = 54
54 ÷ 6 = 9
54 ÷ 9 = 6

7 x 4 = 28
4 x 7 = 28
28 ÷ 4 = 7
28 ÷ 7 = 4

3 x 5 = 15
5 x 3 = 15
15 ÷ 3 = 5
15 ÷ 5 = 3

6 x 8 = 48
8 x 6 = 48
48 ÷ 6 = 8
48 ÷ 8 = 6

Page 127

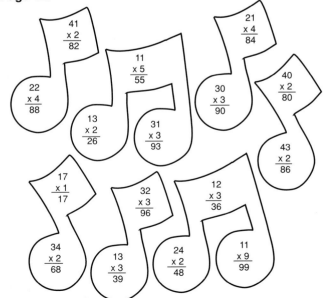

41
x 2
82

21
x 4
84

11
x 5
55

22
x 4
88

30
x 3
90

40
x 2
80

13
x 2
26

31
x 3
93

43
x 2
86

17
x 1
17

32
x 3
96

12
x 3
36

34
x 2
68

13
x 3
39

24
x 2
48

11
x 9
99

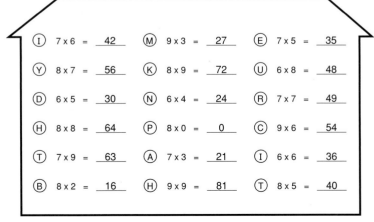

Page 130

A. ²⁄₄ = ½   B. ⁴⁄₆ = ²⁄₃

C. ²⁄₈ = ¼   D. ⁶⁄₈ = ¾

E. ³⁄₉ = ⅓   F. ⁵⁄₁₀ = ½

G. ³⁄₁₂ = ¼   H. ⁴⁄₁₂ = ⅓

Page 131

$\frac{1}{4}$ < $\frac{3}{4}$ $\frac{3}{5}$ > $\frac{2}{5}$ $\frac{4}{6}$ > $\frac{3}{6}$ $\frac{2}{8}$ < $\frac{4}{8}$

$\frac{1}{2}$ = $\frac{3}{6}$ $\frac{3}{4}$ > $\frac{4}{6}$

$\frac{6}{12}$ < $\frac{4}{6}$ $\frac{1}{5}$ = $\frac{2}{10}$

$\frac{2}{3}$ > $\frac{3}{6}$ $\frac{3}{7}$ < $\frac{4}{7}$ $\frac{6}{10}$ > $\frac{4}{10}$ $\frac{6}{8}$ > $\frac{6}{10}$

Page 135

A. 36 cm

B. 26 cm

C. 22 cm

D. 22 cm

E. 16 cm

Page 136

Page 141

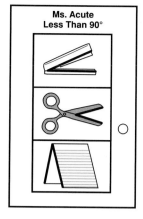
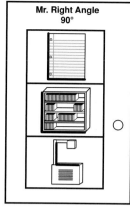
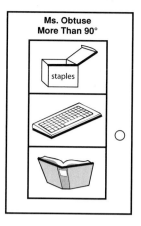

Ms. Acute Less Than 90°	Mr. Right Angle 90°	Ms. Obtuse More Than 90°

Page 146

1. Tetherball
2. Wall Ball
3–4. Answers will vary.

Page 149

Rule: Add 3.

3	6
5	8
8	11
9	12

Rule: Subtract 0.

8	8
7	7
6	6
4	4

Rule: Add 4.

2	6
5	9
7	11
9	13

Rule: Add 8.

5	13
7	15
8	16
9	17

Rule: Subtract 2.

9	7
5	3
3	1
2	0

Rule: Add 4.

0	4
4	8
6	10
8	12

Rule: Subtract 5.

8	3
7	2
6	1
5	0

Rule: Subtract 4.

9	5
7	3
6	2
4	0

Page 150

8 + <u>5</u> = 13   7 + <u>8</u> = 15

4 + <u>7</u> = 11   3 + <u>9</u> = 12

5 + <u>4</u> = 9   4 + <u>4</u> = 8

6 + <u>6</u> = 12   6 + <u>0</u> = 6

2 + <u>8</u> = 10   9 + <u>4</u> = 13

8 + <u>6</u> = 14   5 + <u>2</u> = 7

7 + <u>5</u> = 12   1 + <u>7</u> = 8

3 + <u>5</u> = 8   9 + <u>9</u> = 18

Page 154

A. red, blue, yellow, blue, red

B. orange, orange, yellow, yellow, yellow or yellow, yellow, yellow, orange, orange

C. yellow, yellow, orange, blue, blue or blue, blue, orange, yellow, yellow

D. orange, yellow, red, red, orange or orange, red, red, yellow, orange

E. orange, blue, yellow, blue, yellow or yellow, blue, yellow, blue, orange

Page 157

cooked	living	paper
colors	water	places
leaves	needs	roots
petals	water	trees
soil	stores	boxes
light	green	sound
air	fire	covering
kitchens	rain	doors
sun	matches	towels
vines	light	moons

Page 158

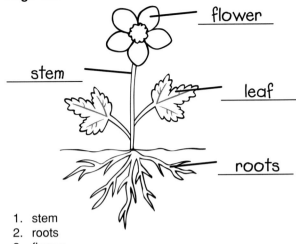

1. stem
2. roots
3. flower
4. leaves
5. minerals
6. sunlight

Page 168

new moon waxing crescent first quarter waxing gibbous full moon waning gibbous third quarter waning crescent

Page 174

1. litter
2. Pollute
3. atmosphere
4. fossil fuels
5. Reuse
6. Earth Day
7. natural resources
8. water

He wanted to grow a <u>power plant</u>!

Page 183

A. 13
B. 2
C. 12
D. 55
E. 81
F. 7
G. 42
H. 39
I. 3
J. 9

Answers will vary.

Page 191

1. red
2. blue
3. blue
4. red
5. blue
6. red
7. red
8. blue
9. blue
10. red

Page 234

1. book
2. write
3. draw
4. like
5. friend
6. water
7. parents
8. color

Page 288

 1. (J)ohnny (A)ppleseed was born on (S)eptember 26, 1774.

 2. (H)is real name was (J)ohn (C)hapman.

 3. (H)e traveled through (O)hio and (I)ndiana planting apple orchards.

 4. (T)here are many stories about (J)ohnny's adventures.

 5. (S)ome people claim he was a medicine man to the (N)ative (A)mericans.

 6. (O)thers say he wore a pot on his head instead of a hat.

 7. (S)till others claim (J)ohnny never wore shoes, summer or winter.

 8. (N)one of these stories about (J)ohnny have been proven true.

 9. (W)e do know that he owned about 1,200 acres of orchards.

 10. (U)ntil his death in 1845, he kept traveling and planting apple trees.

Page 289

1. 125 + 237 = 362
2. 358 + 112 = 470
3. 156 + 129 = 285
4. 160 + 279 = 439
5. 154 + 29 = 183
6. 214 + 159 = 373
7. 136 + 127 = 263
8. 109 + 27 = 136
9. 265 + 225 = 490
10. 237 + 115 = 352
11. 127 + 36 = 163
12. 253 + 186 = 439
13. 197 + 53 = 250
14. 169 + 193 = 362
15. 138 + 126 = 264
16. 371 + 99 = 470

Page 290

1. 2
2. 3
3. 1
4. 2
5. 1
6. 1
7. 4
8. glossary

Page 291

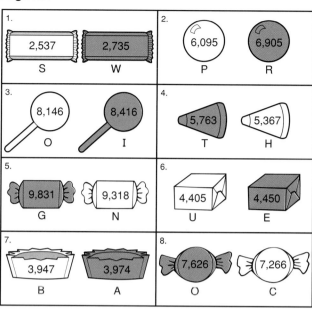

1. 2,537 — S / 2,735 — W	2. 6,095 — P / 6,905 — R
3. 8,146 — O / 8,416 — I	4. 5,763 — T / 5,367 — H
5. 9,831 — G / 9,318 — N	6. 4,405 — U / 4,450 — E
7. 3,947 — B / 3,974 — A	8. 7,626 — O / 7,266 — C

TWIG OR TREAT!

Page 292

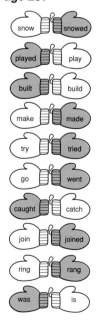

Dates will vary.

Dear Elizabeth,

I hope this letter finds you well in England. I wanted to tell you about the celebration we had this fall. We had a three-day feast to give thanks for our healthy corn crop. We ate wonderful foods such as Fish, geese, and corn bread. Our feast was held outdoors because we had so many guests. Along with the Pilgrims, 90 native people joined in the celebration. They brought deer. I wish you could have been here to enjoy the good food and good company. Please keep in touch!

Your friend,

Mary

The date is missing.

Page 297

snow — snowed
played — play
built — build
make — made
try — tried
go — went
caught — catch
join — joined
ring — rang
was — is

315

Page 298

1. gift
   girl
   give

2. sneak
   sniffle
   snow

3. ribbon
   ring
   rip

4. wrap
   wreath
   write

5. tree
   trim
   trunk

6. sled
   slippery
   slush

7. Prancer
   present
   promise

8. wide
   winter
   wish

Page 299

1. 9:05
2. 9:20
3. 9:45
4. 10:10
5. 10:35
6. 11:05
7. 11:25
8. 11:50
9. 12:00

Page 300

I. 75	T. 294	M. 136
E. 210	H. 248	S. 459
D. 186	W. 78	E. 0
T. 270	O. 87	

She has a lot of <u>WISDOM TEETH</u>.

Page 301

1. $4.75, yes
2. $2.35, yes
3. $4.50, yes
4. $2.80, yes
5. $1.70, yes
6. $6.10, no
7. $6.90, no
8. $3.60, yes

Page 306

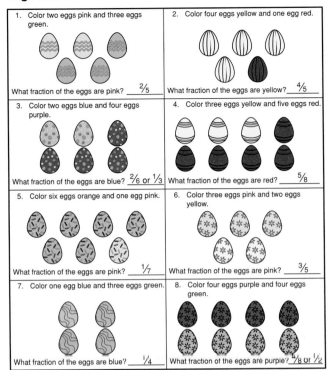

1. Color two eggs pink and three eggs green.
   What fraction of the eggs are pink? 2/5

2. Color four eggs yellow and one egg red.
   What fraction of the eggs are yellow? 4/5

3. Color two eggs blue and four eggs purple.
   What fraction of the eggs are blue? 2/6 or 1/3

4. Color three eggs yellow and five eggs red.
   What fraction of the eggs are red? 5/8

5. Color six eggs orange and one egg pink.
   What fraction of the eggs are pink? 1/7

6. Color three eggs pink and two eggs yellow.
   What fraction of the eggs are pink? 3/5

7. Color one egg blue and three eggs green.
   What fraction of the eggs are blue? 1/4

8. Color four eggs purple and four eggs green.
   What fraction of the eggs are purple? 4/8 or 1/2

Page 307

Page 308

1. great
2. grin
3. glad
4. stream
5. forest
6. construct
7. repair
8. chef
9. intelligent
10. correct

Index